·FEMININ
MASCULINE
—————AND—————
REPRESENTATION

This collection of essays makes an important contribution to
debate on the role of representation in the social construction
of the patriarchal gender order. It deals centrally with
questions about sex and gender, subjectivity and signification.
In her editor's introduction Terry Threadgold confronts the
scepticism of those resistant to the challenge which
poststructuralist semiotics ('that language stuff') poses to all
branches of knowledge. She points out that these discourses
about language, or semiosis, seem arcane only because they
have not yet become part of everyday life, as have similarly
specialist discourses like economics, government, sociology,
biology. Exploring the dynamic intersections of feminist and
poststructuralist enquiry, this work demonstrates powerfully
new possibilities of resistance and transformation.

Susan Sheridan
Editor of *Grafts: Feminist Cultural
Criticism* (Verso, 1988)

In the midst of current and often reactionary nostalgias for
the old analytical categories and political certainties, this lucid
collection deals a timely *coup de grâce* to the unexamined
assumptions which too often prevail in Australian intellectual
debates. Informed by an awareness of global metropolitan
theory and by a passionate committment to political change,
these essays open up a new space beyond the dreary ping-
pong of binary oppositions and separatist politics. No longer
signifying the essentialism of an older dispensation, the
sexed body returns to confound the certainties of
masculine/feminine, to redefine a positive difference, a new
autonomy for women, for men.

Sneja Gunew

·FEMININE·
MASCULINE
—AND—
REPRESENTATION

EDITED BY TERRY THREADGOLD
• & ANNE CRANNY-FRANCIS •

ALLEN & UNWIN
Sydney London Boston Wellington

First published in 1990
Allen & Unwin Australia Pty Ltd
An Unwin Hyman company
8 Napier Street, North Sydney, NSW 2060 Australia

Allen & Unwin New Zealand Limited
75 Ghuznee Street, Wellington, New Zealand

Unwin Hyman Limited
15–17 Broadwick Street, London W1V 1FP England

Allen & Unwin Inc.
8 Winchester Place, Winchester, Mass 01890 USA

National Library of Australia
Cataloguing-in-Publication entry:
Feminine/masculine and representation.
    Bibliography.
    Includes index.
    ISBN 0   04   610018 0.

    1. Femininity (Philosophy). 2. Masculinity (Philosophy).
    3. Femininity (Psychology). 4. Masculinity (Psychology).
    5. Sex differences (Psychology) in literature. I.
    Threadgold, Terry. II. Cranny-Francis, Anne.
305.3

Library of Congress Catalog Card Number: 89-84872

Typeset in 10/11 pt Ballardvalle by Times Graphics, Singapore
Printed by SRM Production Services Sdn Bhd, Malaysia

Contents

Illustrations

Contributors

Jennifer Ash is a postgraduate student in the English Department at the University of Sydney. She is at present researching the religiosity of the late Middle Ages, using a theoretical framework of psychoanalysis, semiotics and French feminisms.

Virginia Blain is senior lecturer in English at Macquarie University. She was a visiting fellow at the Humanities Research at the Australian National University in 1986, during the Feminist year. She is currently completing work on the nineteenth-century section of *A Feminist Companion to Literature in English*, a critical reference to women from 1300 to the present, to be published by Batsford (UK) and Yale (US) in 1989.

Rosi Braidotti has a BA from the Australian National University and a PhD in Philosophy from the Sorbonne. She is professor of Women's Studies and chair of the Department at the University of Utrecht in the Netherlands. She has worked and lived in Paris and has published on issues related to feminism, philosophy and psychoanalysis. She is the author of *Patterns of Dissonance*, an essay on women in contemporary French philosophy (forthcoming with Polity Press). She is on the editorial board of *Women's Studies International Forum*, *Les Cahiers du Grif*, *Copyright* and *Differences*.

Anne Cranny-Francis is lecturer in English at the University of Wollongong, where she teaches in the areas of nineteenth-century fiction, cultural studies and critical theory. She has published in the areas of cultural studies, nineteenth- and twentieth-century fiction, Australian fiction and feminist writing. Her book, *Feminist Fiction*, a study of feminist rewriting of generic fiction, will be published by Polity Press in 1989. She is currently working on an undergraduate text, *En/gendered Fiction*, for New South Wales University Press on the coding of gender into text.

Patricia Palmer Gillard is lecturer in Communications at the Canberra College of Advanced Education. In 1986 and 1987 she worked for the Australian Broadcasting Corporation as head of Research and Development for ABC-TV. She previously worked as a media consultant with her own business, *Audience Views*, as a lecturer in English Curriculum at the University of New South Wales, and as a high school teacher. Under the name Patricia Palmer she has published a book on children and television, *The lively Audience: A study of children around the TV set* (Allen & Unwin, 1986) and a report on TV viewing by teenage girls, *Girls and Television* (Sydney: Social Policy Unit, Ministry of Education, 1986).

Elizabeth Grosz teaches in the Department of General Philosophy at Sydney University. She is the author of *Sexual Subversions: Three French Feminists* (Allen & Unwin, 1988) and has co-edited (with Carole Pateman) *Feminist Challenges: Social and Political Theory* (Allen & Unwin, 1986) and (with Barbara Caine and Marie de Lepervanche) *Crossing Boundaries: Feminism and the Critique of Knowledge* (Allen & Unwin, 1988).

Michael Hurley teaches in the Faculty of Communications at the University of Technology, Sydney. His teaching and research interests are in recent Australian writing, science writing, textual theory and public images of science and technology. Much of that work focuses on gender, sexuality and sexual difference.

Gisela T. Kaplan of the School of Sociology, University of New South Wales, is the current editor (jointly) of the *Australian and New Zealand Journal of Sociology*. She has co-edited a book on Hannah Arendt, entitled *Hannah Arendt: Thinking, Judgment, Freedom* (Allen & Unwin: in press), is a regular contributor to the European journal *Argument*, has written for the *Encyclopedia of the Australian People* (ed. J. Jupp, Canberra, 1988), and has chapters in *Australian Welfare: Historical Sociology* (ed. R. Kennedy, Macmillan) and *Feminist Knowledge as Critique and Construct* (ed. S. Gunew, Methuen, 1988). With major training also in literature, psychology and history, and considerable stage experience in Europe (as an opera singer), she is a defender of interdisciplinary studies. She has a PhD from Monash University and has lectured widely on women's and migrants' issues. At present she is at work on a book on current western European feminism.

Ross Poole was educated at Sydney University, the Australian National University and Oxford University. He now lectures on Marxism and social and moral philosophy at Macquarie University, Sydney. He has published articles in radical and academic journals and collections, and is at present completing a book entitled *Morality and Modernity* to be published by Routledge.

Cate Poynton is lecturer in Communication Studies at the South Australian College of Advanced Education, Magill campus, where she is responsible for the Language Studies component of the BA (Comm. Studies) and also contributes to the Women's Studies Program. She has published on address forms and practices, the semiotics of social relations and language and gender. Her book, *Language and Gender: Making the Difference* (1985) has just been republished by Oxford University Press.

Maryse Rochecouste teaches in the Department of Romance Languages, the Centre for General and Comparative Literature and the Women's Studies Centre at Monash University. Her main research interests are in literary theory, semiotic theory, textual criticism, narrative, the nineteenth century, the hermeneutics of Zola's *Rougon-Macquart*, the semiotics of textual space and the 'Fall'. Her PhD dissertation was recently published by Georg Olms Verlag (Germany, 1988) under the title, *The Role of Parallel Catamorphic Systems in the Structures of Zola's 'Rougon-Macquart'*.

Lesley J. Rogers graduated in science from Adelaide University in 1964. She then spent some four years in the USA studying at the Graduate School at Harvard University and doing research at the New England Medical Centre Hospital. She obtained a PhD at Sussex University, UK, returning to Australia in 1972. In 1985 Sussex University conferred on her the degree of Doctor of Science, for outstanding research in the sciences. She has been active in feminism throughout the 1970s and 1980s, and has written articles on biology and behaviour from a feminist perspective. These have been published in *The Other Half: Women in Australian Society* and *Australian Women: Feminist Perspectives.*

Michelle Royer lectures on French feminist theory and literature in the School of French at New South Wales University. She has completed a PhD on the feminine in Margaret Duras' films. Her current research is on feminist film and literary criticism.

Terry Threadgold is associate professor in Early English Literature and Language at the University of Sydney. Her teaching and research is in systemic-functional linguistics, semiotics, performance studies, language in education, and language and gender. With Elizabeth Grosz, Gunther Kress and Michael Halliday she edited and introduced *Semiotics/Ideology/Language* (Sydney: SASSC, 1986). She has published widely in critical linguistics and social semiotic theory and analysis. She is at present completing two books *Genre: A Study in Power, Pedagogy and Polyphony* with Gunther Kress (for Polity Press) and *Feminist Poetics* (for RKP).

Susan Yell is a postgraduate and tutor in the Department of English, the University of Sydney. She teaches functional grammar, semiotics and performance studies. She is completing a PhD thesis on the analysis of conversation in prose fiction, focusing on notions of conflict and control (character/character and narrator/reader).

Preface

The chapters which now constitute this book were selected from a much larger group of what were originally produced as papers for a conference on the theme 'Feminine/Masculine and Representation'. The conference was intended to provide a multidisciplinary and sexed perspective on the still problematic sex/gender issue and the question of representation. It tried to provide a place and a motivation for men and women to work separately and together on the problems involved. The results were much less homogeneous and sometimes much less harmonious than their representation in the book might suggest.

The book inevitably involved a selection and a reduction of that heterogeneity. The lack of harmony, that is, the contradictions, the debates, the unsolved questions, even sometimes the contemporary confusions over terminologies and methodological frameworks, we hope we have not eradicated. They are important testimony to the currency and the immediacy of the debates and to their openness. We have hardly begun to ask the right questions, let alone answer them: that is one thing we hope this book will say.

The conference was sponsored by the Sydney Association for Studies in Society and Culture (SASSC) and held in Sydney in late 1986. Much of the material has been considerably reworked since then. Some of it has appeared in other places (Braidotti, in *Australian Feminist Studies* and Rochecouste, in her book *Parallel Catamorphic Systems in Zola's Rougon-Macquart* (1988)) in a somewhat different form, and some has been expanded and presented at other conferences (Jenny Ash's chapter was presented in something like its present form at the International

Summer Institute for Structuralist and Semiotic Studies, Vancouver 1989, Cate Poynton's at the same institute in 1988). We are grateful to all the authors who have been so willing to rewrite and reorganise their material for inclusion in the book and for permission to publish what has already appeared elsewhere.

Thanks are due too to all those who worked so tirelessly to make the original conference and thus now the book a success: Susan Elfert, Secretary of SASSC, and her band of postgraduate helpers from the Department of Early English Literature and Language, University of Sydney; Ian Reid, John Lechte, Paul Thibault, Cate Poynton, Jacqueline Rousseau-Dujardin and Jacques Trilling, Rosi Braidotti and Elizabeth Grosz for their many contributions; Anna Gibbs and Lesley Sterne for their participation, and the membership of SASSC for its continued and enthusiastic support of interdisciplinary events of this sort. Thanks are also due to the Vice-Chancellor, Professor John Ward, University of Sydney, for making funds available to help SASSC bring speakers from overseas and interstate.

We are grateful to the following for permission to reprint photographic and visual materials: Ministero per i Beniculturale e Ambientali, Firenze, Italy. Studio Vista, Cassell and Collins Publishers, London. Lund Humphreys, London.

We would like to thank Venetia Nelson for her constructive criticism and help and John Iremonger for his continued support of this and other projects like it.

Terry Threadgold and Anne Cranny-Francis

1 Introduction

Terry Threadgold

Reversing dichotomies and the semiotics of the Lie

It occurs to me that when we formulated the title of this book in 1986, when we reversed the dichotomy masculine/feminine, when we put the feminine in front, on top of the bar, we were suggesting that the masculine might be defined in terms of the feminine, instead of the usual phallocentric definition of the feminine always in terms of the masculine, the other, what she is not. We were trying to make the taken-for-granted nature of the usual dichotomy visible, legible.

We also did something counterproductive. We merely reversed the terms, leaving the dichotomy, the opposition, potentially intact: we did not necessarily redefine the two terms in their specificity and their difference, their autonomy. Nor did we suggest that there might be more than two terms to be considered, that this binarism might be a quite arbitrary division into two of what is actually a continuum. Such are the dangers of speaking, meaning, writing, *inside* phallocentrism. Phallocentrism, located in all our dominant malestream Western ways of thinking and talking about and making our world, is a discursive and representational construction of that world in binary terms such that one term is always regarded as the norm and highly valorised, while the other is defined only ever in relation to it and devalorised. Thus: masculine/feminine, rational/irrational, active/passive and so on.

1

If we start with one of the dichotomies which structure phallocentrism then we are always already in a double bind. We can either reverse it or try to neutralise its effects or insist that the two terms are independent. What we cannot do it seems is to free ourselves from its implications—in this case, that there are just two things, masculinity and femininity, and that they exist in some kind of relationship. Somehow we have to try to start somewhere else, to speak, mean and write *outside* these limitations on what *can* (is possible/is allowed to) be spoken, meant and written. That is one of the things that many of the contributors to this book are trying to do.

In constructing feminine/masculine as a reversal, however, we remained inside the relationship the dichotomy implies. And as well we told a lie . . . the kind of lie that representation always is. Representation—making something appear, to stand for something else, which exists—is real. But does it, is it? What we can say of representation we can also say of signs. 'Semiotics is concerned with everything that can be *taken* as a sign. A sign is everything that can be significantly taken as substituting for something else' (Eco, 1976:7). This something else does not actually have to exist and it does not have to exist in the way in which it is represented as existing. Representation is always a process of signification, of semiosis, of meaning-making, but, like the sign, representations (which in fact are signs) can be 'taken' as *referring* to something else, something 'real', outside signification, something which was not *made* but *is*. This is how a process of construction, of making meaning, comes to be interpreted as reference, referring to something that already exists. It is how representations come to be taken as realities. It is the very problem that Carole Pateman (1988) is struggling with when she argues for the need to understand how it is that slavery has come to be interpreted as freedom in Western civil and capitalist societies.

Semiotics aims to understand this thing that is called representation. This is why Eco (1976:7) defines semiotics as the 'discipline studying everything which can be used in order to lie'. The paradox of the 'lie' is that once structured it may be read as, and thus become, a new 'reality'. The construction of the world and the making of meaning go hand in hand.

It is important to realise that this talk of 'lies', and the whole knotty problem of the relationship between representation and what we think of as reality, is not the old marxist false-consciousness argument in a new guise. There is no sense of semiotics as a 'science' or master knowledge which can somehow get at the 'truth' 'behind' other people's lies. All representations, including semiotics itself, that is including theories and knowledges, are 'lies' in this sense of constructions, fictions. Some writers actually use the terms narrative or story to talk about representations. Thus Lyotard (1984) spoke of the great cultural narratives of marxism and psychoanalysis, Carolyn Steedman (1986) wrote of the 'stories' (that is, the other constructions) of women's lives that cannot be told within those narratives, and Carole Pateman analyses the 'stories' of the social contract that circulate in social and political theory. There is no single 'truth', only different constructions, different representations, some of which are read as 'fact', some as 'fiction', depending on the way they are functionally contextualised and by whom and in whose interests.

What we have is a world constructed in and through discourse, meaning and representation, and the people in that world are constructed in the same way. The semiotic and psychoanalytic and post-structuralist and now feminist story that rewrites the liberal humanist and capitalist narrative of individualism sees subjectivities, too, as a function of their discursive and bodily histories in a signifying network of meaning and representation. This means, among other things, that there is no way for those subjects ever to be outside that network as 'objective observers'. The 'knowing' subject of 'science' is no longer one of the characters in these new stories. In them subjectivities are always inside and sometimes struggling to be also outside the signifying processes and practices of/in which they speak.

That is a paradox about which Teresa de Lauretis has much more to say (1987:24–26), and there are many things in the above that require further definition and explanation. But these are the issues that this book and the voices to be heard within it are debating and constructing as they speak, for, to quote Eco again (1976:29) one cannot speak about the way people speak and mean without affecting, sometimes perpetuating and sometimes changing, the way they do it. The explanations will evolve as they, and I, attempt to grapple with the problems.

I want to carry on a little longer about this business of representation and reality. We need to talk more too, about this 'inside' and 'outside', this positioning of subjects who speak/write and hear/read. These are, it seems to me, some of the singly most difficult concepts for those who are 'outside' semiotic and post-structuralist debates to come to terms with. They are difficult because they run counter to all our commonsense knowledge on the subject, and often, as Tagg (1988) has shown with respect to Roland Barthes, counter to our most profound personal desires.

Let me return to the issue I was discussing above—that of making meanings and then taking the meanings one has made to be reality. When semioticians, post-structuralists, or feminists (and they have much in common with respect to these issues) declare that there are no 'facts', that there is no one single 'truth', no 'reality' that has not been constructed, the commonsense response tends to be in the order of 'stub your toe on that brick and you'll know about reality' or 'if you're poor and hungry you know what reality is'. And, as I will argue later, these responses are not so far removed from the theoretical responses that one finds in the 'hard' and even social sciences to the kinds of questions I am dealing with here. They are responses that take the form of constructing dichotomies, setting up oppositions, between theory or metalanguage and the 'real issues' of·politics and class, or between ideology (usually now in the sense of systems of knowledge or belief, but still related to consciousness) and 'real' structures like the economy, government and so on. These are realisations of oppositions that are still more funda-mental to phallocentric discourses such as fact/fiction, mind/ body, material/immaterial. There are many things happening here, but among these the continuing effects in the discourses of these sciences of the representation/reality problem and of the tendency for meaning-effects to be discounted as irrelevant are paramount.

The problem is that no one takes language, or rather semiosis, the processes by which meanings are *made* in a social system, seriously. This is hardly surprising. Our entire educational process, and the institutions of mainstream linguistics (see Poynton this volume) and philosophy continue to foster and perpetuate a view of language that is 'realist', 'referential' and 'malestream' (Pateman and Gross: 1986). It is a view of language that continues to argue, against all the evidence to the contrary (see Robyn Rowland 1988:chs 1, 2 for a discussion of similar persistences of malestream knowledges, in the face of all the evidence, in biology and science) that meanings inhere in words, that there is a 'true' meaning to be recovered from language, that language is a container for meanings which *it* transmits un-problematically from sender to receiver (and of course sender and receiver are universal, unsexed, ungendered, male?) Language 'refers' to a reality which pre-exists it. People take no part in all of this. Such are some of the dominant metaphors (Reddy: 1979). Little wonder that we think we ought to be simply able to 'say what we mean' or that we believe 'we know what we mean' or that we think we are 'in control' of the meaning process.

The issues are extremely complex and to some extent require a massive deconstruction of the whole malestream linguisitic edifice, something semiotics and post-structuralism and psycho-analysis have been doing for the last twenty years or so, but that is in some ways much more effectively done from *within* linguistics, as Poynton's chapter in this volume demonstrates. That whole long labour cannot be repeated in the space of this introduction, and it has to be said that the institutional edifice of malestream linguistics shows hardly a crack as a result of this concerted onslaught, but it is something that all of us who work with the questions and debates that centre around sex/gender and representation need to be familiar with. I have written at length about these questions elsewhere (Threadgold 1987a, 1987b, 1988a). Suffice to say for the moment that what is at issue here can be viewed metaphorically as a problem of labour and forgetfulness. Rossi-Landi (1973:6ff.) locates the problem in the product/process (or system/use) dichotomy which permeates product- or system-oriented work in the social sciences (and is in fact constructed in and through that work). Cate Poynton (this volume) gives an account of the effects that the product/system, process/use binarism has had in the construction of contemporary mainstream linguistics. Speaking subjects who labour to make meaning inevitably change the system as they work: once the meanings are made they are viewed as 'products' and the processes by which they were produced are forgotten. It is at that point that the 'product', which in this case we might characterise as the representations we have been talking about, 'takes on a sort of apparently autonomous, monstrous life of its own' (Rossi-Landi, 1973:62) and is capable of subordinating 'the capital constituted by the linguistic workers, the speakers, to itself, so that all individuals are, as it were, spoken by it'.

That is, what makes it hard for us to see that the truth-effects of signifying practices are lies, in the sense outlined above, is the fact that the labour of making meanings is forgotten. Meanings are made but they are also reified, 'used', 'consumed' and internalised (or resisted) by speaking subjects. This happens in ways that contribute to the social production of consciousness, and of self-consciousness, and of those commonsense ways of knowing and believing and experiencing that are the very stuff of the transparency and inevitability of representations. Even Roland Barthes, who spent most of his writerly life deconstructing them, was not immune to these truth-effects, as John Tagg has shown (1988:1–3). The example is helpful in many ways, not least because it involves the question of desire. Tagg explains how in *Camera Lucida* Barthes 'leaves us with a poignant reassertion of the realist position', asserting a retrospective photographic realism—the camera is an instrument of evidence—in the face of his mother's death, and his search for a 'just image' of her (Barthes 1981:70). For Barthes what the photograph asserts is the undeniable truth that 'the thing has been there'. It may be a reality one can no longer touch, but it is a reality that once existed (Barthes 1981:76,87). With the personal and very private grief and desire this anecdote expresses we will none of us have any difficulty in identifying. But it raises again all the questions of semiosis, the lie, signification and representation that I discussed above in relation to language. Indeed what was said about language *as semiosis* needs to be said of all semiotic processes in whatever material medium they may be realised.

Thus, to quote Tagg again: 'I need not point out, of course, that the existence of a photograph is no guarantee of a corresponding pre-photographic existent', and later: 'we have to see that *every* photograph is the result of specific, and, in every sense, significant distortions which render its relation to any prior reality deeply problematic and raise the question of the determining level of the material apparatus and the social practices within which photography takes place' (p.2) and finally: 'The indexical nature of the photograph—the causative link between the pre-photographic referent and the sign—is therefore highly complex, irreversible, and can guarantee nothing at the level of meaning. What makes the link is a discriminatory technical, cultural and historical process in which particular optical and chemical devices are set to work to organise experience and desire and to produce a new reality—the paper image which, through yet further processes, may become meaningful in all sorts of ways.' (p.3).

It is in this sense that semioticians and others argue that there is no reality unmediated by semiotic processes. The photograph, as produced (by a labouring subject of semiosis), is not the simple reflection of a prior reality, but a new and specific reality, a two-dimensional, positive paper print from a granular, chemical discolouration on a translucent negative. This new reality is capable of becoming meaningful in certain contexts and has real effects (viz. Barthes) but because of its history as process it cannot refer to a pre-photographic reality as truth. The photograph 'cannot deliver what Barthes desires . . . the repossession of his mother's body' (Tagg, 1988:3).

As for photography, so for language and all other forms of representation . . .

To return to Rossi-Landi's monster, it is not, as Rosalind Coward (1984) explained some time ago, a question of simply seeing women (or indeed men) as being attacked, 'oppressed' from outside, as it were, by practices of representation. The problem is deeper than that. It is the problem that Wendy Hollway (1984:227ff.) was attempting to deal with, the problem of the investments that subjects have in complying with practices of representation, or, as Coward asks, 'what is the lure in the heart of these discourses which causes us to take up and inhabit the female position?' (1985:29). Of course, we do not have to, we can resist, but we can never quite escape the phallocentric libidinal economy of discursive and representational practices within which our sexed identities, our subjectivities, have been and go on being constructed. As Teresa de Lauretis argues (1987:10) the subject of feminism, and we could say also the subject of femmeninism (a term used by Kamuf, 1987 to describe the role of men in feminism), is a theoretical construct whose definition is in progress, inside and outside the phallocentric ideology of gender: and so, (I can only speak as woman) we continue to be cast as woman, we persist with that imaginary relation, even as we know we are not that.

When we constructed this book as a discussion of the issues raised above, and reduced in the process the heterogeneity of the voices of the original conference at which these questions were discussed, we were operating under very specific institutional, economic and ideological constraints. That is, our making of meaning, in and through the construction of this book, was not at all separate from institutional and power relations or from the truth-effects of representation.

We selected materials that enabled, or would enable, the kind of breadth and depth of approach that we ourselves had been looking for in our own teaching and research on the social semiotics of gender and representation. We have therefore included work on the construction and deconstruction and reconstruction of the masculine/feminine dichotomy in visual (Ash, Kaplan and Rogers, Yell), performance (Kaplan and Rogers,

Yell), filmic (Royer) and televisual (Cranny-Francis and Palmer Gillard) and bodily (Grosz, Ash, Yell) as well as verbal media, and we have deliberately tried to bridge and problematise the institutionalised high/popular culture (Ash, Rochecouste, Cranny-Francis and Palmer Gillard, Yell), canonised/non-canonised (Blain, Hurley, Royer), and science/humanism (Kaplan and Rogers) boundaries and the disciplinary/interdisciplinary, theory/application difference by including work on the texts of philosophy (Braidotti, Poole, Grosz), linguistics (Poynton) literature (Ash, Rochecouste, Blain, Hurley, Yell) and drama (Kaplan and Rogers, Yell) as well as those of other domains like soap opera (Cranny-Francis and Palmer Gillard), feminist film (Royer), and the theatrical rehearsal (Yell), work that eludes or exceeds the disciplines of philosophy, literary criticism, English, biology or linguistics, but which in its very *inter*-disciplinarity, begins to construct new and specific generic boundaries.

Thus there is a discernible difference between the kinds of texts produced by the three post-structuralist, feminist/femmeninist, and/or semiotician, and/or psychoanalytic philosophers (Braidotti, Poole, Grosz), the feminist literary critic (Blain), the post-structuralist femmeninist (Hurley), the structuralist semiotician (Rochecouste), the post-structuralist/linguistic and post-structuralist/psychoanalytic semioticians (Yell, Ash), the French feminist semiotician (Royer) and the feminist linguist (Poynton) and the neurophysiologist/sociologist (Kaplan and Rogers). There are also differences between the texts of the men and women in this volume, even within the totally inadequate categorisations that I have deliberately left inadequate and open above. Poole's text is not like that of Braidotti and Grosz, although there are some similarities. His text is not like Hurley's which to some extent exhibits a 'feminisation' that is becoming typical of certain kinds of post-structuralist writing about literature and which Braidotti (this volume) also locates in the work of certain deconstructionist male philosphers.

There are at least two points to be made here.

First there is no way of arguing that theories or genres, kinds of writing and the discourse and stories that they involve, are universally and essentially masculine or feminine, or the property of either men or women. Men and women may have particular kinds of investments in positioning themselves within any genre, discourse or story, although some positions are more usual or more difficult, or more readily allowed, than others

(Hollway, 1984; Kress and Threadgold, 1988b). At the same time it is important to understand that being feminine or masculine in a male body and being feminine or masculine in a female body (Gatens, 1983), and thus writing, or being, in a feminine or masculine way *as* man or *as* woman, are not the same thing. They are not the same because they do not mean the same, either for the writer or for the reader, or for the subject and the 'others' who perceive him/her. Masculinity and femininity are valued quite differently in these bodily and sexed contexts. Thus, for example, Derrida's conception of/evaluation of what he is doing and Braidotti's (this volume) are worlds apart.

These very complex questions about the dialectic or institutional effects, subjective investments, social practices, sexuality and signifying processes in and through which masculine and ''feminine subjectivities are constructed and constrained, allowed freedoms and limited, able to mean differently and silenced, are discussed and analysed in a number of heterogeneous contexts in the chapters of this book but perhaps most explicitly and in some of their most complex forms in the work of Poole, Ash, Blain, Hurley, Palmer Gillard and Cranny-Francis and Yell. The complicity of men *and* women in these processes and the relations of sexual domination which are the linchpin of this complicity are most strongly foregrounded in the work of Ash, Blain and Yell.

The really very different (if not unrelated) issues of discursive positioning and sexuality are frequently confused in feminist arguments about women and language (Spender, 1980 is an extreme example; see Cameron, 1985; Poynton, 1985; Threadgold, 1988a) and the confusion is compounded by misunderstandings or essentialist extensions of the psychoanalytically based arguments of Kristeva (1984) and Irigaray (1985a,b) which would celebrate a 'feminine' language, a woman's language, constituted of all that is opposite to 'masculinity' in phallocentric discourse (Moi, 1985: Part II). Royer's chapter in this book deals with the effects of such a feminist, filmic 'writing' in the work of Marguerite Duras. This is the reversal syndrome with which we began, and this feminist strategy remains entangled in the phallocentric web with which it begins even as it struggles to make that web visible. Woman, women, silenced, disembodied, unable to speak except in intonations. We have to ask—is that how we are?—or is that how we have been made?

The second point to be made in relation to the inter- or transdisciplinarity of the chapters in this book is the one about constructing new generic boundaries (fences, obstacles for readers to jump). What my 'categories' show is something of the intertextuality and discursive incompatibilities that may result from interdisciplinarity and which, quite simply, make it hard for people to talk to one another. It is often hard for the chapters in this book to speak together. It is much harder for those who remain within older generic and disciplinary frameworks, and who do not share the assumptions about the nature of representation, language and meaning that are shared in this book, to speak with us.

There is a need for dialogue, but the questions of language, meaning, representation and the issue of difference, among men and among women, and between men and women, the questions raised by sexed bodies and by the construction of meaning, knowledges and subjectivity in and through those sexed bodies, makes the dialogue, even as the new genres evolve, ever less straightforward. There are only two men in our book, as authors. There are many more in the form of male theory, knowledges, ideologies. There is only one chapter, written by two women, that speaks from the world of science. Why is it that a theme like this should attract so little attention from women or men in the sciences? Are they/the sciences not subject to representation, not implicated in the construction of sex and gender? That too is a question that must be aired.

Our construction of this book/our representation of what was a conference depends on the following beliefs. Sexual difference and masculinity and femininity are not unrelated, but neither can be understood outside the field of representations/significations in which they are constructed and which they construct. Representation *is* construction. The whole of Art and Literature and High Culture is the writing/making of that construction. But the construction of sex/gender goes on, not only in the family, the school, the institutions of the law, religion, politics and labour, through all the many and diverse forms of cultural production, but in the academy, in our theories, in and through our attempts to deconstruct it, to make it visible, to subvert representation, to show that the apparent image is not a reflection of the real, but a construction of it. Even as various femininisms and femmeninisms (Kamuf, 1987:78) seek to deconstruct the sex/gender question and subvert the power of representation and desire (Coward, 1985:25), the process of construction goes on ... That too we cannot not address ... and who is this 'we' in whose voice 'I' seem to speak? (Adrienne Rich, 1985:21). That will do for a beginning ...

Speaking together: intertextuality, discursive conflict and representation.

I hope that what I have said so far may begin to answer the question *why* a book on feminine/masculine and representation. It may also begin to explain why it is that this woman cannot just say what she means, why she has to make it all seem so complicated, so difficult, why she uses that 'jargon' when 'ordinary' words would have done just as well. It might explain the writing strategies of many of the contributors to this book, who also go to great lengths to 'use' 'theoretical frameworks' to 'state the obvious'. Or do they?

What we are using is of course a metalanguage, or several and there are reasons for that too (Threadgold, 1989 forthcoming). If all representations in 'ordinary' language are already constructions then we cannot use 'ordinary' language to talk about 'ordinary' language without forever remaining enmeshed in the contradictions and ambiguities of our own constructions and our own constructedness. For we are also subjects in language, in semiosis. We are, in a sense, what we *can* mean (in both senses of *can*, 'are able to'/'are allowed to') Metalanguages are also constructions but they are constructive of *other* realities and that is their critical function in relation to the complexities of the lived realities in which so-called ordinary language is always implicated (Morris, 1988:34).

There would be far less confusion in feminist work on discourse and language if this were properly understood (Threadgold, 1988a). There would also be far less linguistically naive fear of 'male' metalanguage, and of theory (Toril Moi, 1985). These questions are discussed very cogently in Pateman and Gross (1986) and in Caine et al. (1988), where it is made clear that the issue confronting any attempt to undo the masculine/feminine dichotomy, as a symbol of patriarchal and phallocentric ways of knowing, depends precisely on 'not turning our backs' on contemporary theory, methodology, and the classics of political and social theory, and one might say of linguistic and critical theory as well, but rather on learning how to dismantle and transform this work so as to produce new knowledges, new ways of meaning. Malestream knowledges can be subverted (Pateman and Gross, 1986:4). There is no need to make the whole wheel again each time. This seems to me to be what is wrong with Irigaray's current work on language. The rejection of all linguistic and semiotic frameworks as male metalanguage, with the

11

attendant charges of master-theories and mastery, considerably weakens her own enterprise (Irigaray 1985c).

The problem is a complex one and needs constant rethinking. Maryse Rochecouste (this volume) uses a Greimassien framework to analyse the detailed linguistic realisations of what she calls a patriarchal discourse on femininity, showing how that discourse is perpetuated and constructed as a representation of femininity (this is what women are) in the novels of Zola. Yet the Greimassien theory she makes operate in the service of this deconstruction is founded, precisely, on the phallocentric dichotomies Rochecouste seeks to make visible. Its foundation is the famous semiotic square which Christine Brooke-Rose had such fun deconstructing (1985:9–20). Now Rochecouste, unlike many other writers in this book (Braidotti, Grosz, Ash, Cranny-Francis, Yell, Poynton), does not actually mix theories or tamper with the theory. She uses it, intact, to read with. If male theory really bites, ought she not to have been appropriated by it, so that she could not have spoken except in its terms? Or is that what she is doing? And is that why her feminist reading works?

These kinds of questions make me think that it can be argued, although this is to anticipate a little, that to speak a metalanguage (male or not) as a sexed male or female feminine and feminist (femmeninist) subject, and embodied subject, constructed in and through a historically specific network of signifying practices, social and power relationships and institutional frameworks, can never be to mean, in the same way as that same metalanguage will mean, spoken in the context of malestream knowledges, by a sexed male or female masculine non-feminist subject, constructed in an equally specific, but different network of significations. Essentialist you say, or simply incomprehensible? Think about it . . .

But you see what the problem is. Given the extraordinarily narrow dissemination of linguistic and semiotic concepts, and the equally extraordinary myths and fears that surround their use, to use them at all is to make oneself very hard indeed to understand. But I must insist on the need for the terminology and identify myself here with what Meaghan Morris has dubbed 'the humourless feminist' (1987:176):

> Yet she's really a helpful soul. For humourless
> feminism, unlike philosophy's 'dark unlegislatible'
> femininity, insists on metalanguage: not
> metalanguage understood as a policing of discourse, or

as a primacy accorded to one discourse (say,
philosophy, or 'theory' in literary terms) over others, but
more simply as a critical shift in relation to a given
discourse, in a particular place and time. Such shifts
enable, if they cannot alone achieve, the re-statement,
re-working, re-mapping of the terms of our social
existence. Without the Humourless Feminist's move—
clumsy, indispensible, insufficient—the spriteliest
feminist politics can find itself rapidly blocked.

What is at issue is a need for dialogue, a need for translation—
that need to which my earlier questions about how we are to
speak together was already pointing. But again, before we can
speak together, or even begin to understand why our dialogue is
blocked, there are a number of basic issues about language and
semiotics, about all the 'languages' (the organisation of homes,
cities, transport systems, of sexed bodies and voices, writings) of
daily and institutional life and the ways in which they work, that
have first to be understood. These are generally not understood,
not even to the point of being regarded as problems. This, as I
have said already, is hardly surprising, when language about
language, language about meaning, and discussions of the ways
in which meanings (and therefore 'facts', 'realities' and 'knowledge') are made, not given, are so consistently and systematically eschewed in all our pedagogical institutions.

Let me look for a minute at some of the real effects of these
questions in the reading I have been doing in preparation for
writing this introduction. As I reread the chapters of this book I
realised that almost all of the writers worked comfortably with
the various metalanguages that are available for grappling with
the questions of languages and semiosis, and thus with the
problem of representation. Some writers (Braidotti, Grosz,
Poynton and Kaplan and Rogers) effect quite significant shifts in
the metalanguages themselves, demonstrating my point above
about the phallocentric metalinguistic effects. Yet in reading
around the chapters, outside the book, in a good deal of very
recent feminist writing in Australia and elsewhere, I still find
very much in evidence the strange notion that theory, and by
implication metalanguage, are in some sense quite separate from,
a kind of intellectual game in relation to, 'real' political action.

How then I wonder are the chapters of this book, chapters
which as I have now ordered them in my reading, and for readers,
the co-texts which now come together to articulate something of

an argument about the construction of men and women in and through phallocentric representations—how are they to be understood and read? How are they to dialogue with their intertexts, these other feminist texts which see themselves as somehow 'real', 'political' and straightforward in relation to the 'theory', 'intellectual elitism' and difficulty of what is in this book? What kind of thing are they? Sometimes they look like philosophy, or literary criticism, or linguistics. They talk about things like semiotics, post-structuralism, psychoanalysis, deconstruction and feminism. What are they?

Riddles for readers. The problem of the name. First lesson in semiotics, or post-structuralism or linguistics, if you like. In order to know how to read you have to have been taught, trained in the reading of it. Once you know its rules, you can accept or reject them. Without them you are all at sea. Michael Hurley (this volume) gives a more detailed account of how this works, and his own reading of the institutions of literature and of some texts which they exclude provides explicit, theorised examples of resistant readings. But in a sense there is not a chapter in the book which does not illustrate the power of genre, of generic transformation, and the business of compliance and resistance.

So, you've understood about genre. What you need is a name.

But although you think it is the *name* you need—'this is a book of interdisciplinary x's'—actually as yet there is no name that will subsume and reify them all, turn them linguistically and semiotically into *things*, which you will then know how to handle, use, and make reflect some pre-given reality—the *name* alone is not enough. For contrary to common belief and common sense, language and meaning does not work through names, words, alone, and this despite the ideology realised in the institution of the dictionary, and in reform of sexist language, which beavers away at changing words when it is the whole social system that needs deconstructing.

Language or any other semiotic system is not a set of forms with meanings attached. It is a set of complex, evolved, evolving and open semiotic systems where meanings are realised in and constructed through complex material media, in contradictory and overlapping institutional sites, by sexually, socially and historically positioned speaking subjects, who are subjected to and constructed in and through signifying networks of power and desire.

That is why one cannot simply define one's terms.

To understand what semiotics is (notice the way the language, the grammar of subject, predicate and nominalisation, reifies the term) or what any metalanguage or theory is on about, one has to have been part of its evolution, or be prepared to trace that evolution, by reading, talking, exchanging meanings in dialogue, intertextually, interpersonally, understanding the institutions within which the discourses and genres peculiar to this theory operate, living those institutions and their networks of power and desire, so that one's own subjectivity is partly constructed in these signifying practices.

That is of course the risk and the paradox—and it is where the truth-effects of representation always lie: the point at which the subject who has laboured to understand, to make sense, a subject in process, becomes a finished product, and confuses the semiotic products of her labours, the meanings and the self she has constructed, with some kind of natural, unmade, pre-given reality.

The finished feminist, interdisciplinary, post-structuralist subject who confidently speaks of women's oppression and patriarchy as if the words, the names, constituted some universal reality 'which we all understand', in need of no further explanation or argument, and the finished social science feminist subject, who wants to know what these names have to do with her lived experience as a heterosexual, feminist intellectual—both are caught up in this endless and contradictory semiotic business of being and becoming, of making meaning and knowing, of reality and representation.

But this is the signifying order within which we have to work and it explains, among other things, why Ann Curthoys (1988) writing as a historian, in a book which is full of useful insights, reads the work of radical feminist theory as being uninterested in sociology or history. The need for dialogue, and translation, is very obvious here. Let me quote:

> *Mia Campioni and Elizabeth Gross have argued in an Australian context for a French-influenced radical feminism. They called for a recognition of 'the role of the body in constituting consciousness'. Women's oppression, they suggest, can only be understood 'in terms of the existence of sexually differentiated bodies . . . The point is that we are not disembodied subjects, consciousness distinct from bodies'. Yet Campioni and Gross are not very interested in asking sociological or historical questions, with the result that it*

> *is difficult to apply their perspectives to answering*
> *questions like 'why is it women who mother?'. (Curthoys,*
> *1988:133)*

I would have thought that the question of sexed bodies and of the socially constructed consciousness of the body that might result from the positioning of subjects within a phallocentric order, which is what Campioni and Gross are arguing here, might have *everything* to do with why women mother. Campioni and Gross are absolutely explicit, in their critique of the marxist 'rational subject' that this subject is 'unhinged from lived experience and from the particularity of a position in the world', and in their critique of the related marxist notions of truth and language, that the singular reality which this imposes is incapable of dealing with 'the struggles of women, blacks, gays or youth' (Campioni and Gross, 1983:123,125). This, and the very project of a critique of Marxism's 'insidious politics of representation' (p.119), does not read to me like a lack of interest in sociology or history.

In fact it sounds very like the argument that I read in Curthoys' own book, and indeed in the paragraph which follows the quote above (1988:133). Curthoys is very concerned with the question of why it is women who mother, which she sees as crucial to understanding many other aspects of women's position in capitalist societies. So, after a fascinating analysis of why patriarchy cannot be explained in terms of capitalism, or seen as coterminous with it, a critique of the widespread use of the terms patriarchy and oppression without adequate contextualisation or analysis in terms of class, age, ethnic and gender differences, and an attempt to grapple with the apparent universality of the woman-childcare problem, Curthoys returns to biology and the body: 'When confronted with such a universal pattern, the only basis for universality does indeed lie in the body, in the fact that human reproduction relies on a biological duality between male and female. The only commonality we can be sure of, theorically, is that in all societies this biological duality is given social meaning, is constituted as a basis for sexual division.' (1988:133).

In some ways Curthoys is here arguing from a position that is remarkably close to both Campioni and Gross, and to Carole Pateman (1988) and Poynton (this volume). It is Pateman who puts the sexual back into the *social* contract, refusing the elision of the private and the personal from the public world. [1] Working within and outside social and political theory, in the gaps where it is silent, she 'recovers the story of the sexual contract', showing how patriarchy and oppression have their basis in the sexual contract between sexed men and women, which preceded historically, but continues to have discursive and semiotic effects on the construction of capitalist institutions. The job she does in social and political theory is parallel to the one performed by Cate Poynton (this volume) in recovering the story of the grammar of the interpersonal in the exclusions and the silences of malestream linguistics. The exclusion of the interpersonal is of course complicit with the exclusion and denial of sexuality. Both women's work is complex, fully cognisant of the implications of the operations of language, discourse, and semiosis in the processes of representation. Pateman's, in addition, provides an instance of that proper analysis and deconstruction of 'patriarchy' which Curthoys' book demands.

With all this intertextual agreement then, and apparent evidence to the contrary (neither Pateman nor Poynton is ignorant of or uninterested in French theory; both are concerned with social and historical questions), why does Curthoys think that radical French theory, in the bodies of Campioni and Gross, or in their disembodied textual voices, is not interested in sociology or history and cannot be 'applied' to 'real' questions? It is, I think again, a question of language, or of metalanguage, and of the failure to recognise the way metalanguages can become institutionally naturalised to the point where one does not any longer know that one is speaking them, or being spoken by them, to recall Rossi-Landi's formulation of the problem.

The problem is recognised in Curthoys' and Pateman's books in relation to feminist theory and the reified use of the terms of patriarchy and oppression, terms that have been constructed within the discourses of feminism (Millett, 1977), and then taken for granted as *referring* to some reality outside the process of that contextualised construction. It is recognised in Gross (1986:190ff.) and Grosz (in Caine et al. 1988:98ff.) in the careful attempt to define sexism, patriarchy, phallocentrism and various feminisms and their difference from 'feminist in(ter)ventions' which 'aim at establishing an openly sexualised body of knowledges' that would enable 'a dialogue between knowledges now accepted as masculine, and the 'alien' or 'other' voice of women', and open up the question of the '*ethics of sexual exchange* in knowledges' (Grosz, 1988:103). The latter is something Rosi Braidotti (this volume) is also concerned with.

It is a problem however that is frequently not recognised in the dialogues that go on between feminist 'theorists' and women in the social or hard sciences who see their feminism as somehow not 'theoretical'. It is this difference that Curthoys' comment

17

calls attention to. In some ways, she and Campioni and Gross are saying the same thing; in others, they are saying very different things. Curthoys will never see that while she believes that her language is 'ordinary' and theirs 'arcane' (this is my inter-pretation), or while she believes that 'ordinary' language *can* effect that shift in relation to a discourse, that reworking of our experience, which Meaghan Morris speaks of, and which the metalanguage Campioni and Gross use is trying to effect.

Why should terms like *ideology, biological essentialism, class barriers, segregation of the labour market, capitalism* be regarded as self-explanatory? Why should there be an apparent and taken-for-granted separation between ideological and economic and political effects: 'The courts' wage-setting criteria were not primarily ideological, but economic and political' (Curthoys, 1988:123). Why should terms like *semiotic, discourse, textuality, subjectivity* have the status of arcane mysteries? The following is typical of many reactions: 'There have been a few delightful moments, during my desultory and decidedly non-expert read-ings in semiotics, when the subject made me laugh out loud instead of terrorizing or, same thing perhaps, boring me stupid' (Brooke-Rose, 1985:9). These things are not unrelated to the blocking of dialogue. And the answers are quite simple once one understands that this is a semiotic problem.

Words, terms, only have meanings in relation to the enor-mously complex discursive and semiotic systems (including the sexed bodies and subjectivities) within which and through which they are functional. For a materialist historian, who is not a semiotician, ideology is consciousness, the mind, beliefs, separated from the material, real institutions of economics and politics (mind/body perhaps? theory/reality?). There are frag-ments here of a phallocentric discourse, of the effects of a male construction of knowledge which would always separate con-sciousness and material reality. For a semiotician, and/or a radical feminist philosopher, economics and politics are con-structed in and through discursive and semiotic processes and as such they *are* ideology (not 'false consciousness', but constructed systems of meanings). There can be no separation between them, anymore than there can be a separation between mind and body or theory and reality. So there are then real semiotic differences in the way these women construct the world.

These differences are, at this level, discursive differences, differences related to the circulation and specification of dis-courses, and to the positioning and construction of subjects in a semiotic order. Language about language or semiosis, if it is of the post-structuralist, deconstructive or psychoanalytic kind, is arcane and mysterious because it is rarely ever heard, read or spoken. The terminologies of the discourses of politics, government, sociology, psychology, history, anthropology, even biology and science are, on the other hand, a regular part of everyday life. They circulate in textbooks in the school system, in newspapers, on television, in science fiction, in the documents produced by the bureaucracies with which we all deal daily, in our everyday talk and conversation, to name but a few of the sites and institutions which privilege and support, and continually reconstruct and change, this hegemony of knowledges.

What were once technical 'jargons', metalanguages, have made the transition from theory into the transparent world of the ordinary, the everyday. We forget that these too are constructions, of the world, and of ourselves: and this forgetfulness has 'real' effects in the intertextual arguments I have been deconstructing. It makes extremely difficult a dialogue between women, let alone a dialogue between men and women.

Our attempts to speak together are still enmeshed in a phallocentric order of discourse and representation: and that order, if it is to exist, has to eschew the knowledge of language and semiosis which would enable us to disentangle ourselves from phallocentric constructions or to see the need for autonomy and difference, as articulated by Grosz (1988:103). The very existence of a phallocentric order of discourse and representation depends on a purely representational or referential view of language (Poynton, this volume), a view which sees language as a passive conduit for mental processes and pregiven realities, and denies the dynamic aspects of the interaction between speaking subjects and discursive and representational practices. Only such a realist, individualist view of language can support the conceptual, rationalist basis of phallocentric theory-construction, with its commitment to objectivity and truth, to 'scientific' methods, to the separation of the subjects who know from the things that are known, and to the system of binary oppositions which defines humanity in male or masculine terms (see Grosz, 1988 for a much more detailed account of these questions).

Now the question of binary oppositions and representation was where we began and is indeed central to the story that this book might construct for a reader. If the implications of the masculine/feminine dichotomy are that the feminine has always been constructed in terms of the masculine in phallocentric representations, and that the masculine has been constructed as sexually neutral, universal, and if the implications of that, less often discussed, are that the masculine side of the dichotomy thus also avoids the need to define its own specificity, the specificity of the male body, male subjectivity (Grosz, 1988:97), then it would seem to be very important for men and women to begin to understand why and how that has come about. One way to do this would be to do some really specific and detailed work on the nature of representations, on the details of the realisations of this phallocentric order of discourse, or its transformations and subversions (viz. feminine/masculine) in specific cultural products/processes, under specific historical and social conditions.

There is a good deal of support for, and recognition for the need of, such a critical social semiotic form of cultural analysis (Morris, 1988; Tagg, 1988; Curthoys, 1988:151; Weedon 1987:151; Pateman and Gross, 1986; Keller, 1985), but in fact there is often a great absence where this work should be. This is so particularly in the area of detailed linguistic, discursive and semiotic analysis of the kind that might point to the intricacies of the interrelationships between sex and gender, subjectivity and signification, or discuss the historical relations between representation and subjection, or the discursive and semiotic and institutional complexities of social stasis and social change—and so on. This is not to deny the value of the enormous amount of work that has been done (for example, Pateman, 1988: Schaffer, 1988; Seidel, 1988; Birch and O'Toole, 1988; de Lauretis, 1986, 1987; Diaz-Diocaretz and Zavala, 1985; Coward, 1984; Warner 1985, 1987; Irigaray, 1985a,b,c, to name only a few) but to argue for the need for a great deal more work of this kind.

It is to argue too for a rethinking of the effects of the deconstruction of malestream linguistics by post-structuralism and semiotics. Realist theories of language may need to be deconstructed, even discarded, but that does not mean that we can stop thinking about language, stop trying to make sense of its functions and uses, stop trying to rework, rethink both the real and constructive processes in which language and other semiotic systems participate. There are ways of theorising language and semiosis which are not malestream, even if formulated originally by men (Threadgold, 1987a and 1989 forthcoming; Poynton, 1985, 1988, this volume; Henriques et al., 1984) ways that would fit most of the characteristics of feminist knowledges outlined by Grosz (1986:190ff.; 1988:92ff.)

These are the potential tools for a kind of feminist or sex/gender-conscious work on discourse and representation that feminism and semiotic/post-structuralist analysis on the whole have not yet produced very often. And when I say 'tools' here I do not mean a return to the language of the malestream discourse of 'theory' and its 'application'. I do not mean positioning ourselves as the dutiful daughter in relation to 'master knowledges', and thus, as is so often the case, again making our own work invisible, silencing our own voices (Gatens, 1986:21). I mean to engage in the active deconstruction of those master knowledges in the very process of trying to make them work/labour in the interests of a sex/gender-conscious cultural analysis, so that the process of analysis itself becomes the process of the construction of those in(ter)ventionist theories and knowledges of which Elizabeth Grosz and others speak.

There are many examples of the ways in which attempts to analyse the question of masculine/feminine and representation have fallen short of this aim, simply by failing to recognise and account for their own inevitable positioning inside that phallocentric discursive and signifying order where theory, albeit refused or unidentified, circulates. Chris Weedon (1987:152–56) and Susan Sheridan (1988a, 1988b) present a cogent case for the limitations of much feminist work within the literary institution (Showalter, 1977, 1986; Gilbert and Gubar, 1979) which in seeking to find and valorise representations of women's experience in literature, or in seeking to recover and valorise women's writing, without theorising the construction of gender or subjectivity, or indeed the reading and writing processes, in either post-structuralist or psychoanalytic terms (they are not much concerned with linguistics), simply reproduce the commitment to a theory of the transparency of language and the fixity of subjectivity that is characteristic of much malestream literary criticism.

These are the kinds of problems that make an analysis of representation itself, as an issue, as a signifying and social process, so crucial. There is a world of difference between realist, experience-based accounts of images of women, in literature, art, or film, and an understanding of the way in which those images, and those who produce them, as writers or readers, participate in the signifying and discursive networks of power, desire and representation which actually construct and constitute cultures and social systems.

The problem is even more acute in regimes of knowledge like science or social science, regimes which are constituted by these very representational processes themselves as 'factual', 'truth'-based, mathematically or statistically verifiable. Here, it is hard to come by even the recognition (common in literature because of its construction as fiction) that the stuff of the science is an 'image', which with all its reflectionist connotations of a reality 'out there' which the image truthfully represents, rather than constructing, is at least one step forward from a position which thinks its constructions *are* really itself.

Despite the excellent accounts of these questions in feminist critiques of science (Keller, 1985; Grosz and de Lepervanche, 1988), they remain everyday problems with which we have constantly to deal. The debate between Curthoys and Campioni and Grosz which I discussed (or constructed) above is one kind of 'real' effect that results from our entanglement in representation, our having to speak in the languages, the discourses that we are, even while trying to say other than what they say. It takes other forms institutionally when in discussions of curricula for Women's Studies programs we find women from the social sciences arguing for the 'real' stuff of class and history and politics over what is seen as theory, a course on representation. Is such a course really necessary as a core course they ask . . . We do not escape the truth-effects of representation so easily. We do not emerge unscathed from the patriarchal structures we inhabit; we cannot so readily deconstruct subjectivity discursively produced within a phallocentric order. We should all remember this.

There is a need then for more and other kinds of feminist work, and femmeninist work, on these questions and there is a need for dialogue between and among these positions and for that dialogue to be informed by the kind of understanding of language, signifying practices, discourse and representation and subjectivity that Weedon would call post-structuralism and I called above a critical social semiotic form of cultural analysis (perhaps giving a name to the interdisciplinary x's in this book). One of the interesting aspects of these contributions is that in analysing the way in which the masculine/feminine dichotomy is realised in phallocentric discourse in many media they also often demonstrate the existence of alternative non-binary discursive constructions of the continuum which phallocentrism so arbitrarily divides into two (Braidotti, Grosz, Blain, Hurley, Kaplan and Rogers). More importantly, they are often able to show how patriarchy and the phallocentric network of signifiying practices which it supports manages to elide/exclude/marginalise or silence these alternative discourses and representations which would question and unsettle its own constructions. It is not that we cannot speak, that language is a straitjacket, it is that we are not allowed to speak, and that if we do anyway, what we say is not recognisable to those who read and listen from a position inside the phallocentric representational networks of patriarchy. That is the dialogue and the co-textual and intertextual story that this book, through its many different voices, might construct for the reader who is trained to read it thus or who is ready to listen in new ways.

Sex/gender, feminine/masculine and the body

Why should it be though that a book in which the focus would appear to be the *social, discursive* construction of masculinity and femininity should also have a great deal to say about sex and the body (Braidotti, Grosz, Ash, Rochecouste, Royer, Hurley, Yell, Kaplan and Rogers)? The return of the repressed perhaps?

Surely, in feminism particularly, we have to keep the biology of sex and bodies separate from the social construction of masculinity and femininity, from what has become identified with 'gender' and defined as a social or semiotic construct, not a biological given? Why should this book be so concerned with the discursive construction of bodies and with sexual difference, with sex as a semiotic construct (Grosz, Ash, Blain, Hurley)? Why should there be a certain insistence on the body as a site for the making of meanings (Grosz, Ash, Hurley, Yell)? Why is the strict separation of embodied biological sex (what characterises and differentiates bodies) and socially constructed gender— disembodied (since if masculinity and femininity are social constructs they may attach themselves to, be located in, any kind of sexed body)—suddenly being questioned? What has the sexed body got to do with representation? Why is there a certain slippage, within and among the chapters in this book, between the pairs of terms masculine and feminine, male and female, men and women, sex and gender?

The answers to these questions are not simple. Like the questions raised in the last section of this introduction they have to do with binary oppositions and with the kind of world, the kind of knowledges, those oppositions construct in and through the phallocentric discourses and representations that, in turn, support and maintain the institutions of patriarchy. Unsettling those oppositions is part of the business of dismantling and transforming those knowledges and institutions. It is also part of the business of making new meanings and knowledges, but precisely because new meanings always have to speak in the languages of the old, both inside and outside them, it is a difficult enterprise and one whose ramifications and implications can be extremely hard to understand (Threadgold, 1989 forthcoming).

The argument for looking again at the sex/gender dichotomy which feminism itself has helped to construct is a very complex one. It is complex both because of the contradictions in phallocentric discourses which produce reversals and arguments within feminist debate, and also because it depends fundamentally on an understanding of the metalinguistic metaphoricity of, and the translations that have to be made between, a number of discursive frameworks that speak feminism and which it speaks. A central problem once again, for understanding the arguments, is semiotics, and particularly that kind of semiotics which is not logocentric, or language-centred, and which therefore has no trouble with the concept of a sexed body as a text on and in and through which 'systems of patriarchal morphology may be inscribed' (Grosz, 1988:142; Suleiman, 1986). But that is already to oversimplify, for psychoanalysis is also part of this construction of things, and it is the imaginary body, women's and men's socially and historically mediated experiences of their bodies, which actually bears the marks of these social inscriptions (see Ash and Yell, this volume, for analyses of these processes).

The whole argument then provides a further radical shift in the already radical proposal of social semiotics and post-structuralism that consciousness is socially, discursively constructed, rather than being the prime mover (mind) in the organisation of the world (body). Now, the body and thus sex, is also being represented as a social semiotic construction. The mind/body, material/immaterial, private/public, discursive/non-discursive, text/context, product/process and masculine/feminine dichotomies of patriarchal and phallocentric knowledges are being radically deconstructed. But so now is the sex-gender distinction on which so much work in social science and feminism has depended, and along with it, the priority of *discursive* effects (with its elision of sex/gender and the non-discursive) which has been such a strong tenet of a Foucauldian post-structuralism (Braidotti, Grosz, this volume). What is being argued here is that the socially and historically mediated experience of the *sexed* body, already a semiotic experience, is prior to, different from, and interactive with the *discursive* construction of subjectivity (Grosz, this volume).

24

In part, this seems to be one of those reversals or declarations of independence with which we began. It is what *can* be said or meant next if one wants or needs to say other than what is already being said within a binary phallocentric order. So the *non-discursive* (what for Foucault was bodies, behaviours, practices, all that was not realised in discourse, and what for semiotics, despite its best intentions, remained for a long time also bodies, behaviours, practices, the things it constituted as the *context* for primarily verbal and sometimes visual texts) becomes prior to the discursive, sexual is asserted as prior to social difference, and sexual *difference*, autonomy, is asserted instead of the masculine/feminine binary and subordinating relationship. But there is also something else being said here and it comes from *outside* that phallocentric order and demands and begins to accomplish a more radical dismantling of it.

There are several distinct versions of this new story and they are found in many places. Something similar seems to me to be being argued in some versions of feminist post-structuralism (Henriques et al., 1984; de Lauretis, 1987; Weedon, 1987: 108), although here the semiotic construction of the body is not given priority over the discursive in quite the same way. The work of Poynton in linguistics and Curthoys in history and Pateman's (1988) move in sexualising the private realm and refusing its phallocentric and patriarchal elision from the construction of the public, seem to be translating Grosz's feminist in(ter)vention much more closely into the domains of historical, linguistic and political analysis.

There is much in what I have just said which is cryptic, elusive and dense. My aim was to map out a terrain. Let me now go back to the beginning—or at least to the troubled questions of biology, essentialism, and nature, of masculinity, femininity and sexed bodies, and of equality and difference—and try to follow these arguments through again in different places and in different voices. There is an extensive and growing literature on the subject of the body, some of it emerging from Foucault's post-structuralist emphasis on discourse and the surveillance of the body (Barker, 1984), some of it specifically psychoanalytic (for example Rose, 1986), some of it specifically feminist (Diamond and Quinby, 1988), some of it semiotic and/or linguistic (Scarry, 1985; Suleiman, 1985), some of it mixtures of many of these (Suleiman, 1986; Kroker and Kroker, 1988; Allen and Grosz, 1987; Rowland, 1988:28ff.). I have made no attempt here to be exhaustive or representative and in what follows I am going to be even more selective in tracing some of the argument about the body through a small number of specific but very important Australian texts.

A feminism of equality, in working *within* the current patriarchal order, arguing for equality of women and men within that order, leaves the phallocentric duality of mind and body firmly in place. This happens because in working *against* arguments that the biology of women's bodies both justifies and explains the position of women within that order (see Lumsden and Wilson, 1981 for an extreme example), a feminism of equality is always forced into the position of denying the importance of sexual difference (the body) in order to argue for mental equality (the mind). It is in and through the discursive realisations of these kinds of arguments that the sex/gender distinction as we now know it has been constructed. It has been important to focus on *social* construction, culture, discourse, the *public* sphere of women's activities, and to deny the relevance of their 'other'— the private sphere of women's activities, 'real' biological bodies, nature, the non-discursive (both that which is non-verbal, bodies, behaviours, physical practices and that which is excluded from the discursive, the private, the personal, the emotional, women, giving birth, the sexual). However, in arguing thus, women are actually being totally compliant with the phallocentric order of discourse, even as they struggle to resist it. None of its arbitrary but rigid binarisms is unsettled in the least by any of these arguments: indeed the arguments enlist the very opponents of the system in an elaborate and complex reconstruction of its own binary world of mind/body, private/public oppositions and a new construction of a sex/gender opposition which only further complicates the issue and further reinforces patriarchal and phallocentric structures. It results in a neutering of sexuality which is entirely complicit with the patriarchal construction of the universal (male) subject.

It is not good enough to merely include women in the existing body politic: and the conceptual, for which read linguistic and semiotic, difficulties of arguing *within* this system for a position for women which would be *outside* it are enormous.

It is because of these difficulties that a feminism of difference (for example Irigaray, 1974, 1977, both books translated in 1985) has emerged and that this feminism argues specifically for the foregrounding of sexual difference and the body as a way of clearing a space among the detritus of phallocentrism for a construction of woman and of man that would not be endlessly tied up in phallocentrism's dichotomies—woman as the negative of man, man in terms of the absence of woman, man as the denial of man, woman as the denial of woman. But—and this has to be understood, and is usually not understood—this is *not the same* sexual difference, *not the same* body that we find differently constructed and contextualised in biology and in the biological arguments for the naturalness of women's inferiority, of her childcaring role and so on. Nor is it the kind of essentialist argument for a universal femininity (Kristeva, 1984) which has sometimes resulted from mere reversals of the masculine/feminine dichotomy, so that everything that is devalorised by the phallocentric dichotomy now becomes valorised as the essential, the universal feminine: nature, body, private, passive, emotional, irrational, illogical, hysterical, madness, sexuality and so on.

If the argument is not all these things, then what is it? How does a feminism of difference claim to stand outside the discursive and representational processes of phallocentrism in which a feminism of equality seems to remain entangled? Or must it always be both inside and outside? And is that the difference?

Moira Gatens (1988:59ff.), to whose writing I am indebted for much of my understanding of the above issues, provides a very clear account of what it would be to be both inside and outside and of why, indeed, this might make the difference. Arguing that any account of women's current political and social position requires a coherent theory of the body, she points to the fact that while feminism has shown the masculine bias of the supposedly 'neutral' humanist subject it has paid not nearly enough attention to the congruence between that subject and representations (constructions) of the body politic, of politico-ethical life (1988:62). These stories of the body politic, where that body is defined on the exclusion of women's bodies (p.60) through the fantasy of the man-made (motherless) social body (p.64) which appropriates women's reproductive function to itself, disavowing that function by excluding women from the body politic and restricting them to the private and natural realms, controlling the reproductive female body as a natural resource, explain a great deal about the common ways of thinking and believing that characterise current ideas about the relationship of women's bodies and the state.

These are the stories that we are all inside, that we live daily. Poole (this volume) discusses the implications of the same and related stories for understanding the construction of masculinity. They are stories which inevitably involve the male myth of auto-reproduction that Gatens points to in the sexless and motherless creation of the body politic. Pateman discusses these in relation to the elision of the sexual contract from the story of the social (1988:35–38). Rowland (1988:170ff.) discusses the same myths as they are realised in medical practices, technologies and discourses. Ash (this volume), although her analysis is much more complex than this in the questions it poses about sexuality, the body, institutions and men and women, analyses what seems to me to be a version of the same phenomenon in the 'feminisation' of Christ's body in institutionalised religion in the Middle Ages, an appropriation of the feminine that is not dissimilar to what Braidotti (this volume) describes in contemporary deconstructionist male philosophy. Always the stories are predicated upon the exclusion of women and sexuality, and the incorporation in, or control by, a rational, social, neutered male body, of the feminine, the excluded other.

But there are other stories (Gatens, 1988:67) which are not predicated upon these mind/body or sex/gender (sexed, private women and neutered, public, social men) distinctions. Spinoza's account of the body as a process, which has no 'truth' without contextualisation, and where thought is dependent on the character of the body, instead of mind controlling body as in the other story, provides, Gatens suggests, another place to start, a place that is outside the body-politic story. This might allow a historically specific account of the position of woman as wife and mother which would be autonomous with respect to the dominant frameworks of the other story.

Gatens' paper appeared in print at almost the same time as Carole Pateman's (1988) dismantling and transformation (Pateman and Gross, 1986:4) of the very social and political theory within which stories of the body politic and the original social contract on which it is founded circulate. Her argument is far too complex to repeat here, but there are aspects of it which are crucial to the understanding of that coherent theory of the body that Gatens (1983, 1988), and Grosz (1986, 1988, this volume) and other feminists of difference are arguing for.

First Pateman provides a timely historical criticism and analysis of the meanings and political uses of the term patriarchy, pointing to the fact that according to political theory patriarchy was dead 300 years ago, whereas feminists since the seventeenth century have been arguing that all political theorists have upheld patriarchal right, while in feminist work since the sixties 'patriarchy' has been very much in focus, but with little consensus as to what it is. It refers to a form of political power, but is it literally 'rule by fathers', is it culturally specific or universal, does it exist only in the family or in social life as a whole, and what is the relationship between patriarchy and capitalism? (Pateman, 1988:19–20).

To answer some of these questions Pateman sets about undoing the private/public separation on which the social contract that established 'civil' society as a post-patriarchal construct is based: and this entails putting the sexual back into the social, not only in the rewriting of the contract as sexual, but in our understanding of the way in which what has been represented as *before* 'civil' society and capitalism (patriarchy and sexual domination), what was *excluded* in the stories of their construction (the private, the family, women and heterosexual relations), persists *within* them institutionally and as a particularly modern form of patriarchy. This form is not the traditional 'father as head of the family' version, nor yet the classical paternal theory of the political rights of fathers and the obedience of sons, but a modern fraternal and contractual version which structures capitalist civil society (p.24). However it continues to be read as a patriarchy related to paternal right, partly because of the residual effects of the father-son model (p.32), partly because of feminist retellings of Freud's story of the social structure which is constructed in terms of kinship not contract, and of relations between mothers and fathers, not husbands and wives (p.30). Pateman's argument is that the effect of all these factors is to direct questions at the family and to obscure and avoid discussion of the relations between men and women which precede relations between fathers and mothers and which are institutionalised in marriage (conjugal rights), and employment practices (the master–slave relationship) (p.12,37) within civil society.

In all of this the public sphere which is created by the social contract is seen as replacing nature, and as unrelated to the private sphere which is its necessary basis (p.10–11). This is how the sexual, already in place in 'nature' is evaded, elided from the discussion. Thus the social contract is represented as antipatriarchal and as freedom while in fact being 'a mechanism through which sex-right is renewed and maintained' (p.14). Retrieving the story of the sexual contract, putting the private back in the public, involves, according to Pateman, seeing how the story of the social contract, realised in the institutional practices and discourses of modern law, provides a specifically modern method of creating local power relations of a patriarchal kind within sexuality, marriage and employment. Thus, 'to tell the story of the sexual contract ... is to show how sexual difference . . . constructed as political difference . . . is central to civil society . . . 'individuals' cannot be separated from sexually differentiated bodies . . . the story of the sexual contract is about heterosexual relations . . . and women as embodied beings . . . it is not limited to the private sphere (pp.17–18) . . . One of the advantages of approaching the question of patriarchy through the story of the sexual contract is that it reveals that civil society, including the capitalist economy, has a patriarchal structure. The capacities that enable men but not women to be 'workers' are the same masculine capacities required to be an 'individual', a husband and head of a family. The story of the sexual contract thus begins with the construction of the individual. To tell the story in a way that illuminates capitalist relations and modern patriarchy, the theoretical route through which (civil) slavery comes to exemplify freedom also has to be considered'. (p.38).

I have rehearsed these arguments at length and in detail because it seems to me to be particularly important that we do not misunderstand the position being articulated by feminists of difference, and because it is therefore crucial that we do understand that sexual difference and the sexed body, as they are theorising these, are absolutely central to political, social and historical questions and that none of these things is separable from the discursive, semiotic and representational practices and processes in and through which they are alternately constructed, reified, de-constructed and transformed. Gatens' (1988) and Pateman's analyses provide a necessary and helpful contextual-isation for the theorising of the body in Gatens (1983) and Grosz (1987, 1988 and this volume).

In her critique of the sex/gender distinction (1983) Gatens argues that it perpetuates the ignoring of sexual difference and the foregrounding of class, discourse and power in accounts of the construction of subjectivity. Constructed to enable the claim of equality independent of sex, the dichotomy is based on what she sees as the untenable assumptions of the alleged neutrality of the body and the primacy of consciousness. Masculine and feminine behaviours are then able to be constructed as inscribed as a consciousness that is joined to an indifferent, passive body. It is then possible to argue, as degendering and socialisation feminism does argue, that one can change the effects of 'lived' experience by changing culture (pp.144–7). That is, the social determination of identity is seen to be operating at the level of ideas.

But, as Gatens demonstrates, masculine and feminine behaviours have different personal and social significances when acted out by male and female subjects. The male and female body have different significances and this must, she argues, effect male and female consciousness. What is valorised in patriarchy is not masculinity (gender), but male masculinity. The issue is not gender but sexual difference (p.148).

Thus she insists that there is a non-arbitrary relationship between the male body and masculinity and the female body and femininity. The so-called gender categories actually correspond to the construction of the male and female body in a relation of social and historical specificity. This is very much the same point that de Lauretis is making when she defines masculinity and femininity as the cultural contents given to sexual difference (1987).

That is, theorists of sexual difference are not talking about the physical body, the anatomical body. They are talking about a body which, in Freudian terms, is both biological and psychical, a hinge between nature and culture, and about a biology which is always already cultural (Grosz, 1987:7–8). What is taken as a biological given is, in other words, already a cultural construction (see also Rogers, 1988; Kaplan and Rogers this volume). The meaning the biological body has for human beings, the significance of the body as lived, varies with ideas about bodily functions in a given culture, for example (Gatens 1983:150–51). This significance is learned and developed in a milieu of social meaning and value and constitutes what Gatens (1983) called the imaginary body. The work of Jenny Ash (this volume) on the discursive 'feminisation' of Christ's body points very clearly to that body as a site for the foregrounding of certain bodily functions and processes which cannot be separated from the question of female sexuality—the bleeding wound, the gaping hole; menstruation, childbirth, castration—or the patriarchal Freudian stories in which the making-meaningful of these experiences in the form of the imaginary body is always entangled.

Now this talk of 'ideas' and the 'imaginary' might well seem to be sliding back in the direction of consciousness and the discursive construction of identity, but as the theory has developed it has become clearer that there is a real distinction being drawn here between that and this other notion of bodily and discursively constructed subjectivity. In 1983, Gatens argued against the prevailing socialisation and degendering position in the following terms:

A most common claim made against feminists of
sexual difference is that their theories are essentialist
and <u>a priori</u>, in short, ahistorical. This claim operates
like the infamous blade that cuts both ways. The irony of
the accusation is that feminists who propose
degendering propose it outside of history and without
considering <u>the extreme resilience of expressions of</u>
<u>sexual difference and the networks of language and</u>
<u>other systems of signification that both constitute and</u>
<u>perpetuate this difference</u> (p.150; the italics are mine).

In 1987 Grosz is more specific about the particular psychoanalytic semiotics of the body that she is developing:

The subject's relation to the body is always <u>libidinal</u>.
This is a necessary condition of its ability to <u>recognise</u>
the body as <u>its</u> own. The body, when experienced as-a-
whole . . .—that is, the body and its various organs and
orifices—are always psychically or libidinally mapped,
psychically represented, as a condition of the subject's
ability to use them and to include them in his or her
self-image. <u>These libidinal or eroticised investments are</u>
<u>not simply or clearly psychological rather than</u>
<u>physiological</u> . . . This implies that the body itself, which
is continually traversed by organic-psychical drives, is
both biological and psychical. This understanding of the
body as a hinge or threshold between nature and
culture <u>makes the limitations of a genetic, or purely</u>
<u>anatomical or physiological account of bodies explicit.</u>
If the body is purely natural, an object or form, of
otherness, that has value and status relative to
subjectivity or consciousness, this means that the body's
<u>biological capacity</u> for consciousness and subjectivity
remains uninvestigated. (p.8, extended italics only are
mine).

This is a very different construction, in psychoanalytic and
semiotic terms, of the sexed body and sexual difference from the
constructions of sexual difference that are to be found in
discursively and Foucauldian influenced feminist analyses
which also use psychoanalytic concepts (Henriques et al., 1984;
de Lauretis, 1987; Diamond and Quinby, 1988). And yet the
results are neither totally incompatible nor entirely different.
Thus, for example Hollway (1984:236–38) who speaks of

gender differentiation in relation to discourses concerning sexuality, arguing that men's and women's different subjectivities mean that they do not have equal opportunities of taking up subject or object positions in certain of these discourses, suggests that men and women must also have different 'investments', which she later relates to Lacanian desire (p.239) and a Foucauldian concept of power as productive of knowledges, meanings, values and practices (p.237), in taking up positions in one discourse rather than another. Thus for example it is men who take up the subject position in the discourse of male sexual drive, not women, women who generally read a sexual relationship through the have/hold discourse, not men. The question is why this is so and under what conditions might it change.

While this account speaks in terms of gender as discursively constructed, it does not eschew the question of the historical and socially specific construction of sexuality and biology (men's and women's subjectivities) and it explicity argues for the effects of this on consciousness (in Grosz's sense) when it suggests that men and women, qua men and women, read or position themselves in discourse differently. De Lauretis argues this even more specifically: 'female subjectivity and experience are necessarily couched in a specific relation to sexuality,' (1987:18; and see Ash, this volume).

Both these approaches have affinities with a discursive and social semiotics of the body which would read the body as text, seeing its physical, sexual and socially inscribed attributes, accoutrements and behaviours as the material instantiations of systems of signification, or discourses, which construct and are constructed by a regime of sexual difference, and which participate in the resilience (Gatens, 1983:150) and persistence of that regime (Threadgold, 1988b, 1989 forthcoming; Ash, Yell, Hurley this volume).

As for the body, so for theory, narrative, cinema, television, theatre, literature, literary history, English studies, soap opera, linguistics, biology and feminist deconstruction and in(ter)ventions. These all offer different stories of the body and of sexual difference and they compete and struggle to construct (and sometimes silence) different and heterogeneous and multiple realities, meanings, knowledges, biologies, bodies and subjectivities as they are in turn constructed and silenced or articulated by them. As such they are all technologies of gender (de Lauretis, 1987) and sexuality, producing and reproducing constructions, fictions, with the potential power of the truth-effects of representation. These are socio-cultural practices, the discourses and the institutions, devoted to the production of women and men, producing in the subject those meaning-effects and self-representations which constitute the embodied, lived experience of gender and sexuality.

Some of these effects and representations are extraordinarily stable, static, resilient; others are dynamic, volatile, constantly changing. The reasons for stability and change need analysis. The potential for a different construction of sexuality and gender, outside the sexual contract, at the local level of resistances in subjectivity and self-representation, is possible precisely and only because the self-reflective subject of semiotics is both inside and outside the processes of semiosis and representation (see Yell, Poynton, Hurley this volume).

The work of this book is to try to understand, explain, deconstruct, change and transform some of these processes. In the doing it becomes another construction . . . and we need to keep asking, a construction for whom, in whose interests? Why do we change and subvert a discourse or a representation . . . How? . . . with what consequences? That remains an open question . . . as does the question of sex/gender, masculinity/ femininity and representation . . . but we can only go on asking . . . and the consequences are sometimes surprising:

> It could be said that one of the paradoxical effects of feminism as a political force has been to force the recognition of the diverse and unexpected character of the organisation of sexual differences. It has proved a difficult and contentious problem as to how to analyse the effects of anything from social policy to artistic practices in respect of the organisation of sexual differences. But to reduce these problems to the simplification of an always already antagonistic relation between two social groups who are frozen into a mutually exclusive and jointly exhaustive division is an obstacle both to feminist analysis and to political practice. (Adams, 1979:57)

We hope this book has avoided the last and grappled with the second. We know that what it has to say forces a recognition of the first. Susan Suleiman (1985:60), trying to imagine what the dream of moving beyond the double bind inherent in the binary constructions of phallocentrism might look like, quoted Cixous, whose text, Suleiman says, is inspired by such a dream. That text is not a bad place to end . . . or to begin . . .

And then if I spoke about a person whom I met and who shook me up, herself being moved and I moved to see her moved, and she, feeling me moved, moved in turn, and whether this person is a she [un elle] and a he [une il] and a he [une il] and a she [un elle] and a shehe [une ellil] and a heshe [une ilelle], I want to be able not to lie, I don't want to stop her if she trances, I want him, I want her, I will follow her. (1985a:118)

2 The problematic of 'the feminine' in contemporary French philosophy: Foucault and Irigaray

Rosi Braidotti

M Y ARGUMENT rests on some premises, which are drawn from my work on the problematic of 'the feminine' in contemporary French philosophy (Braidotti, 1981, 1982, 1985): a direct parallel can be drawn between the crisis of the 'knowing subject' of classical philosophy and the elaboration of the theoretical discourse on 'the feminine'.

Over a century ago, Nietzsche stated that all decadent, diseased and corrupted cultures acquired a taste for 'the feminine'—if not for the effeminate. The 'feminine' thus described is nothing more than a very elaborate metaphor, or a symptom, of the profound discontent that lies at the heart of phallo-logocentric culture. It is a male disease, expressing the crisis of self-legitimation which, according to J.F. Lyotard (1979, 1980) is the mark of post-modern societies. This 'feminine' bears no immediate or even direct relationship to real-life *women*; I believe that, as feminists, we should question the rather ancient mental habit which consists in using the 'feminine' as the sign, the metaphor or the symptom of: illness, crisis, discontent. It is a typically masculine attitude which turns male disorders into feminine values. Thinking of Freud's President Schreber (Freud, 1911) who in his delirium declared that he was both male and female and all the more female as he was God's own favourite, well may we wonder at the depths of the 'becoming-woman' as a trend in modern thought—a trend of which Derrida (1967, 1972, 1978) is the main spokesman in France.

What makes me particularly critical of this kind of philosophical thought is that it neglects, in its fascination for 'the feminine' taken as the sign of the crisis of the rational subject, the historical and theoretical impact of the world-shattering event which has been the women's movement.

Isn't it strange that it is precisely at the time in history when women have made their voices heard socially, politically and theoretically that philosophical discourse—a male domain *par excellence*—takes over 'the feminine' for himself?

It seems to me that the relationship between theorisations of the feminine and feminist discourse and practice is to be thought out in terms of power and strategy, and that the coincidence I mentioned earlier between on the one hand the crisis of the phallo-logocentric subject and on the other the renewal of interest for the feminine is in fact a pre-text which conceals the real issue—that's to say the head-on collision between patriarchal assumptions about the feminine and the existential reality of women's lives and thought—which feminism has allowed us to express.

That's what is at stake for me in the post-modern, post-structuralist, 'post-post-card'[1] debate. To demonstrate this I have chosen to displace the debate onto a side issue which is highly significant: the question of ethics and the extraordinary interest that it is receiving in contemporary French philosophy.

Why has the question of 'ethics' come back to the philosophical agenda—after all the years when 'politics' was top of the hit parade of ideas?

My hypothesis is that the so-called 'crisis' of the rational subject, with the related inflation of the notion of the feminine, has had some beneficial effects on *some* male philosophers.

I will juxtapose Foucault's notion of ethics, with the focus on sameness, with the ethics of sexual difference of Irigaray, a woman psychoanalyst and philosopher. It seems to me that Irigaray's critique of the binary structures of philosophical discourse leads to a very intense call for alterity, for otherness, for sexual difference as a sign for multiple differences. I will therefore also argue that we are faced with a fundamental dissonance between on the one hand the discourse of the crisis of the logos and of its feminine, and on the other this project of feminism which demands a focus on sexual difference.

By setting side by side Foucault's and Irigaray's notions of ethics I wish to point out firstly the radically different directions in which their respective thought is moving. I will argue that Foucault elaborates a new ethics that remains within the confines of sexual sameness, whereas Irigaray is arguing for sexual otherness as a strategy allowing for the assertion of feminine subjectivity.

Secondly, I will argue that the profound 'dissonance' between these two thinkers, their variations on the common theme of ethics, demonstrates the lack of symmetry in the discourse of the two sexes. It consequently adds further evidence to the feminist project of positing sexual differences as the central question in the post-modern debate.

The sheer importance of the ethical issue in the work of some male philosophers is an offshoot of the crisis of the rational subject, which has shaken the phallo-logocentric system to its foundations. The question of alterity, of otherness, is receiving renewed attention precisely because of the problematisation of the structures of subjectivity in modern thought. It is my firm belief that the women's movement is one of the primary sources for the dislocation of the rational subject.[2]

Foucault

In the Afterword of Dreyfus' and Rabinow's book *Michel Foucault—Beyond Structuralism and Hermeneutics*[3], Foucault defined the general outline of his thought and stated as his central theme the critical, historical analysis of the modes of constitution of the subject: the ways in which, in our culture, human beings are made into subjects. His analytics of the subject is committed to revealing, denouncing and ultimately undoing the specific form of violence—that's to say the power formations that are at work in the philosophical game. What really interests Foucault is the *materiality* of ideas—the fact that they exist in an in-between space caught in a network of material and symbolic conditions, between what he calls the document, the archives, and the monument, between the text and history, between theory and practice, and never in any one of these poles.

His philosophy is a philosophy of relations, of in-betweens and in that sense he represents the absolute antithesis of sociology.

The central concern of Foucault's work is the criticism of the despotic power exercised by the philosophical text and by the history of philosophy as a monolithic block of knowledge. It seems to me that this critique provides the overall unity of his intellectual project.

As he stated in his introduction to volume 2 of *The History of Sexuality*,[4]

> *There is always something ludicrous in philosophical discourse when it tries, from the outside, to dictate to others, to tell them where their truth is and how to find it, or when it works up a case against them in the language of naive positivity. But it is entitled to explore what might be changed, in its own thought, through the practice of a knowledge that is foreign to it. The 'essay'—which should be understood as the assay or test by which, in the game of truth, one undergoes changes, and not as the simplistic appropriation of others for the purpose of communication—is the living substance of philosophy, at least if we assume that philosophy is still what it was in times past, i.e.: an 'ascesis', askesis—an exercise of oneself in the activity of thought. (p 9)*

The choice of this place of enunciation implies a redefinition of philosophy, the *'exercise of oneself in the activity of thought', 'a test in the game of truth'*. It is a practice which entails a relationship to oneself and to alterity and is consequently an ethical stance.

Foucault's analytic of subjectivity outlines three main modes of objectification, which transform human beings into subjects. These correspond to different stages of his own work.

In the first phase he analyses the type of discourse which claims the status of science, especially in the field of the human sciences; this phase of his work, marked by *The Order of Things* and *The Archeology of Knowledge*, leads him to the critique of the role that the 'knowing subject' plays in the history of Western philosophy.

The second stage of Foucault's work deals with the constitution of the subject through what he calls 'the dividing practices': exclusion, separation and domination within oneself as well as towards the others. This part of his reflection starts with *Madness and Civilization* and *Birth of the Clinic* and continues through to *The Order of Discourse* and *Discipline and Punish*. The central notion is that the modes in which human beings are made into subjects in our culture rest on a complex network of power relations, which he defines in terms of the 'the microphysics of power'. 'Power' being the name we give to a complex strategic situation in a given society, the body is the privileged target of the mechanisms of power relations. Foucault develops a *political economy* of the body—a body defined in terms of *materiality*, that is to say as subject matter which is prone to a variety of symbolic and material operations: it must be made docile, submitted, erotic, usable, productive etc.

These techniques of control and codification of the living body meant as the site of subjectivity also produce 'truth-effects' in that they generate specific types of knowledge about the subject and his/her social inscription. The normative aspects of the power relations in which the body is caught are consequently positive, that is to say productive in terms of *knowledge* in the sense of truth about the living subject. Thus Foucault's notion of the subject rests on a technology of the body as connected to both the rational nature of power and the normative character of the *ratio*.

This idea also provides the link between the second and the third stages of Foucault's work; in the latter he concentrates on the ways in which a human being turns him/herself into a subject: the internal modes of submission and domination by the subject. He takes sexuality as the field in which the proliferation of discursive practices and therefore of normative truth-effects is the strongest in our culture. In the first volume of his *History of Sexuality* he defines Western culture as 'sex-centric': we are the ones who invented *scientia sexualis*, turning sexuality into the site of self-relevation and truth about oneself. His question then becomes: what is this 'sexuality' which we are all so concerned with? And by what means do we become sexual subjects?

In the second and third volumes of *The History of Sexuality* Foucault analyses the ancient Greek and Roman practices of discourse and control of sexuality; he thus points out that the practices which for us come under the general blanket 'sexuality' constituted what Graeco-Roman culture called 'the arts of existence', that is to say, 'these intentional and voluntary actions by which men not only set themselves rules of conduct, but also seek to transform themselves, to change themselves in their singular being and to make their life into an oeuvre that carries certain aesthetic values and meets certain stylistic criteria' (p.10).

Foucault argues that the array of 'arts of existence' in the sense of 'techniques of the self' were later assimilated into the exercise of priestly power in early Christianity and then into educational, medical and psychological types of practices.

It seems to me that the evolution of Foucault's thought traces the progressive sexualisation of his discursive practices: the intersection of the archeological phase with the genealogical decoding of the practices of the self—which produces his *History of Sexuality*—also marks his increasing awareness of his own speaking stance as a man, a male philosopher. It is possible to argue for instance that in his early texts Foucault's androcentric bias is manifest: he uses the term 'man' as a universal form, thus betraying his blindness to sexual difference. In his later works, however, he is conscious of the fact that the system of control of sexuality which he is analysing rests on a profound dissymmetry between the sexes. Speaking of the 'practices of the self', he states: 'Women were generally subjected . . . and yet this ethics was not addressed to women; it was not their duties, or obligation, that were recalled, justified, or spelled out. It was an ethics for men: an ethics though, written and taught by men, and addressed to men—to free men, obviously.' (p.22)

The point Foucault makes here concerns not so much the exclusion as the *disqualification* of women as ethical agents and consequently as subjects. He stresses the interconnection between entitlement to moral status and the right to citizenship in the social, political and judicial sense of the term. The rules and regulations of a moral life—which also transform the subject into an ethical substance—are implicitly connected to sociopolitical rights, and women are kept on the margin of both.

Arguing that governing oneself, managing one's estate and participating in the administration of the city were three practices of the same kind, Foucault emphasises the key value of 'ethical virility' as the ideal on which the system as a whole rests. In turn this implies perfect coincidence between one's anatomical sex—male—and the imaginary construction of masculine sexuality; moreover, he stresses the accordance of both to the ruling social representations of what ought to be the *universal* ethical standard: symbolic virility. Thus the male body is all one with the body politic.

If we read Foucault's project in this sense, it can be taken as the critical anatomy of phallocentric structures in discourse; the practice of 'ethical virility' in fact also lays the foundation of the philosophical game as such, that is to say that it provides the basic parameters of the political economy of truth, as submitted to the authority of the *logos*. Moreover, the phallo-logocentric economy thus analysed also reveals the male homosexual bond which constitutes the basis of the social contract as well as the discursive practices which society adopts for itself: it is a world for and by men.

Whatever the female 'use of pleasure' may have been like, with its truth-effects and production of knowledge about the female subject, remains a matter of speculation. The discursive gap translates into historical absence; thus, the whole history of philosophy, as we have come to inherit it, has been conjugated in the male masculine and virile mode. History—rather than anatomy—is destiny.

According to this reading of Foucault, it can be argued that he is a male philosopher who is bringing out the highly sexed rules governing philosophical discourse. Far from being universal, the scene of philosophy rests on the most sexual-specific premises: those which posit the primacy of masculine sexuality as a site of social and political power. In Foucault's latest work phallo-logocentric discourse is a specific political and libidinal economy—one which assigns the sexes to precise roles, poles and functions, to the detriment of the feminine.

Irigaray

As a feminist, a psychoanalyst, a powerful writer and a philosopher, Luce Irigaray cannot be situated very easily; she is forever in between different fields, disciplines, levels of experience and places of enunciation. Her work on the philosophical subject is related to the crisis of the logos mentioned above, and in many ways it is a positive, non-reactive response to the masters of the crisis of philosophy. Irigaray addresses the same tradition of classical Western ontology which Derrida, Foucault, Deleuze and other contemporary French philosophers have also focused on. But there is a fundamental difference in the very place of enunciation which she adopts: for Irigaray the crisis which for Foucault spells the death of philosophy is already over—she is standing among the ruins and already sees what is to come to replace the old order.

There is a visionary, utopian and at times even prophetic quality in Irigaray's writing, which expresses her faith in the force of the feminine as a new symbolic and discursive economy.

A comparable force of affirmation and quality of intensity is found in the work of feminist theology (M. Daly), of lesbian poetry (A. Rich) and in the work of Italian radicals (C. Lonzi, 1974, 1977 and more recently Luisa Muraro 1984)[5] on the question of the female symbolic system.

Women can see the light where men just stare into empty space watching the downfall of the phallic monuments and documents they had erected by and for themselves. Women have something to say—failing to say it would amount to an historical abortion of the female subject.

For Irigaray the crisis which spells the death of the logocentric subject opens the condition of possibility for the expression of female subjectivity. The crisis is merely the death of the universal subject—the one that disguised its singularity behind the mask of logo-criticism. That men should be greatly shaken by this is no wonder, but the crisis allows us to ask at long last the question which for Irigaray is fundamental: that of sexual difference.

What makes Irigaray's critique of modernity very significant is that she attacks the complicity between rationality and masculinity. The subject of discourse is always *sexed*; it can never be pure, universal or gender-free.

Irigaray's work rests on a double purpose:

1 to undo the association of masculinity with rationality and universality—through the rereading of the history of Western ontology;
2 to voice and embody in her own texts women's own 'feminine', as distinct from the kind of 'feminine' which is implicitly annexed to the logocentric economy.

What is at stake in Irigaray's project is the double urge to express the radical novelty of a feminine corporeal reality which has never been adequately represented and also not to interrupt the dialogue with the masters of Western philosophy. This is particularly true of her first phase: *Speculum* and *This Sex which is not One*,[6] where her very special style mediates the intense effort of critique and creation which marks her work.

Irigaray's textual strategy is eminently political: it consists of refusing to separate the symbolic from the empirical, to disso-ciate the discourse on 'the feminine' from the historical realities of the condition and status of women in Western culture. In other words, the fact that 'the feminine' is the 'blind spot' of all textual and theoretical processes means that women's voices are buried underneath someone else's, man's own words. There is therefore a direct equivalence between the process of metaphorisation of 'the feminine' and the phenomenon of the historical oppression of women. Irigaray's project is to recover, unveil and express that voice, starting from the major texts of Western philosophy.

'The feminine' she is after is a woman-defined feminine and as such it is still a blank; it is not *yet*, we are to think of it in the conditional mode: how can the feminine of/in/by women come into being in the sexually indifferentiated (indifferent/undifferentiated) system of our culture? What are the conditions that would make the first coming of the female subject possible? The strategy Irigaray proposes in response to this challenge consists in claiming as her place of enunciation the position to which 'the feminine' is assigned in various texts of classical philosophy. Thus she reads, or rather unreads the texts as a function of their representation of and relation to the 'feminine': it is a game of specular/speculative reflection of the inner logic of phallologocentric discourse. This game of strategic repetition of throwing back to the text what the text does to the 'feminine' becomes a highly subversive practice of critique of discourse.

Irigaray's project of redefining the parameters of subjectivity and the very understanding of what thinking is all about rests on one major assumption: the belief in the ontological basis of sexual difference. In other words, the difference between the sexes is *radical* and it is *constitutive* of the human experience; it should be listed alongside mortality as the ineluctable frame of reference of the human being. Just like death, sexual difference is *always already there*, whether we acknowledge it or not. The ontogical claim for sexual difference is what makes Irigaray so important theoretically and politically; the essentialist belief in ontological difference is a political strategy aiming at stating the specificity of female subjectivity, sexuality and experience while also denouncing the logic of sexual indifferentiation of phallologocentric discourse.[7]

The now famous image of the lips of the female sex—close together and yet apart—stands for the multiplicity, the excess and the unique combination of plurality and singularity which characterises the bodily, sexed reality of the female experience. This highly suggestive image, with its implicit reference to the psychoanalytic theory of female narcissism, is however very ambivalent. Irigaray is not a theoretician of homosexuality and of the lesbian experience; on the contrary she has made it quite clear that she aspires to genuine heterosexuality in the sense of full recognition of sexual difference by each sex. The process must start with each woman recognising other women in a system of symbolic reference, of mutual and auto-recognition of 'the woman as other'.

Another way of exploring the polyvalence of the images Irigaray proposes is the mother–daughter relationship which exemplifies the specificity of the female libido and of female desire while being both unexplored and misunderstood in psychoanalytic theory and practice. The emphasis that Lacanian psychoanalysis places on the Name-of-the-Father and the primacy of the Phallus is such that the mother–daughter couple is simply left aside, foreclosed. Irigaray reads this couple in terms of a woman-to-woman relationship which phallocentric power separates and denies; recognising the bond of women is the first step towards the elaboration of another symbolic system, one in which the patterns of separation would be mediated differently.

The Ethics of Sexual Difference is one of the clearest manifestations of Irigaray's notion of 'otherness' in relation to the project of expressing female subjectivity. In comparison with her earlier works, this book marks a shift that was already visible in *Amante Marine; La croyance meme;* and *Femmes Divines*—namely that the double-layer structure of address, the fact that Irigaray was addressing *both* the great masters of classical ontology and women who are existentially involved in the process of transformation of the 'feminine' in our culture, becomes streamlined. In *The Ethics of Sexual Difference* Irigaray is addressing almost exclusively the great masters, and this narrowing of the interlocutor, combined with the vocative mode of speech, produces an intense *poetic* text which reads as a major treatise on love.

The focus of Irigaray's text is the politics of heterosexuality; she argues that the mystery of alterity, of relationship to the other and especially to the Other that is the Divine Being, is summed up in the other who is sexually different from me, that is to say *the other sex for each sex.* Emphasis is laid on the classical Cartesian passion of 'wonder' as the perfect mode of encounter of men and women, each sex in its specificity: the perfection of two sexually different beings. And while the feminists cried out in horror at what reads at first sight as a monumental step backwards towards monogamous heterosexual couples, Irigaray has been quite adamant, particularly in her work on female goods and the female experience of the divine, that the politics of heterosexuality as the underlying theme of the thought of sexual difference is a necessary step in order to ensure the emergence of female subjectivity and of an imaginary and symbolic system morphologically suited to the female corporeal reality.

Ethics is for Irigaray a move towards the other (sex) as the paradigm for a new mode of relation to the other, including the other woman who, while sexually the same-as me, remains nevertheless an-other, a mystery.

Of dissonance and other games

If you set side by side the two projects of ethics which I have briefly summarised here, you will see quite clearly the opposite directions in which the respective thoughts of Foucault and Irigaray are moving. Foucault elaborates a critique which remains within the confines of sexual sameness; Irigaray emphasises sexual difference as a way of asserting female subjectivity.

Foucault's account of classical Greek and Roman ethics, of the use of pleasure and the apprenticeship of the arts of subjectivity in all its political and symbolic connotations—as direct from the Christian form of ethics—is not meant as an apology for either discursive system. The focus of his work on ethics is the discontinuity between the modern predicament and earlier, both Christian and Classical, ethics. What ultimately interests him is to try and elaborate a modern ethics, one which would be historically and conceptually suited to the *here and now* of our place of enunciation. The question is: how can we move beyond the historicity of our modern condition? Foucault argues that the age of modernity is one for which no morals is possible: we are historically condemned to rethink the basis of our relationship to the values that we have inherited, especially from the nineteenth century.

Irigaray's project of redefinition of the basis for interpersonal relationship, her ethics of sexual difference is another response to the same historical challenge: *how can we learn to think differently about human subjectivity and alterity?* This question has been on the philosophical agenda ever since Heidegger, and it seems to me that feminism as a movement of thought is caught up in this problematics and it has a major role to play within it.

And yet, it may well be that the feminist reply to the challenge of modernity is radically different from the response of male philosophers; the case of Foucault and Irigaray tends to prove that on the conceptual level, patterns of great dissonance are emerging between male and female philosophers. It may well be that we differ as to the nature and structure of difference; it may well be that sexual difference as a movement of thought will open the door to the recognition of multiple differences which spell the death of the One and Only logic of phallo-logocentrism.

The lack of symmetry in the thought of difference—such as it emerges in the work about ethics—also confirms Irigaray's insight that conceptual thinking is not neutral but rather very sexual-specific. That major divergences should appear between male and female thinkers on the question of difference is therefore rather reassuring; I would even argue that the fundamental asymmetry in the thought of sexual difference as elaborated by men and women is precisely what makes the intellectual dialogue between them possible.

Dissonance is related to sexual difference as one of its modes of expression. If we are to take seriously the notion that the philosophy of sexual difference is the central question for modernity and one which we are historically condemned to come to terms with, we should grow accustomed to playing the game of dissonance as a mode of relation.

Lacan's witty remark that love means giving what you have not got to someone who does not want it anyway adds a further dimension to this debate: dissonance as a mode of relation is also the theme of encounter and of *desire*. It is quite clear that desire is the one concept behind the philosophy of sexual difference, but that is another story...

3 Modernity, rationality and 'the masculine'

Ross Poole

> Reason has always existed, but not always in reasonable form
>
> Marx 1975: 143

> Faust to Mephistopheles: 'Yours is the bread that satisfieth never'
>
> Goethe 1951:87

GENEVIEVE LLOYD, has recently argued that the various ideals of reason which have concerned Western philosophy have involved an exclusion of what have been taken to be feminine characteristics, and that the conception of what it is to be feminine has been in part constructed through this process of exclusion (Lloyd, 1984: esp. ch.7). A corollary to this is the thesis that the various ideals of reason have included what have been taken to be masculine characteristics, and that masculinity is in part constructed through this process of inclusion. To be a masculine subject ('to be a man') is to recognise oneself in the ideals of reason and to aspire to the norms of rational thought and action.

An important implication of Lloyd's argument is that even within Western philosophy there has been no single ideal of reason. While there has been general agreement that reason defines both the goals and the practices of philosophy, there has been a great deal of variety in the manner in which this goal and these practices have been conceived. Reason is not, except in a very abstract or perhaps a utopian sense, a universal. It has been constructed, and contested, in accordance with different conceptions of the world, of social existence and of morality. Corresponding to these different conceptions have been different constructions of masculine and feminine identity.

My focus in this chapter will in one sense be much narrower than Lloyd's in that I will only be concerned with one cluster of conceptions of rationality. But in another sense it will be broader. I will be concerned with forms of rationality, not as these have been deployed in the discourse of philosophy, but as they are constructed in certain practices which are characteristic of modern social life. I will be concerned, in other words, with reason as it is constituted by modernity. But not just with reason: I will also be concerned to delineate the forms of masculine and feminine identity which are defined, through complementary processes of inclusion and exclusion, by these concepts of reason.

I

The thesis that the modern world is characterised by a particular concept of rationality is associated with Max Weber. According to Weber, the development of modern Western civilisation has been a process—undoubtedly uneven and incomplete—of 'rationalisation'. Which is to say that certain principles of rationality have come to be embodied in the dominant institutions and practices of the modern world—especially in the capitalist market, the capitalist labour process, the bureaucracies and the establishments of science. Rationalisation in this institutional or objective sense generates corresponding modes of rationality and the thought and behaviour of those subject to it.

The account of rationality which I provide here will be Weberian in spirit rather than in detail. Weber's own account is complex and defies easy summary (for systematic attempts to display Weber's views on rationalisation and rationality, see Levine, 1981 and Brubaker, 1984). In what follows, I will select from, simplify, interpret and often go beyond Weber's account as suits my purposes.

There are, I suggest, three pervasive modes of rationality in the modern world:

1 'Instrumental' or 'Means/End' rationality (see Weber 1922/ 23:293, 1964:115).

2 'Juridical' rationality (Weber does not clearly distinguish this from instrumental rationality; but see Weber, 1922:216–21).
3 'Cognitive' or 'scientific' rationality (see Weber, 1919; 1922/23:293).

Instrumental rationality

This form of reason is most clearly present in the marketplace, the labour process and capitalist accounting procedures, but it informs a wide range of other activities as well. It is almost certainly the dominant form of reason in the modern world, and in many discussions is simply identified with rationality per se.

Individuals are rational in this sense if they select from the range of possible actions open to them that action which on the best evidence available is most likely to achieve a given end. Where ends conflict, this rationality selects those ends which are most likely to be achieved, taking into account the intensity and duration of the desires involved. It abstracts from consideration of immediacy and considers future ends as being as important as present ones. This concept of reason treats all desires as having a right to gratification. It functions to point to the ways in which they might be gratified and, by taking into account their strength, duration and the contingencies of the world, it introduces a ranking among them.

Instrumental reason is concerned above all with efficiency and its only measure of efficiency is quantitative. It is most effective where its material—the potential means available to maximise nett satisfaction—is also conceived quantitatively. Instrumental reason's preferred form of existence is as calculation of quantitative input and quantitative output, and this is paradigmatically exemplified by capitalist accounting procedures.

Instrumental reason characteristically takes one of two kinds of end. The first concerns the consumption needs of the individual. The second, which is characteristic of capitalist enterprise, concerns not consumption but profit. According to Weber, 'Capitalism is identical with the pursuit of profit and forever renewed profit, by means of continuous, rational capitalistic enterprise' (Weber, 1984:17). What this involves is acting in such a way as to maximise one's returns, not in order that one might consume the proceeds, but in order that they might be used to further one's returns in the next round of activity; and so on, indefinitely. This is a form of rational behaviour, which is directed toward an end where the end is always a means towards a further end of exactly the same kind. In so far as individuals are conceived of as having ends of this kind, they must be supposed to have desires which are never satisfied and are indeed insatiable.

Weber's analysis of the Protestant ethic was intended to show how this kind of insatiable desire, rationally pursued, came into existence, and in so doing gave the psychological impetus necessary for capitalist development to begin. However, once capitalist institutions and practices are established then society is objectively rationalised in this sense, and individual behaviour must conform to it (see Weber, 1984:45–55). This is clear in the case of the capitalist entrepreneur. Unless such individuals are prepared to reinvest a competitive proportion of profit into improved and expanded production, then they will not be able to continue as capitalists, and will be replaced by others who do reinvest. For capitalists, therefore, as against say feudal lords, consumption wants must be subsumed under the rational pursuit of ends which are only means to further ends. What is pursued in other words are not ends, but the capacity to pursue ends. This is identical with the pursuit of power, not as a means, but as an end in itself. It has long been noted, especially by theorists of the Frankfurt School, that the operation of instrumental reason involves power in the sense of control (see for example, Marcuse, 1968). It needs also to be stressed that instrumental reason in the form in which it is especially characteristic of the entrepreneur, but which is much more pervasive than this, is the same as the pursuit of power for its own sake. (We might have called this 'the will to power' if this term had not already been appropriated in a rather different sense by Nietzsche.)

In a capitalist society, the effective pursuit of profit through increased productivity is only possible where there is a corresponding increase in consumption. This may be achieved through expansion of the available market. More characteristically, however, it is achieved through an intensification of consumption. Thus, complementary to the pursuit of power for its own sake is the drive towards increased consumption. Just as the former is conceived as insatiable, so too are the consumption needs of the individual. These come to be directed not at specific objects of consumption but at the act of consumption itself. Wants of this kind are insatiable, and the attempt to satisfy them involves the unending repetition of acts of consumption. In this way, instrumental reason as directed towards the consumption need of the individual comes to assume the same repetitive and insatiable structure as that form of instrumental reason concerned with profit maximisation.

Juridical rationality

This form of reason is instantiated in the practices of the judiciary and some parts of the state bureaucracy. Weber noted it, but seemed not to have conceived of it as distinct from instrumental reason (a surprising oversight given his familiarity with Kant). However it is at least prima facie distinct. Individuals are rational in this sense if they conceive of their actions as instances of general principle which they are ready to apply to all actions which are relevantly similar. If instrumental rationality is concerned with efficiency, juridical rationality is concerned with consistency. In its exemplary form, for example, the government bureaucrat or judge dealing with an action, it is concerned to establish the appropriate description of the act, and then to apply to it the relevant principle. In so far as it informs the behaviour of individuals, it does so by constraining the operations of instrumental reason to actions which instantiate principles of behaviour which apply to all actions which are relevantly similar.

Cognitive rationality

This form of reason is instantiated in the practice of modern science. Its concern is with truth, in some realist sense of that term (the 'correspondence' theory of truth being the most familiar realist account). Individuals are rational in this sense if their beliefs and judgments are arrived at or tested by methods which are more likely than available alternatives to produce true beliefs and judgments. These methods are those of experiment, repetition and quantification, and the construction of concepts which are abstract and allow for the use of mathematical procedures. The individual who is rational in this sense is, if not in possession of the truth, at least oriented towards it. Which is to say that he is on the path towards conceiving the world as it is and not, for example, as he might want it to be.

These three forms of rationality have certain common features. Each is characterised by a certain impersonality. Each abstracts from relationships of kin, emotion and empathy, and deals with its material in terms of efficiency, consistency or objectivity. Each involves a separation of rational subjects from the objects of their rational concern. What is dealt with is other. And finally, each has a penchant for the mathematical: what is rationally conceived is quantity, and quality only exists to demarcate the distinct spheres of rational attention. But there are significant distinctions also between the various forms of modern reason, and some tensions between them (as, for example, between the entrepreneurial drive toward instrumental efficiency and the bureaucratic demands for consistency). I shall return to some of these issues later.

II

For Weber, a necessary condition for the rationalisation of the market, production, administration and knowledge was the institutional separation of these spheres of activity from the household, the familial, the erotic and the emotional (see Weber, 1984:21–22; 1922:197, 215–216). It is the exclusion of these from the domain of public life which allowed for the impersonal and calculative otherness which is essential for the operation of reason. This does not mean—could not mean—the elimination of the domestic, kin relationships, sexuality and the passions from social existence. But it does involve a kind of conceptual quarantine, so that these disorders do not infect the domain of the rational.

I am not here so much concerned with the blurred and uncertain social distinction between a public world of rationality and a private realm of its opposite, as with the ways in which this conceptual—or perhaps symbolic—distinction enters into the construction of masculine and feminine identity. What is at issue is not the social fact that men—largely—dominate the public world and that women—largely—inhabit the private. What is at issue is the fact that this distinction informs our conception of what men and women are.

Masculinity is constructed within the ideals of reason. This is not to say that to be a man is to be rational. It is, however, to re-cognise oneself within the conception of reason, and it is to aspire, however unsuccessfully, to its ideals. The relationship between masculine identity and reason involves both the 'is' of identity and the 'ought' of obligation. It is my identity as a rational subject, which means that I am inscribed within the norms of reason. I recognise that they are addressed to me and inform me as to what I ought to be and do.

To be instrumentally rational in the specifically modern sense is to pursue efficiency and ultimately power on the one hand, or consumption on the other. It requires a capacity to abstract oneself as an agent from the particular social relationships in which one exists, from specific others, and even from one's own activities. All these must be evaluated in terms of their effectiveness in pursuing one's ends. Where other relationships, individuals and activities are more effective as potential means towards those ends, they must be selected. Whatever comes within the scope of rational calculation must be conceived as other. Correspondingly, the identity of the rational agent must be achieved through abstraction and separation from particular individuals, relationships and activities.

If instrumental rationality presupposes abstract individuals as its subjects, the operation of juridical reason serves to constrain the activity of such individuals. An individual is rational in this sense when he conceives of his behaviour as subject to universal principles binding upon himself and all others like him. It is a requirement of a certain kind of equal treatment and impartiality. It is, in other words, a principle of formal justice. The legal system and the bureaucracy are the external embodiment of these principles, and impose themselves on the behaviour of individuals subject to them. The internal representation of this principle—and thus the internal constraint on instrumental action—is the voice of morality.

Feminity is constructed, at least in part, through exclusion from the ideals of reason. It is constructed, not through abstraction and separation, but through relationships. To be a woman is to exist within specific relationships to specific others and it involves specific activities with respect to those others. It is to be wife, mother, nurturer and so on. These activities, relationships and others are not subject to the norms of instrumental reason, because they are not replaceable means to independently specifiable ends. They are rather expressive of a certain relational form of identity, and are necessary to sustain that identity. Morality does not here take the form of an impartial and impersonal consistency but of working through one's specific responsibilities to specific others. (Hence the lack of a sense of justice—as a characteristic of this kind of morality—which has worried such moral theorists as Rousseau, Hegel and Freud).

There are quite different moral structures involved here. For the abstract relentlessly insatiable individual which is one aspect of masculine identity, morality takes the form of law and duty. It is the necessary constraint—either external or internal—on its behaviour. From another perspective, it is the containment of instrumental rationality by bureaucratic reason. Things are quite different for that relational form of identity which is, in part, constitutive of femininity. Here, morality is a form of character. To be moral is to be a certain kind of person, to know how one should act in order to express that identity, and so to act. Somewhat paradoxically given the etymology of the word (ultimately from *vir*, man), the morality appropriate to feminine identity is one of *virtue* (for a fuller discussion of this, see Poole, 1985a).

I have so far supposed that masculine identity is constituted through the public sphere. This, however, cannot be the whole story. Masculinity exists in both spheres: the private as well as the public. It is plausible to suggest that masculinity is doubly representative. In the public sphere, masculinity represents the private; hence masculine identity is not merely abstract, but also that of bearer of family responsibilities ('breadwinner'). Within the sphere of domesticity, it is the role of masculinity to represent the wider public realm of reason, order and duty. Indeed, as we shall see in a moment, without such representation, the private world could not produce and reproduce the kind of identity required by the public world.

III

Rationality is produced and reproduced through the structures of public life—the exchange of commodities, the workplace and so on. This is what Weber meant by rationalisation: individuals in carrying out their daily lives must subordinate their activities to the logic of the institutional framework within which they exist. There is no once and for all constitution of the rational masculine subject. Still, it is clear that there must be a primary process in which the elements of masculinity are put into place.

I will only discuss one stage in this process here, though it is one which is of particular significance to my theme. This is the resolution of the Oedipal situation for the male child. There are two aspects of this which are important. First is the moment of separation: the child repudiates the mother and breaks out of that identity formed in relationship to her, Second is the moment of incorporation: the child takes into himself the figure of the father. These moments are not parallel. The loss of the first identity is total. What is left, and what is henceforth the identity of the male child, is a void. What is left is the capacity to abstract from any given context, i.e. any relationship or activity, and—eventually—to bring the norms of instrumental reason to bear on it. The superego which is formed by taking in the figure of the father remains other, even if an internalised other. As such, it represents the demands of impersonal consistency and justice. It is the law both within and external to the self. This is at least one reason why the familial world in which the Oedipal drama takes place must contain a representation (perhaps in the superego of the father) of the demands of public and juridical rationality.

The abstract subjectivity which is brought into existence through the resolution of the Oedipal situation is a highly vulnerable one. It exists only by constituting everything with which it comes into contact as other, and thus separating itself from everything which could give it content. Generalised otherness, however, must also pose a threat to that identity: it invokes a world which is not the self, but which might also engulf it. Consumption presents itself as one way in which this threat may be evaded. It is an activity which both affirms the self and which negates otherness. But it is a form of consumption which is literally infinite in scope, since it must take everything which is not the self as a potential object. A complementary strategy involves bringing that externality under control: it involves the quest, not for consumption, but for power. In these two strategies lie the psychological basis for the insatiability of consumption wants and of the desire for power which operate through the grid of instrumental reason.

There are two (at least) more specific threats to this form of identity. It seems highly likely that the identity of any given subject of experience is crucially dependent upon a measure of recognition by other subjects. Our individual existence must find confirmation in our experiences of others. That is to say, some form of intersubjectivity is a necessary condition for subjectivity. Hence, if one fails to recognise the existence of others *as subjects*, one eliminates a condition necessary for one's own subjectivity. But the instrumental rationality to which masculine subjectivity aspires has no place for the subjectivity of those others who fall within its scope. Others exist only as means or as impediments, not as subjects in their own right. Even where instrumental rationality is constrained by the demands of justice (the superego), it does not allow for genuine intersubjectivity. The second problem confronted by the masculine subject is the threat—and the attraction—of that relational form of identity associated with the feminine. If it was the repudiation of the mother which allowed entry into masculine subjectivity, this repudiation is never in practice complete, and collapse back into that relationship is an ever present possibility. Such a collapse is both a desire and the ultimate threat: the complete loss of self. This emerges most clearly in the domain of erotic love, and encapsulates the problem of (hetero-)sexuality for masculinity. (In the last two paragraphs, I have drawn on Hegel, 1977:104–119.)

Modern social life offers a number of partial resolutions of these problems. There are, for example, forms of identity which are constituted through relationships of mutual recognition. Often, these build on the relationships embodied in the family. Nationalism is the most familiar and pervasive of these (see Poole, 1985b). There are also various rituals through which some of the tensions embodied in masculinity are held in suspension and the underlying desires gratified, at least in fantasy. Thus, to take an example explored by Jessica Benjamin (1984), in fantasies of erotic domination, and more especially the sadomasochistic rituals celebrated in much pornography, the practices of instrumental reason are extended to the erotic. Through the fantasy, the agent confirms his identity through the exercise of power over the other (who will usually be, but need not be, a woman). What is crucial is that the victim's submission to the power be (or come to be) voluntary and that her or his eventual annihilation be indefinitely deferred. Hence, it involves and indefinitely prolongs the moment of recognition but remains within the canons of instrumental reason. Further, the exercise of ritual violence against the woman is both a revenge against the mother and also a confirmation of that identity gained by repudiation of her.

It is important, however, that the resolutions offered in modern social life to the problems of the masculine subject are partial and depend heavily on fantasy and illusion. The abstract identity which is a precondition for the operation of the modern form of reason is a highly vulnerable one, and the main direction of the desires which move that subject—towards consumption, towards power—only recreates that vulnerability.

IV

According to Nietzsche (1968:9), nihilism comes on the scene when the highest values devalue themselves. On this account, nihilism is the consequence of the turning in on itself and self-destruction of a value system. It is in this sense that modern forms of reason are nihilistic.

Instrumental reason promises, if nothing else, the efficient realisation of an individual's goals. However, in its modern form it takes as its goals ends which are essentially unrealisable. The goal of consumption, for example, has come to be located, not in the satisfaction of one's consumption needs, but in the act of consumption itself. Thus the gratification achieved with a particular act of consumption is evanescent, and must immediately give way to the quest for further acts of consumption. What is achieved is not satisfaction but endless repetition. The goal of power is equally unattainable. In part, this is because power is always relative: to have it means to have more than others. Hence, one's own achievements are always liable to be undermined by the achievements of others (cf. Hobbes, n.d.: chs. 10–11). But the unattainability of power is also due to the internal logic of the quest. Whatever is achieved must always be used as a means for further achievement of exactly the same kind. In other words, whatever is achieved as an end only has value in so far as it can be used as a means to further ends. But, as Aristotle pointed out (1976:ch.1, section 1), means are only valuable in so far as their ends have value. Somewhere, there must be ends which have value as ends, not as means. Yet this is precisely what the conception of instrumental reason directed towards power rules out. As a consequence, the rational individual finds his energies directed toward ends which are of their nature unattainable. As was the case with consumption, what is achieved is not the efficient realisation of goals, but endless and compulsive repetition.

The incoherence of instrumental reason is not diminished by the operations of juridical reason. The demands of justice and impartiality do import new values, indeed values which are often at odds with those of instrumental reason. These demands place limits on the instrumental activity of any given individual by imposing some principles of equal treatment (or perhaps equal right) to others. What this does not provide is any further principle which might validate the restless endeavours of instrumental reason. It is silent about ends.

Weber's own worries about nihilism had a slightly different origin. For him, modern scientific reason revealed a world which is devoid of human or quasi-human meaning and purpose. We thus find ourselves in a world in which the only values are those posited by us, values which are therefore a matter of subjective choice, not rational argument. Weber was aware of a paradox here. For if it was science which revealed a world in which values can only exist as non-rational choices, the commitment to science itself becomes just such a matter of non-rational choice. Science cannot validate itself, and the choice of science as a way of life is no more or no less rational than the choice of religion (Weber, 1919).

Weber's worry here is that the subjectivism and arbitrary nature of value which is revealed by scientific reason threatens to encompass science itself. This worry may be deepened. For while Weber assumes that there is a tendency towards both scientific rationality and instrumental rationality in the modern world, he is aware that these two 'types of rationalism are very different, in spite of the fact that ultimately they belong inseparably together' (Weber, 1922–23:293). The problem is that there is an insuperable tension between the two forms of rationality.

One might treat scientific reason as a form of instrumental rationality by positing as its specific end the appropriation of the true—a conception and understanding of the world as it is in itself. No doubt there are those who do take this as an aim in life. Probably it was this lonely commitment to 'science as a vocation' which Weber was, against all his principles, advocating. But one cannot help hearing at this point Nietzsche's mockery of those 'objective' men whose desire it is to reflect the world like mirrors. They are 'precious instruments' who need to be taken good care of but whose role must be to be used by those who are mightier (1973:115–116). In the modern world, it is instrumental reason, i.e. that form of reason which in its dominant forms is directed towards power, which does and must dominate that other form of reason directed towards truth.

It might be suggested that herein lies the place and the justification of scientific reason: that as the necessary means for the efficient pursuit of one's ends, one needs an understanding of the world as it is, not as one would want it to be. But the connection is contingent at best. There are far too many cases where ideology and self-deception are necessary components in the achieving of certain goals for it to be plausible to hold that there is some essential relationship between instrumental reason and the pursuit of truth.

Indeed, the argument here can be reversed. It is plausible to claim that the institutions, practices and discourses of modern science exist largely within the space provided for them by the dominant forms of instrumental reason—that which is directed towards power. But if this is so, precisely for that reason, science cannot make good the claim to 'truth' in any realist sense, for example to provide an account of the world which corresponds to how it is. Compare the situation with prescientific world views such as those of religion. From the perspective of modern science, these appear to construct a world which involves an objectification of the desires and fears of the human subject but which are not recognised as such. But the same analysis can be provided of modern science itself. The world displayed by modern science appears as an objectification of those desires which are served by that science particularly the desire for power. The world lacks meaning (is 'disenchanted' in Weber's poignant phrase) just because it is conceived as a means to ends which are independent of it. In other words, the meaningless world revealed by science has no more claim to be the 'real world' than has the meaningful world revealed by religion. Both worlds are the objectification of the desires of the subjects involved in the construction of the discourse. So just to the extent that scientific rationality is subsumed within instrumental reason it loses its status as a purveyor of objective truth.

A critique of modern conceptions of reason should not be confused with an affirmation of the non-rational. The critique I have provided here is largely an auto-critique: it makes use of certain principles of reason in order to show the limited, partial and ultimately self-defeating nature of the conception of reason which contains them. It is by its own criteria that instrumental reason in its characteristically modern form fails: it does not provide for the efficient pursuit of human goals. It is because scientific reason claims to pursue objective truth that those forms of science which are subsumed within the logic of instrumental reason can be shown to fail in this aim. It is a mistake criticised by Hegel (1977:50–51) to think that the result of an effective auto-critique is a mere nothingness: a complete denial of the claims of reason. To reject modern conceptions of reason is in some way and in some form to go beyond them. Such a going beyond only appears to be a form of unreason if one accepts the claims of modern reason to be identical with rationality itself. From a more critical and historically informed perspective, it is part of the process of constructing new and more adequate conceptions of rationality (cf. Lloyd, 1984: especially 109–110).

Similar remarks can be made about the construction of masculinity and femininity associated with modern conceptions of reason. To assert the feminine has point as a reminder of the significance of certain norms and ideals which have been subordinated or excluded. But ultimately, the present construction of femininity exists as the symbiotic opposite of masculinity: it presupposes and is presupposed by it. Hence it does not provide an independent set of principles to set up against dominant masculine norms. Corresponding to the nihilistic tendencies of modern reason are certain obsessive, repetitive and ultimately self- and other-destructive features of masculinity. Its claims to represent the human condition as such are invalidated by the existence of the feminine; its implicit claim to represent and realise some ideal of human existence is invalidated by its own criteria. It is by reference to its own standards and ideals that masculinity is driven to go beyond itself.

4   Inscriptions and body-maps: representations and the corporeal[1]

Elizabeth Grosz

. . . books are only metaphors of the body . . .

—Michael de Certeau 'Des outils pour ecrire le corps'
Traverses 14–15,1979, p.3

The book has somehow to be adapted to the body.

—Virginia Woolf *A Room of One's Own* Penguin,
1963, p.78

THE BODY has figured in many recent texts as a writing surface on which messages can be inscribed. The meta-phorics of *body-writing* poses the body, its epidermic surface, muscular-skeletal frame, ligaments, joints, blood vessels and internal organs, as *corporeal surfaces* on which engraving inscription or 'graffiti' are etched. The metaphor of the *textualised body* affirms the body as a page or material surface on which messages may be inscribed. The analogy between bodies and texts is a close one: tools of body-engraving—social, surgical, epistemic or disciplinary—mark bodies in culturally specific ways; writing instruments—the pen, stylus, or laser beam—inscribe the blank page of the body. The 'messages' or 'texts' produced by such procedures construct bodies as networks of social signification, meaningful and functional 'subjects' within assemblages composed with other subjects. Each gains a (provisional) identity from its constitutive relations with others. Inscriptions of the corporeal differences between bodies can be seen to produce body-subjects as living significations, social texts capable of being read or interpreted.

I want to explore and evaluate this metaphor of corporeal inscription. The metaphor does not, of course, originate with those associated with it today—Foucault, Deleuze, Irigaray, Lyotard, Lingis et al.; it is anticipated in considerable detail in Nietzsche's writings, and is strikingly evoked in Franz Kafka's short story, 'The Penal Settlement'[2]. Both Nietzsche and Kafka conjecture about the ways in which social power, especially punitive and moral systems, mark bodies in more or less violent, brutal and socially sanctioned ways, through institutionalised cruelty and torture. It is not my aim to encourage sadomasochism (though an analysis of cultural sadomasochism would be well worth undertaking) but to re-examine various presumptions within current feminist and leftist theory about the ways in which power functions to construct subjectivity.

This chapter will explore the following theses:

1 that, as a *material* series of processes, power actively marks or brands bodies as social, inscribing them with the attributes of subjectivity. (This is intended to challenge a prevailing model of power conceived as a system of ideas, concepts, values and beliefs, *ideology*, that primarily effect consciousness);

2 that consciousness is an *effect* or result, rather than the cause of the inscription of flesh and its conversion into a (social) body; and

3 that while relying on the work of a number of male theorists of the body (Foucault, Nietzsche and Lingis), feminist assertions of sexual difference simultaneously problematise their work. Thus, although this chapter focuses on male theorists, my objectives remain feminist: to see what in their works may be of use for a feminist account of sexed bodies.

Writing bodies

Foucault is probably the most well-known theorist of the body today. His disparate works cluster around a thematics of carnality and its relations to subjectivity, around, that is, the intricate history of the link between pleasure/pain/sensation/knowledge and power. Foucault's account of the internal relations between power and knowledge relies on a belief that power functions *directly* on bodies by means of disciplinary practices, which, while relying on knowledges, operate without mediation of *conceptual* or intellectual processes—that is, without resort to a concept like 'ideology'. He bypasses a primarily marxist-psychoanalytic-semiotic understanding of social power, which sees ideology as a system of representations, signs received by subjects regarding the social world and their place within it. For him, power is not a set of signs, or texts, meanings or conceptual functions. Power is a material force that *does* and *makes* things, it is a substrate of forces *in play* within a given socio-personal constellation. The body is its primary object. In *Discipline and Punish* (1977) and the first two volumes of *The History of Sexuality* (1977; 1985) he argues that power is inscribed on and by bodies through modes of social supervision and discipline as well as self-regulation. The bodies and behaviours of individuals are targets for the deployment of power, and they are also the means by which power functions and proliferates.

Power-knowledge is invested in producing determinate types of bodies, with correlative psychical, economic and socio-moral attributes. Bodies are objects of knowledges, which then reinvest the body in increasing spirals of knowledge-pleasure and power: 'The body is moulded by a great many distinct regimes; it is broken down by the rhythms of work, rest, and holidays; it is poisoned by food or values, through eating habits or moral laws; it constructs resistances' (Foucault, 1977:153). If power is primarily *ideological*, that is, a system of conceptual distortion, if ideas, beliefs, ideologies, values—some kind of soul—are to be attributed to the human subject, this is an effect of a certain mode of corporeal inscription. For this reason, Foucault is irresistably led in his accounts of the history of knowledges and of truth to accounts of punishment, torture, medicalised observations, sexuality and pleasure—all processes that mark the body in specific ways of specific rituals and practices. But if the body is the strategic target of systems of codification, supervision and constraint, it is also because the body and its energies and capacities exert an uncontrollable, unpredictable threat to a regular, systematic mode of social organisation. As well as being the site of knowledge-power, the body is thus also a site of *resistance*, for it exerts a recalcitrance, and always entails the possibility of a counterstrategic reinscription, for it is capable of being self-marked, self-represented in alternative ways.

Within our own culture, the inscription of bodies occurs both *violently*—in prisons, juvenile homes, hospitals, psychiatric institutions—keeping the body confined, constrained, supervised and regimented, marked by 'body-writing-implements', such as handcuffs, traversing neural pathways by charges of electricity in shock therapy, the straitjacket, the regimen of drug habituation, chronologically regulated time-and-labour divisions, cellular and solitary confinement, and deprivation of mobility, the bruising of bodies in police interrogations etc.; and by *less openly aggressive* but no less coercive means, through cultural and personal values, norms and commitments. The latter involve a psychic inscription of the body through its adornment, its rituals of exercise and diet, all more or less 'voluntary' inscriptions by lifestyle, habits, and behaviours. Makeup, stilettos, bras, hairstyles, clothing, underclothing, mark women's bodies in ways other than the ways in which hairdos, professional training, personal grooming, body-building etc, mark men's. There is nothing natural or a priori about these modes of corporeal inscriptions: through them, bodies are marked so as to make them amenable to the prevailing exigencies of power. They make the body into a particular kind of body—pagan, primitive, medieval capitalist, Italian, American, Australian. What is sometimes loosely called 'body-language' is a not inappropriate description of the ways in which culturally specific grids of power, regulation and force condition and provide techniques for the formation of particular bodies.

Body-writing relies on the one hand on extraneous instruments, tools for marking the body's surface—the stylus, or cutting edge, the needle, the tattoo, the razor; and on interior, psychical and physiological body-products or objects to remake the body—moisturising cremes, makeup, exercise, the sensations, pleasures, pains, sweat and tears of the body-subject. The subject is *named* by being tagged or branded on its surface, creating a particular kind of 'depth-body' or interiority, a psychic layer the subject identifies as its (disembodied) core. Subjects thus produced are not simply the imposed results of alien, coercive forces; the body is internally lived, experienced and acted upon by the subject and the social collectivity. Messages coded onto the body can be 'read' only within a social system of organisation and meaning. They mark the subject by, and as, a series of signs within the collectivity of other signs, signs which bear the marks of a particular social law and organisation, and through a particular constellation of desires and pleasures.

The subject is marked as a series of (potential) messages

from/of the (social) Other, the symbolic order. Its flesh is transformed into a *body*, organised and hierarchised according to the requirements of a particular social and family nexus. The body becomes a 'text' and is fictionalised and positioned within those myths that form a culture's social narratives and self-representations. In some cultural myths, this means the body can be read as an *agent*, a contractual, exchanging being, a subject of the social contract; while in others, it becomes a body-shell capable of being overtaken by the Other's messages, (e.g. in shamanism, or epilepsy). Social narratives create their 'characters' and 'plots' through the tracing of the body's biological contours and organic outlines by writing tools. Writing instruments confine corporeal capacities and values, proliferating the body's reactions and capacities, stimulating and stifling social conformity (the acting out of these narrative roles as 'live theatre') *and* a corporeal resistance to the social. The consequences for the social are twofold: the 'intextuation of bodies', which transform the discursive apparatus or social fiction/ knowledge regimes, 'correcting' or updating them, rendering them more truthful, and ensuring their increasingly microscopic focus on bodies; and the *incarnation* of social law in the movements, actions and desires of bodies.

Social inscription

For Nietzsche, civilisation instils its basic requirements only by branding the law on bodies through a *mnemonics of pain*. Morality, shame and guilt are not the causes but the consequences of the subject's incorporation into collective memory or history. Nietzsche conditions history and social life on the provision of a kind of corporeal memory for each subject, a memory fashioned out of the suffering and pain of the body. For example, economic and social law functions only if the relation between debtors and creditors is founded on some sort of contractual *guarantee*, ensuring the payment of debts. For Nietzsche, justice does not originate in economic equivalences or some kind of mathematical computation, but from a compensatory equivalence of the economic with the corporeal. This equivalence ensures that, even in the case of economic bankruptcy, the debt is repayable corporeally. Nietzsche cites examples from Roman law where

> The creditor . . . could inflict every kind of indignity
> and torture upon the body of the debtor; for example,
> cut from it as much as seemed commensurate with the
> size of the debt—and everywhere and from early times
> one had exact evaluations, <u>legal</u> evaluations, of the
> individual limbs and parts of the body from this point of
> view, some of them going into horrible and minute
> detail. (Nietzsche, 1969:64)

Damages are not measured by equivalent values which are substitutable for each other, but by forces, organs or parts extractable from the debtor's body—a recompense by sanctioned cruelty. Contractual relations are thus the foundation of justice, and are themselves founded on *blood*, suffering and sacrifice. Within such a corporeal economy, the creditor gains both the benefit of a value equivalent to the debt, and the pleasure of extracting it from the debtor's body.

> It was in <u>this</u> sphere, the sphere of legal obligations,
> that the moral conceptual world of 'guilt', 'conscience',
> 'duty', 'sacredness of duty' had its origin: its beginnings
> were, like the beginnings of everything great on earth,
> soaked in blood thoroughly and for a long time . . . this
> world has never since lost a certain odor of blood and
> torture. (Not even in good old Kant: the categorical
> imperative smells of cruelty.) (p.65)

If morality and justice share a common genealogy in barter and cruelty, social history and memory are also instilled in individuals by being branded on flesh. The law functions because it is tattooed indelibly on the subject:

> Man could never do without blood, torture and
> sacrifices when he felt the need to create a memory for
> himself; the most dreadful sacrifices and pledges
> . . . the most repulsive mutilations . . . the cruellest rites of
> all the religious cults (and all religions are at the
> deepest level systems of cruelty)—all thus has its origin
> in the instinct that realized that pain is the most
> powerful aid to mnemonics . . . The worse man's memory
> has been, the more fearful has been the appearance of
> his customs; the severity of the penal code provides an
> especially significant measure of the degree of effort

> needed to overcome forgetfulness and to impose a few
> primitive demands of social existence as present realities
> upon these slaves of momentary affect and desire.
> (p.61).

These inscriptive processes may be more easily recognisable in those forms of body-engraving designated as 'savage' or 'primitive' rituals and practices. In his two books, *Excesses: Eros and Culture* (1984), and *Libido* (1985), Alphonso Lingis sketches an account of the body as a surface of erotogenic intensity, a product of and material to be further inscribed by social norms and ideals. The processes by which the 'primitive body' is scarred seem to us barbaric and painful. Lingis argues that the incision of or writing on the body surface functions to intensify, proliferate and extend the body's erotogenic sensitivity. Welts, cuts, scars, tattoos, perforations, incisions, inlays, function to increase the surface space of the body, creating locations, zones, hollows, ridges: places of special meaning (in some cases) and libidinal intensity (in all cases). What he describes is the creation of erotogenic orifices, rims or libidinal zones. These produce erotic zones potentially at all points on the surface of the skin and within the body's skeletal and muscular frame, a kind of weaving of inscriptive incisions with the sensations, sexual intensities and pleasures of the body. This *creates* erotogenic surfaces, not simply through the displacement of pregiven libidinal zones (as occurs in the 'civilised' neurosis, hysteria—where, say, in Dora's case, the meaning of the phallus is displaced from the genitals to the throat and oral cavity):

> *The savage inscription is a working over the skin, all
> surface effects. This cutting in orifices and raising
> tumescences does not contrive new receptor organs for
> a depth body . . . it extends an erotogenic surface . . . It's
> a multiplication of mouths, of lips, labia, anuses, these
> sweating and bleeding perforations and puncturings . . .
> these warts raised all over the abdomen, around the
> eyes . . . (Lingis, 1984:34)*

Primitive initiation ceremonies and our own more 'civilised' forms of permanent and semi-permanent social body-markings, designate the body as a socio-cultural and sexual body, a body positioned in relation to the social body, an environment, mythic affiliations with animals, plants, locations, sites etc. They not only mark the kind of individual, the position he or she may occupy, but also *the ways* in which these positions may be occupied.

Our own cultural practices are no less barbaric and no more civilised than those operating in so-called 'savage' or 'primitive' cultures. Primitive inscriptions, it seems, can be differentiated from so-called 'civilised' body-inscriptions in two broad ways: the 'savage' body is marked on its naked surface by signifiers, patterns, arrangements or organisations of marks, welts, cuts, perforations and swellings; and the 'savage body' does not presuppose, as does the 'modern' body, a latent or secret 'private' *depth*, a depth beneath the body's superficial or manifest surface. The 'modern body' is a body read symptomatically, in terms of what it hides. The primitive body, by contrast, is all surface: it is a proliferation or profusion of zones, indefinitely extending libidinal intensity unevenly over the body's surface, using pleasure and pain to somato-psychically mark the body (like the Medusa's Head) through a multiplication of phalluses that are peculiarly non-phallic because of their profusion. The processes of initiation and tattoo designated as 'primitive' intensify and unevenly spread over the whole of the body, along the lines marked by incisions of social position, location, name and function. These lines are inscribed in the case of the 'civilised body' as the lines of incision of surgical and chemical intervention, sites of social and personal remaking.

Primitive body-marking does not merely spread out a surface of sexual intensity across the subject's body, creating orifices, hollows, plateaux, rims where previously there were smooth spaces and unbroken surfaces. It divides up, or maps, the body in regular ordered sequences carefully specified in ritual form. Cicatrisations and scarifications mark the body as a public, collective or social object—as a map of social needs, requirements and excesses; and as a legible, mean-receiving, interiority, a subjectivity experiencing itself in and as a determinate form. The body and its privileged zones of sensation, reception and projection are coded by objects, categories, affiliations, lineages, which engender or make real the subject's social, familial, marital or economic position and/or identity within a social hierarchy: 'It is the incision and tumescence of new intensive points, pain-pleasure points, that first extends the erotogenic extension. What we have then, is a spacing, a distributive system of marks. They form not representations and not signifying chains, but figures, figures of intensive points, whose law of systematic distribution is lateral and immanent, horizontal and not traverse' (Lingis, 1984:38). The primitive body is distinguished from the civilised body not by degrees of barbarism or pain, nor in terms of the writing implements and tools used, but by its *sign-ladenness*. In the case of the civilised body, bodies are created as sign-systems, cohesively meaningful and integrated into patterns that can be read in terms of personality; and above all, by the construction of a *depth* body, a body within which resides an interiority, a psyche or self. Ours is not a *superficial* identity but an enigma to be explored by reduction of the body to a symptom of the self: 'All that is civilised is significant . . . We find the ugliness of tattooed nakedness puerile and shallow . . . The savage fixing his identity on his skin . . . Our identity is inward, it is our functional integrity as machines to produce a certain civilised, that is, coded, type of action' (Lingis, 1984:43). Inscriptions on the subject's body coagulate corporeal signifiers into signs, producing the effects of meanings, depth, representations within or subtending our social order. The intensity and flux of sensations traversing the body become fixed into consumable, gratifiable form, become needs, requirements and desires which can now be attributed to an underlying psyche or consciousness. Corporeal fragmentation, the unity and disunity of the perceptual body, becomes organised into the structure of an ego or consciousness, which marks a secret or private depth. These mark the 'modern' or civilised body as use and exchange-value, the production and exchanges of messages.

Sexed bodies

Do differently sexed bodies require different inscriptive tools to etch their different surfaces? Is it power which inscribes bodies as sexually different? Or does sexual difference simply require sexually differentiated regimes of power? Is *sex* or *gender* the object of power? These remain central dilemmas for feminists working on the texts of the male theorists of the body I have been discussing. Their work remains problematic, even if highly suggestive for feminists, in describing the interventions of power on *women's* bodies.

Foucault, for example, in certain texts (especially *The History of Sexuality*) implies that the divisions between the sexes, and the different characteristics attributed to them by knowledges, institutions and practices, are effects of power. He implies that, outside the deployments of power, there is nothing other than 'bodies, organs, somatic locatizations, functions, anatomo-physiological systems, sensations and pleasures' (1978:152–53). For him sex, not gender, is the object of power. Women's medical, moral, psychological and domestic position is specified only as part of a regime which creates the category of 'sex', bringing together a heterogeneity of hitherto non-specific, disparate and not always commensurable elements of bodies and pleasures: 'Sex—that agency which appears to dominate us and that secret which seems to underlie all that we are, that point which enthralls us through the power it manifests and the meaning it conceals, and which we ask to reveal what we are, and to free us from what defines us—is doubtless but an ideal point in the deployment of sexuality and its operations' (1978:155).

In spite of his brilliant evocation of corporeal inscriptions, Lingis also remains committed to a paradoxically sexed yet neutral (neutered?) body underlying or forming the surface to be incised. It is as if the body were a pure plenitude of undifferentiated processes and functions that becomes sexed only by social marks: 'circumcision castrates the male of the labia about his penis, as the clitoridectomy castrates the female of her penis. It is through *castration of the natural bisexual* that the social animal is produced' (Lingis, 1984:40, emphasis added). If these male theorists of the body are still relevant to feminist theory—as I think they are—then it seems essential that feminists distinguish their own positions as feminists from this commitment to a neutralised, non-specified corporeality; and also that they make clear what the raw materials and basic units of inscription are, that is, sexed, carnal, specific bodies: male, female, black, white, etc.

To conclude, I would like to make some suggestions about how feminists may use these conceptions of the body to articulate women's lived experiences and their potential for autonomy. These suggestions are, I think, consistent with the insights of these (male) philosophers of corporeality, and also with feminist commitments to explore and question prevailing categories of sexual polarisation. I will outline these briefly.

1. Biological, anatomical, physiological and neuro-physiological processes cannot be automatically attributed a *natural* status. It is not clear that what is biological is necessarily natural. Biological or organic functions are the raw materials of any processes of production of determinate forms of subjectivity and

material, including corporeal, existence. If this is the case, universal or quasi-universal physiological givens, such as menstrual, anatomical and hormonal factors, need to be carefully considered as irreducible features of the writing surface, distinct from the script inscribed: a kind of 'texture' more than a designated content for the 'text' or the 'intextuated body' produced. The raw materials themselves are not 'pure' in so far as culture, social and psychological factors intervene to give them their manifest forms: it is well known, for example, that menstrual patterns can be severely disrupted or stopped according to diet, exercise patterns, anxiety etc. Biology provides a *bedrock* for social inscription but is not a fixed or static substratum: it interacts with and is overlaid by psychic, social and signifying relations (see Grosz, 1987). The body can thus be seen not as a blank, passive page, a neutral ground of meaning, but as an active, productive, 'whiteness' that constitutes the writing surface as resistant to the imposition of any or all patterned arrangements. It has a texture, a tonus, a materiality that is an active ingredient in the messages produced. It is less like a blank, smooth, frictionless surface, a page, and more like a copperplate to be etched.

2. The anatomical differences between the sexes must be distinguished from the ways in which sexed bodies are culturally classified. *Differences between bodies* can be represented on a vast continuum which could include bodies typical or representative of each sex, but also, all those who fit into both categories (for example, hermaphrodites) or neither. Conceived on the model of 'pure difference', corporeality is potentially infinite in form, no mode exhibiting a prevalence over others. However, within our social and signifying systems, this plenum is divided and categorised according to binary pairs—male/female, black/white, young/old etc.—which reduce ambiguous terms not amenable to binary hierarchisation, back into this polarised structure (hence Foucault's analysis of the hermaphrodite Herculine Barbin, who is legally required to change 'her' sex from female to male; there is no possibility of adopting a sexual position that is neither male nor female). From *pure differences* of a biological type, *distinctions* and *oppositions*, binary categories and mutually exclusive oppositions are formed. It is thus *not* simply a matter of the socially variable issue of *gender* being imposed on a biological neutral body, but rather, a *social mapping* of the body tracing its anatomical and physiological details by social representations. The procedures which mark

male and female bodies ensure that the biological capacities of bodies are always socially coded into sexually distinct categories. It is the *social inscription of sexed bodies*, not the imposition of an acculturised, sexually neutral *gender* that is significant for feminist purposes (see Gatens, 1983).

3. While the sexes are represented according to a binary structure that reduces *n-sexes* to two, the binary structure itself reduces one term within the pair to a position definitionally dependent on the other, being defined as its negation, absence or lack. This is a *phallocentric* representational system in the sense in which women's corporeal specificity is defined and understood only in some relation to men's—as men's opposites, their doubles or their complements. This means that women's autonomously defined carnal and bodily existence is buried beneath both male-developed biological scientific paradigms, and a male-centred system of social inscription that marks female bodies as men's (castrated, inferior, weaker, less capable) counterparts. In other words, not only is the corporeal surface to be inscribed differently, the social regimes of body-tattoo, incision and marking, the tools of body writing, are oppositionally used to produce male bodies as virile, strong, phallic, hierarchised, structured, teleological, in relation to women's passive, weak, castrated, disorganised bodily structure.

4. Inscriptive procedures marking the body and producing it as sexually determinant and coded are active in transforming the anatomo-physiological structure of the body as socially located *morphology*. Body-morphologies are the results of the *social meaning* of the body. The morphological surface is a retracing of the anatomical and physiological foundation of the body by systems of social signifiers and signs traversing and even penetrating bodies. Morphological differences between sexed bodies imply *both* a traced, 'biological' difference which is transcribed or translated by discursive, textual representations, *and* corporeal significations. It implies a productive, *changeable*, non-fixed biological substratum mapped by a social, political and familial grid of practices and meanings. The morphological dimension is a function of socialisation and apprenticeship, and produces as its consequences a subject, soul, personality or inner depth. This has direct implications for the beloved feminist category of 'gender' and its relation to its counterpart, 'sex'. Masculinity and femininity are not simply social categories as it were externally or arbitrarily imposed on the subject's sex. Masculine and feminine are necessarily related to the structure

of the lived experience and meaning of *bodies*. As Gatens argues in her critique of the sex/gender distinction (1983), masculinity and femininity *mean different things* according to whether they are lived out on and experienced by male or female bodies. Gender is an effect of the body's social morphology. What is mapped onto the body is not unaffected by the body onto which it is projected.

5. Whereas morphological *oppositions* between sexed (male or female) bodies are prevalent in contemporary Western cultures (at the least), their oppositional or phallocentric representations are now capable of being challenged so that we need no longer accept an unchangeable natural basis for their social status. Their morphological status, as an effect of the transcription and transmission of meanings and values for the body and its specific parts and processes, can now be addressed by the kinds of theoretical, literary and cultural representations of an autonomously conceived and defined femininity, or woman-centredness, that feminist work has provided. The oppositional form of this morphology, moreover, can be contested, even if not readily overthrown, by demonstrating the ways in which male self-definitions require and produce definitions of the female as their inverted or complementary counterparts. This implies, among other things, an analysis of the ways in which masculine or phallocentric discourses and knowledges rely on images, metaphors and figures of woman and femininity to support and justify their speculations. It also, and perhaps more importantly, implies an exploration of the disavowed corporeal and psychic dependence of the masculine, with its necessary foundation in women's bodies, on the female corporeality it cannot claim as its own territory (the maternal body).

5 The discursive construction of Christ's body in the later Middle Ages: resistance and autonomy

Jennifer Ash

T HIS chapter is an investigation into the religiosity of the late Middle Ages, with its focus on the bleeding, dying body of Christ crucified. I am interested in the discursive construction of that body, and the relationship which existed between that body and (the body of) the medieval worshipper. However, I would like to stress that what I am presenting here is work which is in progress; I am not offering final conclusions or solutions, only possibilities.

I must also specify the methodological equipment I am using in this investigative enterprise: a combination of semiotic theory, French feminist theorising, and Lacanian psychoanalysis. For many who are working in the area of medieval studies there is a problem with this, that I use twentieth-century theory to analyse and interpret discursive material—texts and textuality—from this other period. Does the application of contemporary theorising to the past constitute an anachronistic interpretative practice, an act of analytic and interpretative violence against the cultural integrity, the cultural specificity of an historical other?

For the semiotician, objections such as these are irrelevant.

The semiotic enterprise has demonstrated the relativity which necessarily constitutes both textual production and textual reception. The text is not an autonomous entity, but is, rather, historically specific, bound to the signifying network, the cultural context which produced it. And when in the twentieth century we are confronted with a medieval text, we must be aware of and respect its difference, its cultural specificity. Yet we will never be able to read that text from a position within the culture which produced it. My reading of medieval texts and textuality will necessarily be constrained by the discourses which inform my own position within late-twentieth-century Western capitalism, those discourses which have constructed me as thinking, speaking subject.

For this investigation, I have made use of both visual and verbal texts. By visual texts I mean sculpture, painting, drawing and manuscript illuminations; by verbal texts I am referring to several specific generic types: religious prose and poetry, hagiography, sermons and prayers, and (selections from the) Cycle plays. The dates of the texts used range from the twelfth to the fifteenth centuries; provenance extends across linguistic and geographical boundaries: England, France, Italy, Germany and the Low Countries. I should stress that not all of these verbal texts were written in vernacular languages; many were produced in Latin, the 'universal language' of the educated, the official language of ecclesiastical discourse.

It is possible to locate shifts within Christian consciousness quite simply through the (re)construction of that event central to Christian faith and cosmology: the (re)construction of the Crucifixion which also works to construct Christianity's distinctive and distinguishing signifier. The originary moment of Christianity is located in the Incarnation, the enfleshing of the Divine Word, the paradox of the Christian God-man. The purpose of the Incarnation was redemptive, and this was effected through another paradox: that of (the) Divine death. Late Medieval Christianity turned its attention to the events of the Passion, obsessively focusing on the battered and bleeding body of Divinity dying. The Crucifixion, rather than the Resurrection, was situated at the centre of Salvation History. The late Middle Ages constructed a Christian discourse which venerated, as its object of worship, a body—passive, suffering, bleeding, dying. The Christianity of the later Middle Ages was a discourse constituted through a rhetoric (both visual and verbal) of violence and death, of pain and suffering: a discourse of the body and the bodily, revelling in the fleshliness of the Word.

Transubstantiation was made official doctrine in 1215. The

Wood carving, first half of the fourteenth century. Alps, Salzburg
(*Schiller, 1972 no. 486*)

Wood carving, c. 1300, Y-cross. Friesach (*Schiller, 1972 no. 484*)

Wood carving, c. 1300, Y-cross. Cologne (*Schiller, 1972 no. 483*)

Wood carving, c. 1370, Pietà, Western Germany, Bonn (*Schiller, 1972 no. 628*)

celebration of the eucharistic sacrament was symbolic no longer: to take communion was to participate in a communal, ritual feasting, was to eat God's flesh and drink His blood. The constituent elements of the Eucharist were metaphoric no longer; Christ's body and blood was a real and actual presence in the bread and wine.[1] A feast day dedicated to God's body, to Christ's flesh and blood, was instituted in 1264, although it was not universally celebrated until 1311–12. This was Corpus Christi, the feast which led to the creation of the English Cycle plays—a drama dedicated to the enfleshing of the Word, the corporeal carnivalisation of the Divine.

From the year 1200 onwards, within the mass, the priest elevated the host at the moment of consecration. When transubstantiation became doctrine, this celebratory, ceremonial gesture was invested with power and meaning: to see the host was enough. The communicant could consume the body of God simply by looking, by (greedily) gazing upon Divine flesh held in the hands of the priest. And, as the body of God, the host was worshipped and adored, was treated as the most sacred relic of all. Stories circulated: fantastical narratives of bleeding hosts, wonder-working hosts, stories 'authenticating' and providing popular 'proof' for the actuality of Divine presence (Ward, 1987:13–18). The body of Divine humanity was the object of orthodox and institutionalised Christian devotional consciousness and practices. But more precisely, it was this body in its moment of dying which was the object of veneration and adoration; that is, the body of God as sacrificial victim, silent in His suffering, patient in the pain and shame of crucifixion.

There is a set of discursive statements which, in late medieval Christianity, work to construct God's (human) body in a very specific way, crossing boundaries of media and genres. But the specificity of this construction of Christ's body functions on the level of the metaphoric as well as the manifestly literal. That is, the construction of Christ's body—battered, bleeding, dying—is the production of a polysemous signifier: Christ's body means and signifies differently in different contexts; Christ's wounded body can signify a range of different signifieds simultaneously. Christ's body is plural, polyvalent, polysemous. The relationship between Divinity and the human subject who worships Divine-Other can be apprehended, and signified through different discursive and rhetorical possibilities. For example, in her *Revelations of Divine Love* Julian of Norwich discusses the visions of the crucified Christ she experienced while desperately ill, and supposedly dying: 'And thus I saw that god enjoyeth that he is our fader, and god enjoyeth that he is our moder, and god enjoyeth that he is our very spouse, and our soule his lovyd wyfe. And Cryst enjoyeth þat he is our broder, and Jhesu enioyeth that he is our savyour' (Colledge and Walsh, 1978:546). The speaker here identifies the range of possible signifiers which might be used to encode the relationship of each Christian with Divine-Other. And there are other texts, which, like Julian's speaking, use the rhetoric of a familial discourse to signify the relationship between self and Divinity. These texts metaphorically encode the intensely, exclusively private and personal nature of this relationship with the Divine. In the above statement, Julian makes chaste reference to her (Divine) 'spouse', while other speakers and other texts use a more passionate and aroused language. But whether or not He is specified as 'spouse', the Divine here functions as a very beloved other; it is Christ constructed as lover in the tradition of the 'sponsa motif'— metaphoricity originating in the great biblical lovesong of Solomon.

Texts such as the Middle English Passion lyrics, Richard Rolle's *Meditations on the Passion*, *The Book of Margery Kempe*, but especially those (extraordinary) texts of poetic prose—*þe Wohunge of Ure Lauerd, On Ureisun of Oure Louerde*, and *A Talkyng of þe Loue of God*—these texts verbally (re)construct the spectacle of the bleeding, dying body of Christ.[2] This body is made a site for speculation, contemplation and adoration; the crucified body is the object of worship, but it is also the object of desire. The bleeding wounds are privileged, invested with meaning which is not only salvific but also erotic. That is, the verbal (re)construction of the Crucifixion is the construction of Christ as beloved other. In each of the poetic prose texts, speaking begins with an ecstatic rhapsodising to Christ. The opening utterance of *A Talkyng of þe Loue of God* is the most spectacular.

Ihesu soþ God. Godes sone.
Ihesu. soþ God. soþ mon. Mon
Maydenes child. Ihesu myn
holy loue.Mi siker swetnesse.
Ihesu myn herte.my sele. my
soule hele. Ihesu. swete Ihesu.
Ihesu. deore Ihesu.Ihesu.
Almihti Ihesu.Ihesu mi lord. my
leof.my lyf.myn holy wey. Myn
hony ter.Ihesu. al weldinde
Ihesu.Ihesu þou art al þat
I.hoþe. Ihesu mi makere. þat me

Jesus, true God, God's son!
Jesus, true God, true man! Man,
virgin's child! Jesus, my holy
love, my sure sweetness! Jesus,
my heart, my happiness,
health of my soul! Jesus, sweet
Jesus! Jesus, dear Jesus! Jesus,
almighty Jesus! Jesus, my lord,
my beloved, my life, my balm,
my nectar! Jesus, all powerful
Jesus! Jesus, You are all that I
hope. Jesus, my maker, who

madest of nou3t.And al þat is in heuene.and in eorþe. Ihesu my Buggere.þou bou3test me so deore.wiþ þi stronge passion. wiþ þi precious blod and wiþ þi pyneful deþ on Roode. Ihesu my saueour.þat me schalt sauen.þorw þi muchele Merci. & þi muchele mi3t Ihesu my weole.& al my wynne. Ihesu þat al my blisse is inne. Ihesu al so.þat þou art. so feir and so swete.3it art þou so louelich.Louelich and louesum.þat þe holy Angeles.þat euere þe bi holden. ben neuere folle. to loken on þi face. Ihesu þou art al feir. whon þe sonne a3eyn þe. nis bote a schade.And schomeþ a3eyn þe brihte leor of hire þesternesse. þou þat 3iuest hire liht.and al þat liht haueþ.Lihte my þester herte. Graunte þat þi brihtnesse clanse my soule. þat is vnseliche. wiþ sunne foule I. fuiled.Lord mak hire worþi. to þi swete wonynge. Cundele me wiþ þe blisse. of þi brenninde loue. Swete Ihesu my leoue lyf.Let me beo þi seruaunt.and lere me for to loue þe.&mak me for to serue þe.louynde lord. so þat onliche þi loue.be euer al my lyking my þou3t and my longyng.Amen.

made me of nothing and all that is in heaven and on earth. Jesus, my Redeemer, You bought me so dear with Your grievous passion, with Your precious blood and with Your painful death on the cross. Jesus, my Saviour, who shall save me through Your great mercy and Your great power. Jesus, my weal and all my delight! Jesus, in whom is all my bliss! Jesus, besides that You are so fair and so sweet, You are moreover so lovely; lovely and lovable that the holy angels, who always behold You, are never weary of looking at Your face. Jesus, You are all-fair, the sun being but a shadow in comparison with You and ashamed of her darkness in the presence of Your bright face. You, who give her light and all that has light, light my dark heart. Grant that Your brightness cleanse my soul, which is miserably defiled with foul sin. Lord, make her worthy to be Your sweet dwelling. Kindle me with the bliss of Your burning love. Sweet Jesus, my dear life, let me be Your servant, and teach me to love You and make me serve You, loving Lord, so that Your love alone be ever all my delight, my thought and my longing. Amen. (Westra, 1950: 2–5)

But the construction of Christ as Lover is also the construction of Christ as mother.

a ihesu louerd þi grip. hwi abbe ich eni licung in oþer þing þene in þe. hwi loue ich eni þing boten þe one. hwi ne bi-hold ich hu þu strabstest þe for me on þe rode. hwine warpe ich me

Ah! Lord Jesus, thy succour! why have I any delight in other things than in thee? why love I anything but thee alone? O that I might behold how thou stretchedst thyself for me on the

bitweone þe ilke earmes. swa
swiþe wide to-spradde. he
openeþ swa þe moder hire
earmes hire leoue child for to
cluppen.ȝe soþes and tu
deorwurþe louerd. gostliche to us
and to [þine] deorlinges wiþ þe
ilke spredunge gest. as þe moder
to hire child. hua leof. hwa lif.
hwa deþ him þe bitweonen. hwa
wule beo bi-cluppet. a ihesu
þin eadmodnesse and þin
muchele milce. hwi nam ich in
þin earmes. In þin earmes swa
istrahte. and isprad on rode.

A. Ihesu þin ore. whi haue
I.likyng.in oþer þing þen in þe.þat
bouȝtest me so deore. Whi ne
be holde i. algates. wiþ eȝe of
myn herte. hou þou henge for
my loue streyned on Roode. þin
Armes wyde I. spradde. þi
derling to cluppe.wiþ toknyng of
trewe loue.þat sprong out of þi
syde. Whi nul I.beo þi derling
and loue þe ouer alle þing and
comen to þi clupping.to cleuen in
þin armes.and cluppen þe
swete. A derworpe lord muchel
is þi myldeschupe. þat
spraddest so þin Armes.
bodiliche on Roode. and in
toknyng of þat openest þi
grace.þat sprad is so wyde.wiþ
loueliche tollyng.& open is and
redi to alle þat in synne beop
gostliche storuen.Clepeþ him to
lyue.and to loue cosses. As
Moder doþ hire deore sone.þat
hereþ hit wepen. Takeþ hit in
hireArmes.and askeþ him so
sweteliche. Ho leof. Ho lef heo

cross! O that I might cast
myself between those same arms,
so very wide outspread! He
openeth them as doth the mother
her arms to embrace her
beloved child. Yea, of a truth!
And thou, dear Lord, goest
spiritually towards us, thy
darlings, with the same out-
spreading (embrace) as the
mother to her children. Each is
beloved; each is dear; each places
himself in thy arms; each will
be embraced. Ah! Jesus, thy
humility and thy great mercy!
O that I were in thy arms, in thy
arms so out-stretched and
outspread on the cross! (Morris,
1886:184,185)

Ah Jesus, of Your grace! Why
do I take pleasure in other things
than in You, who bought me so
dear? Why do I not continually
contemplate with the eyes of
my heart how You hung for the
love of me, stretched on the
cross, Your arms wide-spread to
embrace Your darling in token
of true love that sprang from
Your side? Why do I not wish
to be Your darling and love You
above everything and come to
Your embracing to cling in Your
arms and clasp You sweetly?
Ah dear Lord, great is Your
clemency, who thus spread
Your arms bodily on the cross
and, as a token of that, open
Your grace, which is so widely
spread, with sweet inviting,
and is open and ready for
everyone who is spiritually
dead in sin, calls him to life and
to love-kisses, as a mother
does her dear son, who hears
him cry and takes him in her

doþ him. hire bi twenen.Ho wole
be bi clupped.and cusse me
swete.who haþ do my deore.who
haþ do þe so.Heo ʒeueþ him
hire pappe. and stilleþ his teres.
Þat pappe beo my lykyng.my
mournyng.my longyng. swete
Ihesu heuene kyng. to souken
of my fulle.þat þorw þe speres
openyng.in feole mennes
gounyng.wiþ dewing of þi deore
blood.stilleþ alle bales.And
wher eny mon wene þat he
schal.haue part of þat ilke
sok.of þi deore herte in heuene
riche blisse. and þere be þi
derlying.in þi deore
cluppying.bote he þe heere
cluppe.hongynge on Roode. And
parte of þi passion. þorw holy
meditacion.wiþ loue lykynde
þouʒt.and reuþe of his herte.
Nay sikerliche nay.ne trouwe þat
no mon. Whose euere wol
haue part. þer of þi blisse. he mot
dele wiþ þe. heer of þi pyne.

arms and asks him so sweetly:
'Hush, darling; hush, dear'. She
takes him in her arms. 'He wants
to be embraced and to kiss me
sweetly? Who, my darling, who
has done this to you?' She
gives him her breast and stops
his tears. That breast be my
pleasure, my care, my longing,
sweet Jesus, King of heaven, to
suck to satiety, which through
the opening by the spear,
while gaped at by many men,
with the moistening by Your
precious blood relieves all
sorrows. And if anybody
should think that he will share
that same suck of Your
precious heart in the bliss of the
heavenly kingdom and there
be Your darling in Your
affectionate embracing,
without embracing You here,
hanging on the cross and
sharing Your passion through
holy meditation with love-
liking thought and heart-felt
pity...No, certainly not, let no
man believe that. Whosoever
wants to share Your bliss
there, he must share Your
suffering with You here.
(Westra, 1950:6,7)

In these texts Christ is lover, yet is simultaneously mother. The
body of Christ, wounded and bleeding, is the eroticised and
desired body of the lover, yet it is also the maternal body which
nurtures and feeds (Lagorio, 1985; McLaughlin, 1975; Bynum,
1982, 1986a, 1986b, 1987). In these particular texts two separate
systems of metaphoricity conflate, two distinct discourses merge
in Christ's dying body. So that when the speaker says,

hwi nam ich in þin earmes. In
pin earmes swa istrahte.*and*
isprad on rode.

O that I were in thy arms, in
they arms so outstretched and
outspread on the cross!
(Morris, 1886:184,185)

there is deliberate ambiguity, erotic tension in the play of signification. Does the speaker yearn for the loving (but 'chaste') embrace with the maternal body, or is it the erotic lover's embrace which is desired?

The construction of Christ as mother, of Christ's body as the maternal body, is founded on the association of women's bodies and food, women's bodies as food in their maternal functioning (see especially Bynum, 1986b, 1987). So the bleeding body of Christ crucified can be recognised as maternal in its functioning; the bleeding wound in Christ's side functions as a lactating breast. The speaker in *A Talkyng of þe Loue of God* says,

þer wol I.souken of þi syde.	There I shall suck of Your
þat openeþ a ʒeyn me so	side, which opens towards me so
wyde.wiþ outen eny	wide, without moving at all,
fluttying.þer wol I.a bide.as	and there I will stay. When it
As hit was opened for me.so	was opened for me, so blessed
blessed be þat tyde.	be that time. (Westra, 1950:68,69)

Bleeding is lactation. This maternal functioning of Christ's body is metaphorically constructed in visual texts with eucharistic significance. Here Christ's naked, wounded torso bleeds profusely; the blood spurts from His side wound (=breast)—and in some texts, from all His wounds—into the chalice (of the Eucharist). According to scientific theorising in the Middle Ages, breast milk was actually blood; the blood of the mother which was used to nourish the unborn child in the uterus was, after the child's birth, converted into breast milk.

So the crucified body of Christ is constructed as the maternal body in its capacity to nurture and nourish the human soul, or— as we shall see when metaphoricity is made literal, material, and actual—in the eucharistic capacity of Christ's corporeality to sustain also the body (usually a woman's body), to provide the basic requirements necessary for (physical) survival. The bleeding (side) wound as a source of nourishment is a lactating breast; but it is more than this, it is also a womb. The agonising pain of the crucifixion, the suffering of Christ in His passion, was the suffering, the 'passion' of a woman giving birth. Marguerite of Oingt, a fourteenth-century Carthusian prioress, wrote:

> *My sweet Lord...are you not my mother and more than my mother? The mother who bore me laboured in*

delivering me for one day or one night, but you, my
sweet and lovely Lord, laboured for me for more than
thirty years. And my sweet and lovely Lord, with what
love you laboured for me and bore me through your
whole life. But when the time approached for you to be
delivered, your labour pains were so great that your holy
sweat was like great drops of blood that came out of
your body and fell on the earth...Ah! Sweet Lord Jesus
Christ, who ever saw a mother suffer such a birth! For
when the hour of your delivery came you were placed on
the hard bed of the cross...and your nerves and all
your veins burst when in one day you gave birth to the
whole world (Bynum, 1986a:266)

Painting, 1331, Crucifixion, at the back of the Klosterneuburg Altar,
by the Vienna Master (*Schiller, 1972 no. 516*)

Painting, c.1510, Eucharistic Man of Sorrows, by Jacob Cornelisz, Antwerp (*Schiller, 1972 no. 708*)

Other texts use the side wound to signify different maternal possibilities. For example, in the Middle English lyric 'Quia Amore Langueo', the speaker who is the crucified Christ refers to this particular wound first as a 'neste' (verse 8), and then as a 'chaumbir' (verse 14). In His poetic speaking, Christ, textually constructed as the lover who is made to languish with the burden of His love in the tradition of the Song, becomes Christ the protective mother:

(8)
In my side y haue made hir neste;
　Loke in! how weet a wounde is heere,
þis is hir chaumbir, heere schal sche reste,
　þat sche & y may slepe in fere.
　　Heere may sche waische, if only filþe were,
　　Heere is sete for al hir woo;
Come whanne sche wole, sche schal haue chere,
　Quia amore langueo.

(14)
My loue is in hir chaumbir: holde ȝoure pees,
　Make ȝe no noise, but lete hir slepe:
My babe, y wolde not were in disese,
　I may not heere my dere child wepe.
　　With my pap y schal hir kepe.
　　Ne merueille ȝe not pouȝ y tende hir to;
þis hole in my side had neuere be so depe,
　But quia amore langueo.

(Furnivall 1866: 182,186)

The beloved bride becomes the speaker's beloved baby, is the speaker's child-bride.

To construct Christ as mother, Christ's crucified body as the maternal body, is to construct Christ's body with the attributes of the feminine. A male body might signify the maternal through means of metaphor, but there were other discourses working to construct this body, a male body, as 'feminine'. To begin with, the dichotomous processes of classical philosophical discourse had been thoroughly internalised by medieval theology: man/woman, soul/body, spirit/matter, life/death, transcendent/immanent, and so on (Bφrresen 1981; McLaughlin 1974). The twelfth-century visionary and theologian Hildegard of Bingen wrote in the *Liber Divinorum Operum*: 'Man...signifies the divinity of the Son of God and woman his humanity' (Bynum, 1986a:274). And to Elizabeth of Schönau, another twelfth-century visionary, the humanity of Christ appeared in a vision as a female virgin (Bynum, 1986a:273–74, 1986b:420). So the enfleshing of the Divine Word came to be metaphoricised in terms of marriage between Divinity as groom, and humanity as bride. But it was also the physiological theories of Aristotle (and to a lesser extent those of Galen), which both informed medieval scientific discourse and provided strong support for this metaphoric expression of the Incarnational mystery (Børresen, 1981; Bullough, 1973; Lemay, 1982; 1985; Rousselle, 1988; Bynum, 1986b).

In the Aristotelian theory of procreation, the paternal function is primary, providing the form which potential life will take, and as well, the spirit or soul which will inhabit the newly-created being. The maternal however, provides matter, human fleshliness; the maternal body is simply a vessel, a space where the not-yet-born might develop. The woman's body, the feminine, comes to be associated with the matter of human flesh; and so humanity, the bodily aspect of the Divine, can be understood in this sense as 'feminine'. The fleshly matter of incarnated Divinity was inherited from His mother Mary. Christ's flesh was Mary's flesh, was quite literally feminine fleshliness; for Christ's conception was without the participation of earthly paternity: in the bodily being of Christ, the Divine met with woman without masculine mediation. And in its bleeding and feeding the male body of Christ participated in the bodily functioning of the feminine and the maternal.

In the second half of this chapter I want to explore the relation constructed between the heavily coded body of Christ and that of the medieval Christian who worshipped and adored that body. Exploration begins with the metaphoricity of the Song of Songs, which perhaps functions as the key text for medieval Christianity. Medieval exegetical practices used this Song's metaphoricity to construct the discourse of Christ as lover/groom/husband. Read allegorically, the Song tells of the passionate love-longing which exists between each human soul and her beloved-other, the Divine Word. That is, each human soul is feminised, becomes the bride of Christ. This is the metaphoricity used by the discourse of affective or 'positive' mysticism, 'cataphatic' mysticism. The Song's erotic metaphoricity was used to signify the mystery which constitutes mystical experience: union with the Divine.

The saintly Bernard, abbot over the Cistercian monks at Clairvaux, spent the final twenty years of his life sermonising on this particular text, developing a system of mystical theology based on it. But Bernard died in 1153, and his strategic use of the Song's metaphoricity was transformed—the mystical marriage metaphor ran quite out of control. Bernard had produced his sermons, his mystical reading of the Song, for a masculine, monastic audience. For him, these were the true 'brides of Christ'. But since Christianity's first centuries women religious had been identified as the intended of the Son, destined for nuptial bliss with the Divine. Women religious could identify themselves as the 'brides of Christ' at the level of the literal and the actual, an identification not accessible to male religious (Bugge, 1975). The phenomenon of mysticism increased dramatically in the later Middle Ages; Bernard's mystical theologising had been only the beginning. But it was the irruption of a 'feminine' mysticism which disturbed church authorities. For these women took the language of mysticism, the language of the Song, and made it their own; these women appropriated the metaphoricity intended for the monastic mysticism which was produced within the bounds of institutionalised orthodoxy. These women took the metaphoric from Bernard's texts and made it literal (Bugge, 1975). But to make metaphor literal was to materialise the immaterial: theirs was 'a very material mysticism' (Beckwith, 1986), a discourse obsessed with fleshliness and actuality, the substantiality of bodily being, a discourse which focused on the bleeding, dying body of the God-man.

These mystical women identified with the Divine body they worshipped and adored. Being women, they could identify with Divine immanence, the fleshly substantiality inherited directly from the maternal body, a woman's body. And they could identify with that crucified body in its capacity to bleed and feed—for these are the functions of a woman's body. That is, these women recognised something of themselves, their bodily experience in the body of the crucified Christ. These mystical women identified with that body in a manner which can best be explained, I think, through psychoanalytic theorising.

Hagiography is the narrativisation of this bodily identification, the relation which existed between the body which was worshipped and adored and the body of the worshipper. These narratives present the lived experience of late medieval sanctity in terms of an extraordinarily vigorous asceticism. But I want to stress that I am referring here not only to the lifestyle of saintly women, for since Christianity's inception there has always been a select minority of both men and women who chose to live out their lives through the heroic ordeals of Christian asceticism. But hagiographical evidence constructs the mystic discourse of the later Middle Ages as fiercely ascetic, and as a discourse dominated by women.

Christianity in the later Middle Ages was a penitential practice; the focus on and identification with Christ's dying body
produced a religiosity and a lifestyle with an emphasis on
passivity, patience, pain and suffering (Kieckhefer, 1984), all of
which proved to have redemptive effect. That is, for the body to
bear pain and suffering passively and patiently, was for that body
also to participate in the salvific achievement of Christ's body.
To suffer bodily pain in this life was penitential, was to bear
purgatorial punishment for sinfulness in this life rather than in
the next. Bodily suffering could also be substitutive: the penitential suffering of a saintly body could release some other body
from its earthly pain, or liberate a soul from purgatory's punish-
ments (Bynum, 1987). The Christian lifestyle was conceived of as
an 'imitatio Christi', a 'via crucis'. In its most extreme form this
'imitatio', this mimicry of and identification with the Divine
body, became a literal experiencing of the same. The body of the
worshipper, the mimic, would be inscribed with the pain and
suffering of Christ's dying body; the stigmatised body of the
worshipper would be marked in total identification with the
body of the Divine Other, would participate in the hol(e)y
wounding of (a) grand Passion.

Freudian psychoanalytic theorising names such a display of
mimicry of bodily identification with an-Other, hysteria. I want
to stress that in late medieval Christianity, both men and women
participated in this lifestyle of imitation, this heroic if hysterical
lifestyle of spiritual athleticism. There were men whose bodies
expressed total identification with that of the Divine: St Francis,
Peter of Luxembourg, Henry Suso (see Kieckhefer, 1984, but cf.
Huizinga, 1965). Yet their masculine feats of imitative fervour
were somewhat more restrained, were always somehow less
than the imitative strategies of mystic women. It would seem that
if Christianity in the later Middle Ages was a discourse increasingly mysticised, it was also a discourse increasingly feminised, a
discourse hystericised.

In the discussion which follows I will be focusing on the
bizarre behaviour of these women; and I will be using the
Freudian paradigm of hysteria because it enables interpretive
access to what would otherwise function as an indecipherable
code, an impenetrable system of signification. The theorising of
contemporary French feminists—Helene Cixous, Catherine Clement, but especially that of psychoanalyst Luce Irigaray—has
been founded on the Freudian model of the (feminine) hysteric; it
is a theorising which itself participates in and reproduces the
hysteric's discourse. For the psychoanalytic investigation into
hysteria—an investigation which was the founding moment of

psychoanalysis—has demonstrated that hysteria functions as strategem.[3] Hysteria constitutes a woman's psychical resistance, her unvoiced rebellion against patriarchy, against the functioning of Symbolic Law and Order. For in hysteria it is the body which speaks, the body is used to encode, to articulate psychic pain, psychic suffering. The hysterical body signifies dramatically, for in patriarchy, woman's relation to language—to representation, and symbolisation—is problematised.[4]

Within psychoanalytic theory—and I am using a Lacanian framework here—entry into the Symbolic Order, into language and subjectivity, is by means of the resolution of the Oedipal drama. Theorising has provided a paradigm of this process in the case of the boy, but for the girl-child there has only been conjecture, sheer speculation. Woman, her body, her sexual difference, constitutes an enigma for psychoanalysis; she is the 'dark continent'. But within the Symbolic Order, the dominant discourses are congruent, isomorphic with phallic sexuality. So the woman with her bodily and sexual difference is alienated, is excluded by and from language, by and from a system of signification where the signifier of signifiers is the phallus (Lacan, 1977:281–91; Gallop, 1985:133–56). For a woman to speak at all, it seems that she must of necessity mime the man's relation to language, she must participate in a masquerade. However Luce Irigaray proposes an alternative: the possibility of an-other discourse, an-other language which would be a 'feminine' language able to express the difference of woman's bodily being, and her sexuality. Such a language would speak, would in fact produce and make possible the morphological plurality of woman's sex, the multiplicity of her body's polymorphous pleasure(s)—a polyvalent and playful speaking.

The hysteric's discourse signifies woman's excessive disquiet under the dictates of the Father's Law, enunciating her alienation and exclusion from symbolisation and the workings of phallic signifying processes. The mystic's program of bodily 'imitatio' was a bodily 'acting out' which constituted and consecrated her status as holy; it was a process of bodily signification— ascetic achievements which from the contextual distance and difference of the twentieth century seem to demonstrate an excess which disturbs, and which has at times been identified as pathology. Asceticism has always been an integral part of Christianity: activities such as heroic fasting, sleep deprivation, the wearing of hair shirts and plates of metal next to the skin, binding the body with ropes and chains, self-flagellation, immersion into freezing water, extraordinarily long periods of prayer and psalm-reciting accompanied by innumerable genuflexions and bodily contortions. But hagiography from the later Middle Ages cites acts of extraordinary self-abasement and humiliation, acts of self-immolation, acts of gruesome and grotesque violence carried out by the saint on her own body. For example, Mary of Oignies (thirteenth century) hacked off pieces of her own flesh while immersed in a vision of the Crucifixion (Bynum, 1984:190); St Catherine Benincasa of Siena (fourteenth century) attempted to overcome physical disgust and nausea by drinking pus from the putrifying, cancerous breast of a dying woman. To Raymond of Capua, her confessor and biographer, she said, 'Never in my life have I tasted any food or drink sweeter or more exquisite' (Bynum, 1987:171–72). Similarly Angela of Foligno (thirteenth century) drank the water used to wash the sores of lepers, and when a scab stuck in her throat she commented that it tasted as 'sweet as communion' (Bynum, 1987:144–45). Francesca de' Ponziani (fourteenth to fifteenth century) would prepare herself for sexual relations with her husband by pouring boiling pork fat or candle wax over her genitals (Bell, 1985:137).

But it was fasting, food deprivation, which dominated the intensely ascetic Christianity lived out by these mystic women. Often it was a fasting against the advice of confessors, or against the explicit orders of religious superiors. Even within the context of medieval Christianity, the fasting of these women was perceived as excess, was, even then, identified as pathological, or more dangerously, as diabolical (Bell, 1985; Bynum, 1987). It became a fasting 'out of control', a fasting which went beyond the control of church authorities, the male priestly caste. And it could be a fasting to the death—as with St Catherine of Siena, who died in 1380 at the highly significant age of thirty-three.

Evidence, both biographical and autobiographical, suggests that these fasting women were acting out a form of hysteria which has again irrupted in the patriarchal society of the late twentieth century. I am speaking of anorexia, and again there will be those who will be troubled here at what might seem to be the inappropriate application of contemporary terminology, the imposing of contemporary medical—or at least psychiatric discourse—onto this historical other, wilfully disregarding, and deliberately annihilating, cultural specificity, cultural alterity. But this is to wilfully misrecognise the meaning and function of hysteria, and in particular of anorexia. For neither hysteria nor anorexia should be reduced to the discourse of late-twentieth-century medical science; hysteria/anorexia is not a disease so much as the expression of profound social and psychic dis-ease (which, I suggest, occurred back in the fourteenth and fifteenth centuries just as it does now, in the twentieth century). And it is psychoanalytic theory which enables access to the meaning and function of the hysteric's body, the anorexic's body; for the hysteric, the anorexic, speaks the 'unheard-of' language of the body which only psychoanalysis can decipher (Ulmer, 1980).

Psychoanalysis has demonstrated that anorexia, like other forms of hysteria, functions as a strategy by means of which the anorexic acts out her resistance to the workings of the Symbolic Order, which has locked her into a position of passivity within a patriarchal construction of the feminine. Anorexia is a woman's strategic play for autonomy within a system which both defines and constructs her in terms of lack and castration, a state of being which is 'not-all'.[5] The anorexic stages her refusal of and rebellion against such a definition and construction of her 'self' through direct action; and it is action effected with her body, the Symbolic body, the 'castrated' body of patriarchal femininity. Destruction of the Symbolic body, however, enables the reconstruction of an-other body, an 'autonomous' body liberated from the controls and constraints of phallic signification and phallic Law. Anorexia is a discourse dealing directly with power and control. The records of female sanctity in the later Middle Ages provide evidence which supports this. There are, for example, St Catherine of Siena, Umiliana de' Cerchi, Francesca de' Ponziani—mystical women whom the historian Rudolph Bell has called 'holy anorexics' in order to distinguish them from the outbreak of fasting women in our own time (Bell, 1985).

But to return to the Middle Ages: women in ever-increasing numbers were choosing to dedicate their lives to God, to live the penitential lifestyle of a religious—a choice which often necessitated remarkable determination in order to fight against frequent familial opposition.[6] And as we have already seen, this female religious was very likely to participate in a very literal and ascetic 'imitatio Christi'. Her religious experience often reached the ecstatic extremes of a flamboyant mysticism. The religious life functioned for these women as an alternative to the subject(ed) position(s) enforced upon them by the workings of the patriarchal ordering of society. It provided a space where women might locate 'solutions' to the crises engendered by the patriarchal construction of femininity. The ascetic practices of the religious woman, her mystical experiences, constituted the radical refusal of her own 'self' as the 'patriarchal female', and a reconstruction of subjectivity and sexuality beyond the strictures of the Law. And this constituted her own 'inquiry into femininity',[7] her attempt to locate a different 'self', a bodily being beyond the Name/No of the Father.

Yet historical evidence of the strict claustration imposed on medieval religious women by the male church hierarchy, the extent of the dependence of the female religious house on male religious for sustenance both spiritual and physical, seems to suggest that the religious lifestyle would not and could not provide these women suffering severely from Symbolic constraint(s) with anything different (Schulenburg, 1984). The institution of the church in the Middle Ages was a patriarchal construct, and operated according to the dictates of the Father's Law. Women religious were able physically and materially to resituate themselves with the development of the Beguine movement and the mendicant tertiary orders. However, it was only when a woman religious—whether or not she was bound by vows or rules of enclosure—adopted a strategy of mysticism and asceticism that excess worked to liberate her from the limits imposed by the masculinist discourse of institutionalised religion. Her excess(es) took her beyond arbitrary limitation and man-made boundaries; her excess was ecstatic, an ex-stasy, a being beyond herself where she might meet with the Divine. The excess of her rapturous relation with the Divine-Other bypassed her need for priestly mediation, male mediation which also functioned as male containment and male control. Her ex-stasy took her way out of control, beyond the control of the Other.

Patriarchal discourse, as we have seen, identifies woman as the 'not-all', yet simultaneously perceives in her 'lack', her 'castrated' (Symbolic) body, a disturbing excess which resists symbolisation. As excess, as that which exceeds, woman is located by male discourse as Otherness; her difference (of excess) makes woman an object of fantasy for (a) masculine subjectivity. But the site of the Other is also the site of God and Truth: that which has been submitted to an intense process of mystification, positioned behind a veil, a 'cloud of unknowing'.[8] That is, the site of the Other is the site of excess, of that which exceeds symbolisation and Symbolic processes. Woman and Divinity meet in and through unmediated excess.

Julia Kristeva theorises such excess in terms of 'semiotic' irruptions into the workings of the socio-symbolic order. *Holiness* can be the site of such an irruption, also poetry and madness (Kristeva, 1976, 1980, 1984). However, *institutionalised religion*—and in this specific instance I am referring to the monolithic machinery of the medieval catholic church—works on behalf of Law: the institutionalisation of holy excess is Symbolic control and containment. The mystic woman on the other hand, ruptures religious discourse, the institutionalised Christian discourse of the later Middle Ages. Excess exceeds (and succeeds); her holiness is a (strategic) madness which transports her beyond, is a pleasure which takes her out of herself. Her excess, unsymbolisable, unspeakable, is her 'jouissance': excess beyond the phallus.

The hysteric (it has been said) suffers from reminiscences (Freud, 1912:5, 156); but (more specifically) the anorexic suffers from nostalgia for maternal corporeality, the plenitude of the pre-Symbolic body (Celemajor, 1986, 1987). The medieval woman mystic, the 'holy anorexic', through her intense devotion to and excessive identification with Christ's crucified body, attempts to relocate, reconstruct her Symbolic body (and being). But this is also her attempt to recreate the wholeness, the completeness of the mother-child relation in the Imaginary state of being. That is, mystical union with the Divine can function as fusion with the maternal body. Christ's body, the human body of the Divine, has become of the body of the phallic mother. Longed-for union/fusion could be achieved, quite literally, through the celebration of the Eucharist, the ingestion of the host, which was to incorporate the body of Christ in a fleshly and substantial way. To eat Christ was to 'fuse' with him physically and actually, was to recreate and re-experience the bodily pleasure(s) of the Imaginary dyadic existence. Intense eucharistic fervour was a basic constituent element in the feminine mysticism of the late Middle Ages. It functioned as yet another manifestation of feminine excess: a holy madness. But it was most extreme in those women who exhibited heroic eating austerities, women who would not eat. For these women the only form of nourishment acceptable, the only form of bodily sustenance permitted, was the host (for example, St Catherine of Siena). For these women, the host was enough, was itself sometimes experienced as 'too-much'. For the eucharistic meal was, for many of these women, the occasion for rapture and ecstasy. So much so that church authorities litigated against the communication of ecstatic women (Bynum, 1987:328, n.116). It was a desperate attempt to reassert control, to confirm (male) authority, to contain the excess so visible, so obviously present in the woman's body as pleasure took her quite beyond herself, rapt into ecstasy. The bodily pleasure of her ex-stasis was total, the polymorphous pleasure located in the pre-Oedipal body, in the unsymbolisable excess(es) of woman's body.

The body of Christ then, functions as the woman's object of desire, a body discursively (re)constructed as both lover and mother. There is textual evidence of the eroticisation of Christ's wounded and bleeding, dying body; but it is an eroticisation which is quite primal, which signifies a return—or at least the desire to return to the longed-for body of the first love-object: the body of the (phallic) maternal. So Catherine of Siena, when she had drunk the pussy offering from a dying woman's cancerous breast, was able, in a vision, to take both nourishment and comfort from Christ's bleeding side wound; Christ speaks:

> 'As you then went far beyond what mere human
> nature could ever have achieved, so I today shall give
> you a drink that transcends in perfection any that
> human nature can provide...' With that, he tenderly
> placed his right hand on her neck, and drew her
> toward the wound in his side. 'Drink, daughter, from my
> side,' he said, 'and by that draught your soul shall
> become enraptured with such delight that your very
> body, which for my sake you have denied, shall be
> inundated with its overflowing goodness.' Drawn
> close...to the outlet of the Fountain of life, she fastened
> her lips upon that sacred wound, and still more eagerly
> the mouth of her soul, and there she slaked her thirst.
> (Bynum, 1987:172)

Her lips meet the lips of his wound in the kiss of (a) union which is mystical, yet also physical, sensual. So too the speaker in *A Talkyng of þe Loue of God* enunciates holy desire:

þenne ginneþ þe loue.to springen at myn herte.and glouweþ up in myn brest.wonderliche hote. þe loue teres of myn neb.rennen ful smerte.my song is likynge of loue.al wiþ oute note. I.lepe on him raply.as grehound on herte.al out of my self.wiþ loueliche leete.And cluppe in myn armes.þe cros bi þe sterte. þe blood I.souke of his feet.þat sok is ful swete. I.cusse and	Then the love begins to well up in my heart and glows very hotly in my breast. The tears of love run plentifully down my face. My song is delight of love without any melody. I leap at Him swiftly as a greyhound at a hart, quite beside myself, in loving manner, and fold in my arms the cross at the lower end. I suck the blood from His feet; that sucking is extremely sweet. I kiss and embrace and

I.cluppe and stunte oþerwhile.as mon þat is loue mad.and seek of loue sore. i loke on hire.þat him bringeþ.and heo bi ginneþ to smyle.as pauȝ hire likede wel.and wolde i dude more. I lepe eft þer i was.and auntre me þore.i cluppe and I. cusse as I.wood wore. I.walewe and i souke.i.not whuche while. and whon I.haue al don.ȝit me luste more.þenne fele I.þat blood.in pouȝt of my Mynde. as hit weore bodilich.warm on my lippe. and þe flesch on his feet.bi fore and beo hynde.so softe and so swete.to cusse and to cluppe.

occasionally stop, as one who is love-mad and sick with love-pain. I look at her, who brings Him, and she begins to smile, as if it pleased her and she wanted me to go on. I leap back to where I was and venture myself there; I embrace and I kiss, as if I was mad. I roll and I suck I do not know how long. And when I am sated, I want yet more. Then I feel that blood in my imagination as it were bodily warm on my lips and the flesh on his feet in front and behind so soft and so sweet to kiss and to embrace. (Westra, 1950: 60,61).

But if mystical 'inedia'[9] was the strategy deployed by Catherine and others like her to locate possible alternatives to the patriarchal construction of the feminine, it was, as the realisation of an 'autonomy' (of being) situated in dangerous excess, as dangerous excess, beyond the phallus.

And now, in the late twentieth century, this mystical discourse of late medieval women becomes the privileged site of contemporary theoretical explorations into femininity. The French psychoanalyst Jacques Lacan theorises the feminine by means of Bernini's spectacle in stone, his spectacular representation of the rapt body of St Teresa in ecstasy: the representation of excess in stone. Lacan constructs his theory on and of the feminine using a masculine reproduction, a masculine reconstruction of the same. The male artist and the male theorist intrude upon an excessively, intensely private moment, that moment when the mystic woman achieves union, experiences union with the Divine. Like the church authorities in the later Middle Ages, a male priestly class threatened and outraged by their exclusion from this relation between the mystic woman and the Divine, the male artist and male theorist attempt to enforce and inflict masculine presence, a presence which works to effect (male) dominance and control.

But in 'La Mysterique', Luce Irigaray (1986) posits resistance to phallic discourse which works to reappropriate and constrain that which exceeds. 'La Mysterique' is a coming together of the

Bernini's *St Teresa in Ecstasy*

mystic, the hysteric, mystery and woman (through 'la'—signification of the feminine): femininity, holiness and madness conflate in this discourse. Irigaray liberates (the mystic) woman from
the binding restraints of male theoretical discourse, the male
construction of the feminine. The discourse of feminine mysticism, the feminine relation with the Divine, is again used
strategically as a site for (feminine) resistance as it is also a site for

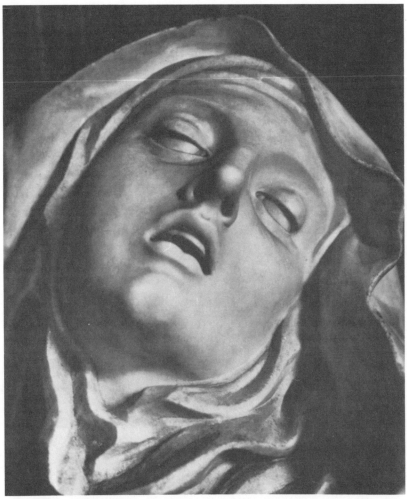

Detail of Bernini's *St Teresa in Ecstasy*

feminine (self-)knowing, a site for the realisation of an autonomous being.

To bring to an end this brief exploration of the religious
experience and expression of the late Middle Ages, I would like
to consider a few final texts: visual (re)constructions of Christ's
crucified body, and a short passage from 'La Mysterique' (Irigaray, 1985), a text which speaks (of) the relation which was/is

101

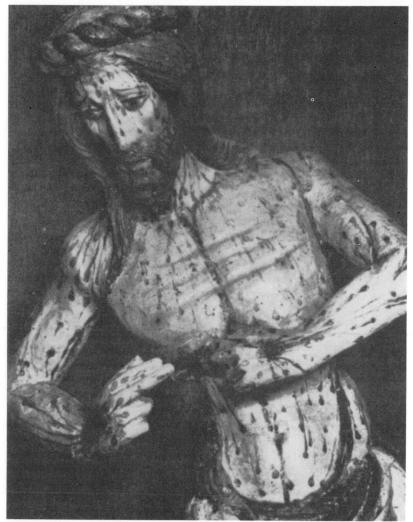

Wood carving (detail), 1370–80, Man of Sorrows. Southern Germany, Frauenworth (*Schiller, 1972, no. 698*)

Painting, first third of the fifteenth century, Man of Sorrows, with symbols of judgment, by Master Francke, Hamburg (*Schiller, 1972 no. 711*)

Painting, c. 1425, Pietà with angels, by Master Francke, Leipzig
(*Schiller, 1972 no. 758*)

between the mystic woman and the wounded, bleeding body of
that man who was/is also Divine.

*And if 'God' who has thus re-proved the fact of her
non-value, still loves her, this means that she exists all
the same, beyond what anyone may think of her. It
means that love conquers everything that has already
been said. And that one man, at least, has understood
her so well that he died in the most awful suffering. That
most female of men, the Son.*

*And she never ceases to look upon his nakedness,
open for all to see, upon the gashes in his virgin flesh, at
the wounds from the nails that pierce his body as he
hangs there, in his passion and abandonment. And she
is overwhelmed with love of him/herself. In his
crucifixion he opens up a path of redemption to her in
her fallen state.*

*Could it be true that not every wound need remain
secret, that not every laceration was shameful? Could a
sore be holy? Ecstasy is there in that glorious slit
where she curls up as if in her nest, where she rests as if
she had found her home—and He is also in her. She
bathes in a blood that flows over her, hot and purifying.
And what she discovers in this divine passion, she
neither can nor will translate. At last, she has been
authorized to remain silent, hidden from prying eyes
in the intimacy of this exchange where she sees (herself
as) what she will be unable to express. Where she sees
nothing and where she sees everything. She is closed
over this mystery where the love placed within her is
hidden, revealing itself in this secret of desire. In this
way, you see me and I see you, finally I see myself
seeing you in this fathomless wound which is the source
of our wondering comprehension and exhilaration.
And to know myself I scarcely need a 'soul', I have only
to gaze upon the gaping space in your loving body.
Any other instrument, any hint, even, of theory, pulls
me away from myself by pulling open—and sewing
up—unnaturally the lips of that slit where I recognize
myself, by touching myself there (almost) directly.*
(Irigaray, 1985: 199–200).

6 'The feminine' as a semiotic construct: Zola's *Une Page d'Amour*

Maryse Rochecouste

SEMIOTICS PROVIDES highly functional analytical tools with which to explore textual dynamics. The aim of this chapter[1] is to demonstrate the use of these tools in the exploration of textual communication in prose narrative, more specifically to look at the representation of the feminine in Zola's *Une Page d'Amour*. My analysis of this will show how the multiple components which contribute to the representation of the feminine in the novel are intimately and obsessively linked with the theme of the Fall, or the 'catamorphic', as I shall refer to it.

The term 'catamorphic' thus pinpoints the major recurrent theme of the 'Fall' in the novel and it highlights the generality of the theme through *all* its manifestations. Zola's work is centred around notions of the Fall, of falling, crumbling and decaying. He manipulates verbal and semantic systems to do with both descent and ascent. Consequently, space—within which actantial representations occur—plays a major role as a textual signifier.

In the novel *Une Page d'Amour* images of the Fall are related to the representation of *one* facet of feminine identity, namely female sexuality. One consequence of this is that the representation of the heroine's sexuality gives us some insight into patriarchal values; her sexual identity as constructed in the novel can be seen as a discourse through which we can decode the patriarchal ideology of the nineteenth century.

One cannot use the tools of semiotics without using a certain amount of basic terminology. Since this may not always be familiar to all readers let me first define some basic terms relevant to this analysis. Sign, signifier, signified and signification are crucial concepts in semiotics, as Saussure and his many followers have shown. A sign—which consists of a signifier and a signified—is a simple material object, for example a sound, mark, shape, gesture or colour, which by a *natural* or *conventional* relationship is held in a given society to take the place of a complex reality (Fiske, 1982:ch. 3). The signifier is 'the sign's image as we perceive it' and the signified 'the mental concept to which it refers' (Fiske, 1982:47). Signification is the 'process' or 'act which binds the signifier and the signified' (Barthes, 1981:48), whereas the referent is the external 'reality' to which the signifier refers and through which the signified acquires meaning.

Associated with the sign and signification are the notions of denotation and connotion. The former is the 'first order of signification' and 'describes the relationship between the signifier and signified within the sign, and the sign with its referent in external reality . . . [It] refers to the commonsense obvious meaning of the sign' (Fiske, 1982:90–91). The latter 'describes the interaction that occurs when the sign meets the feelings or emotions of the user and the values of his culture' (Fiske, 1982:91).

There is, further, a triadic classification of signs—icon, index and symbol—which is derived from the work of the philosopher C.S. Pierce. I use it in the generally accepted literary sense, described as follows by Hawkes: ' . . . the *icon*, something which functions as a sign by means of features of itself which resemble its object: the *index*, something which functions as a sign by virtue of some sort of factual or causal connections with its object: and the *symbol*, something which functions as a sign because of some 'rule' of conventional or habitual association between itself and its object' (1977:127).

When we come to deal with the way signs are used in texts we need two other equally important concepts: paradigm and syntagm. A paradigm is a 'set of signs from which the one to be used is chosen' (Fiske, 1982:105), that is, it consists of sets of elements which are interchangeable on the basis of discontinuity, similarity or variation. The use of a paradigm involves selection, association and substitution of elements belonging to these sets. A syntagm is 'the message into which the chosen signs are combined' (Fiske, 1982: 105). That is, it consists of elements which unfold along the linear axis of combination, contiguity and succession, and it involves the structuring, organising and ordering of signs.

The 'actantial model' (already referred to above) is a Greimassian typology inspired by Sourian's and Propp's work on recurring character types in narrative. Greimas (1987) defines and classifies narrative performers or 'actants' according to the roles they perform in the action. The term 'actant' refers to units of narrative grammar, that is, categories of protagonists (and of course the protagonists themselves) defined by their function in the intrigue. Greimas, attempting to develop a 'grammar' of narrative, isolated six fundamental functions which he grouped in the following pairs: subject–object, sender–receiver, helper–opponent. The focus of any narrative varies according to which character one elects as the actantial subject (and this is not necessarily the hero). (See Greimas, 1987:ch. 4).

Since my analysis also looks closely at space, I will use the term 'proxemics': here I prefer the exact definition of Hall who coined the word and defined 'proxemics' as 'the study of man's perception and use of space' (1980:83). My use of the term 'anamorphic' (the opposite of catamorphic) referring to anything pertaining to height, elevation or altitude, is related to my interest in the way space is constructed in the novel. The term 'valorisation' means the attribution of worth, value or quality, but is used as a technical term in the discussion of the attribution of value to members of binary semantic oppositions (Ubersfeld, 1987:189).

Zola's *Une Page d'Amour* is marked by striking dichotomies, and the text unites, juxtaposes and sets up parallel systems of opposites. There is a disparity and an interplay between these. Every pattern or cluster of images constructs two antithetical yet complementary spatial configurations: one is real, the other imaginary: the 'real' is in fact one face of a coin whose metaphoric and inseparable reverse side is constructed by the imaginary. The dialectic between them is crucial to the representation of female sexuality in the novel. Zola uses vocabulary and imagery strongly based in the semantics of language of the physical senses: sight, touch, hearing—above all smell, movement and colour. One of the fundamentals of any semiotic analysis of text is the interpretation of paradigmatic clusters—the variables of themes and imagery—and their syntagmatic organisation or structuring in the sequence of the text. By examining the visual, auditory, olfactory and kinetic paradigms or systems of meaning in the text I have found that underlying structures relevant to the Fall are specifically associated with the representation of the feminine: the heroine's Fall in *Une Page d'Amour* is directly related to her sexual trangression. Embodying both stereotypes of woman as 'damned whores *and* God's police' (Summers, 1975) at a crucial stage in her life, she has to choose between the two contradictory codes of behaviour mediated or conveyed to her through her positioning in specific social and cultural contexts; none of the accepted sexual stereotypes allow 'whore' *and* 'saint' to co-exist within the one individual.

The catamorphic structures within which these polarised stereotypes occur must manifest themselves within space. They must form part, either of the textual space itself, or of the various spaces described in the text. They may appear as abstract or concrete, as acted upon or acting, as icons, indices or symbols. As part of the textual space itself, the catamorphic semantics of falling/the Fall, and its various associated connotative values, along with its antithetical anamorphic pole, the semantics of ascent/transcendance, together constitute an aspect of the paradigmatic/syntagmatic structuring of the text. Spaces described within the text, such as the apartment and Paris, the Passage des Eaux, never escape Zola's manipulation of these semantic systems of descent and ascent: nor do objects within these spaces, like the swing, which constructs a new spatial semantics of its own based again on this same catamorphic/anamorphic opposition.

Une Page d'Amour depicts a brief love affair. Oppressed and frustrated by her past dull life, and now widowed and trapped between the subconscious incestuous affection of her daughter Jeanne and her own 'bovarysme'[2]—Hélène, the main female actant, rebels. In her effort to free herself and find self-fulfilment, she yields to sexual passion offered to her by Henri—a married man; but she (mis?)interprets Jeanne's death which follows soon after as punishment for her adulterous transgression. Unable to cope with her shame and guilt, she decides, in self-abnegation, to return to her former life pattern: she engages in yet another loveless, but legal, marriage.

Based on the story structure, the following basic actantial models can be drawn to establish the areas of conflict more clearly:

Figure 1

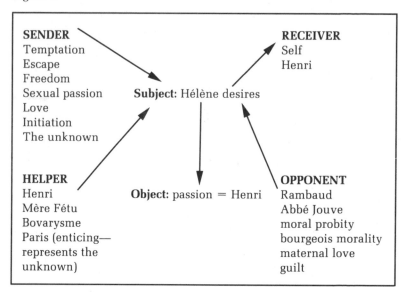

Figure 2

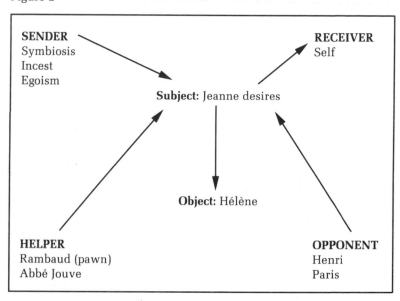

The opening chapter is carefully structured so as to emphasise Hélène's psychological dilemma. On the one hand for instance, paradigms of purity and respectability abound, seemingly depicting Hélène's dominant trait of character. A whole range of stereotyped values associated with the female gender, such as passivity, innocence, emotional sensitivity and maternalism are directly attributed to her. In other words, she seems to display the appropriate gendered psychological and social attributes pertaining to the 'Saint'.

On the other hand, many other elements contradict this surface representation, suggesting that all is not well; for example, the theme of drowsiness, the nocturnal scene itself, her daughter's sudden epileptic fit;[3] plus also the theme of closed and open spaces, of suffocation and freedom to breathe, the disorderly layout of her bedroom, the symbolic white shroud formed by the fallen snow. These have many connotations, among which are ignorance, psychic stagnation, even death.

Most telling of these are perhaps the involuntary and probably unconscious kinetic indices associated with the hairstyle and vestmental codes,[4] functioning as 'attitudinal markers.'[5] For instance, the opposition between Hélène's neatly tied up or dishevelled hair, between her shawl hanging neatly on her shoulders or slipping down, between Henri's fastened or unfastened jacket all contribute to the production of meaning.[6] Here they reveal the characters' metamorphosis. As in travesty or exorcism rituals, the ritual of undressing and dressing is linked with the dialectics of appearance and reality, death and rebirth: by undressing, the actants symbolically signify that they are dropping their social masks and defences to reveal their true selves.

The purely functional role of all these conflicting signs is soon superseded, as the more important role ascribed to them in defining the nature of the space they occupy—that is, the referential space of Hélène's private environment and in turn Hélène herself—emerges. It soon becomes apparent through the conflict constructed through these patterns of opposites that Hélène longs to free herself from her bourgeois morality and to find self-fulfilment; she is in fact sexually unawakened despite having experienced marriage. Her first arranged marriage is described thus: 'She had been . . . tormented with fever neither of the body nor of the heart . . . Good heavens! Was there nothing else? Did that sum up everything?' (Zola, 1895:59, 1857:49 modified). Now widowed and obviously experiencing a lack, she

Figure 3

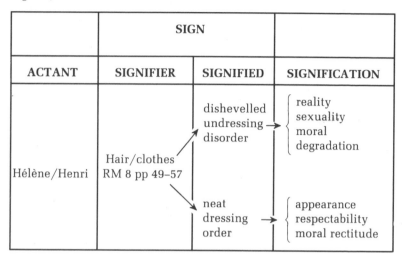

asks herself while indulging in Walter Scott's *Ivanhoe*: 'What did the book mean when it spoke of a love so powerful that it could give meaning to one's whole existence?' (Zola, 1857:49).

Representations of female sexuality can be further deciphered through one of the novel's catamorphic foci, namely Hélène's 'Fall' from virtue in moral and socio-cultural terms, and through her failure to come to terms with her libidinal drives.[7]

The battle triggered by her psychological dilemma is encapsulated in a key sentence describing her and Jeanne contemplating *Paris* from the *window* of their *apartment* in *Passy*:

> It was as if they had stopped on the THRESHOLD of a world that lay forever outspread before them, and refused to enter it. (Zola, 1895:65, my emphasis)

This sentence makes explicit the literal *and* figurative threshold upon which Hélène vacillates, torn between her secure but claustrophobic existence and the unknown but intoxicating adventures she craves for. As the link between exteriority and interiority, the window which ambiguously symbolises separation and alliance makes concrete a critical phase in Hélène's sexual development.

The notion of threshold in turn connotes initiation (liminality) and rites of passage. In another context, Eliade stressed the sacredness of such initiations and the personal growth they lead to (Beane and Doty, 1975:169); and one could expect them to be positively valorised. But, as will be seen, that is not the case with Hélène's initiation[8] to sexual emancipation,[9] which can certainly be regarded as a liminal experience. Plagued by her ignorance of life, symbolised by Paris—as spelt out by the sentence: 'Paris-...was life' (Zola, 1973:349, my translation)—she has an intense desire for knowledge; and although hesitant, she is nonetheless prepared to explore her true sexuality and sexual identity—or rather, Zola's conception of her sexuality; the social, cultural and sexual constructs of her patriarchal society have become too constricting.

The sentence about the window/threshold is the first major indication that the binary spatial opposition between Paris and Hélène's apartment is a hierarchical one, and that it plays a vital role in the representation of woman, and also forms part of a catamorphically oriented semiotic system.

In any proxemic analysis, the point is not merely to 'identify oppositional spaces and the closely woven interplay of their network of meaning . . . the point is to see if space organizes itself, and how it organises itself oppositionally' (Ubersfeld, 1978:190 my translation).

Zola exploits the binary function of the potential paradigm 'above/below' by semanticising it: one automatically associates this type of spatial hierarchy with the symbolism related to concepts of 'high' and 'low', various scenes in the text being divided according to these two symbolic levels. As Ubersfeld (1978:189) points out, traditionally, 'the valorisation of *height*, sign of spiritual and social elevation, is linked to culture and the image of the sky as the source of values and of authority' (my translation).

Hélène's apartment, apparently symbolic of her moral probity, appropriately occupies a towering position *above* Paris:

> The two windows of Hélène's room were wide open.
> Down below the vast plain of Paris stretched out, in the
> abyss that lay at the foot of the house, perched right
> on the edge of the hill. (Zola, 1895:56)

Through this sharp contrast whereby Paris is spatially positioned down below, the capital city acquires negative connotations. Indeed, the spatial relationship of Passy and Paris is the concrete realisation of the opposition themes of superiority and inferiority, or of virtue and transcendence as opposed to sin and the Fall respectively. Through this positive valorisation as 'high', Passy becomes the metaphor for inaccessibility—at least until the process of devalorisation is set in motion.

Let us see, through two selected extracts juxtaposed to the two sentences quoted earlier, how the textual semantics, based on conflict and opposition, proceeds to construct Hélène's psychological dilemma:

> *Upstairs in her room, in that familiar atmosphere of cloistered quiet, Hélène felt herself stifled. She was amazed to find the room so calm, so confined, so drowsy under its blue velvet hangings, while she herself was panting and afire with turbulent emotion. Was this really her room, this lonely, lifeless, airless place? Then, violently, she threw open a window and leaned there to look out at Paris. (Zola, 1895:94)*

> *Paris . . . was unsoundable and various as an ocean, innocently bright in the morning and aflame at night, assuming the joyous or melancholy mood of the skies it reflected. A burst of sunshine would set it rippling with floods of gold, a cloud would darken it, awakening stormy turbulence. It was constantly new; in a dead calm it would glow orange, under a sudden squall turn leaden grey from end to end, bright clear weather would set the crest of every house-top sparkling, while rainstorms drowned heaven and earth and wiped out the horizon in chaotic disaster. For Hélène it held all the melancholy and all the hope of the open sea; she even fancied she felt the sharp breath and the tang of the sea against her face; and the very sound of the city, its low continuous roar, brought her the illusion of the rising tide beating against the rocks of a cliff. (Zola, 1895:47–48).*

As demonstrated in Figure 4 below, entitled 'Apartment vs. Window vs. Paris',[10] when the convergence and opposition of signifieds are tabulated, a clear pattern emerges: superiority and virtue, linked to the apartment in Passy, are paradoxically associated with a comatose state instead of a transcendent one—and indeed, Hélène does lead an impassive and indolent life. By opposition, action and adventure, linked to Paris, are associated with change, instability, disorder, disaster and destruction, as well as ecstasy. At a semantic level, the window which defines the boundaries between these two opposite worlds—the apartment and Paris—is a mere demarcation point which permits the elaboration of these conflicts. The effects of devalorisation of the 'high' and oscillation between 'high' and 'low' are largely achieved through the inversion of the symbolism of verticality (see Figure 4).

The connotations so far described are further expanded through a process of association, to include the following paradigmatic relations and syntagmatic features. The antitheses in the syntagmatic sets (the linear associations that structure the text as it develops), marked by the vertical arrows in Figure 5, pull in opposite directions to the paradigmatic sets associated with the meanings *apartment*, *window* and *Paris*, listed on the horizontal axis in Figure 5. The graphic organisation of Figure 5 illustrates this semantic conflict and the mediating role of the window:

Hélène's psychological oscillation, constructed through these antitheses and oppositions, may be explored from two other semiotic perspectives: first through the proxemics of the swing in the garden sequence, and second through that of another connecting artery between the two major oppositional spaces, namely le Passage des Eaux—the Water Passage. Through its mediating capacity as an ambiguous signifier, the window has an obvious affinity with both the swing and le Passage des Eaux.

Hélène's psychological oscillation, like a pendulum going to and fro, is evoked by the swing on which she sways, literally suspended in midair between heaven and earth; the reader cannot help wondering whether she will gather enough momentum to attain the desired height and thereby achieve mutation. In this context the swing sequence is a key one, the swing's symbolism being very rich and complex. The swing's sharp and natural focus on upward and downward motion, mirroring Hélène's irresolution, allows the symbolism of verticality to be exploited once more. At a metaphysical level, swinging, isomorphic to flying, symbolises spiritual elevation and purification by air.

This semantic shift converts the swing scene into a clear allegory of the initiatory scenario with dominant, positive valorisation. At a more physical level, the swing's rhythmic motion which evokes the movement of coition makes it a sexual symbol linked to fertility rites; it is therefore a signifier of Hélène's and Henri's future liaison.

Figure 4

MODES OF PERCEPTION (REAL/METAPHORIC)	ACTANT	SIGN		SIGNIFICATION	CONVERGENCE OF SIGNIFIEDS	OPPOSITION OF SIGNIFIEDS
		SIGNIFIER	SIGNIFIED			
URANIAN	APARTMENT	En haut / la maison, bâtie à pic sur / la hauteur	height	superiority / strength / inaccessibility		
CLOSURE		douceur cloîtrée / si bien close / coin mort de solitude	seclusion / enclosed space / tomb	alienation / imprisonment / nothingness	DEATH	
CLAUSTRO-PHOBIC		Hélène se sentit étouffer / elle manquait d'air	airlessness	suffocation		
STATIC		si endormie / [Hélène & Jeanne] arrêtées / la pièce si calme	drowsiness / halt / tranquility	torpor / immobility—stagnation / peace	VIRTUE	
KINETIC		[Hélène & Jeanne] refusant d'y / descendre	control	order / constraint		
PROXEMIC	WINDOW	Seuil / deux fenêtres [...] grandes / ouvertes / elle [Hélène] ouvrit une fenêtre, / elle s'accouda en face de / Paris	threshold / demarcation point / [implied closure] / vs. / opening / exclusion / vs. / admission	interiority/exteriority / separation/alliance / constraint/self abandonment / asphyxiation/ventilation / darkness/illumination / ignorance/knowledge / opacity/vision	FLUCTUATION	

		new realm / exhibition	discovery—knowledge / adventure—thrill
VISUAL	Un monde / Spectacle		
CHTHONIAN and CATAMORPHIC	Paris, dans l'abîme qui se creusait au pied de la maison / insondable	depth / mystery	inferiority / vertigo
OLFACTORY and GUSTATORY	Senteur amère	obnoxiousness	evil
AUDITORY	Souffle fort grondement	breath rumbling	ferment—activity
KINETIC (PARIS)	marée montante battant contre les rochers d'une falaise / averses noyant / coup de soleil / coup de vent / changeant / se renouvelait / débâcle d'un chaos	unleashed fury / engulfment / assault / change / confusion/disorder	cataclysm / action—mobility / Hell—Babel—Bedlam
PROXEMIC	Paris [...] déroulant sa plaine / immense / l'étendue / [le] large	open space	freedom / escape
AQUATIC	océan / flots / tempêtes / averses / marée	flood	calamity / Valley of tears / destruction
COLOUR	incendié / flots d'or / coup de soleil / couleur orange / temps vifs et clairs allumant / une lueur / assombrissait	gold / flames / light / darkness	temptation / Hell / good—knowledge—salvation / evil—ignorance—doom

DISASTER

PASSION

Figure 5

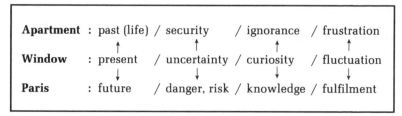

At a psychological level, flight is also symbolic of mental escape, as suggested by the familiar imagery of letting the imagination take flight to release thought. Hence the act of swinging is a signifier having Hélène's 'bovarysme' as signified. It could also be argued that at a semantic level, Hélène's 'bovarysme' is a form of masturbation or 'plaisir solitaire'.

However, despite this positive anamorphic emphasis on ascent and light, the kinetic rise and Fall imagery of swinging and flying makes these actions, paradoxically, potentially catamorphic, that is, symbols of falling: hence, they are most appropriate vehicles for the metaphorisation of Hélène's Fall, more particularly so since her Fall stems from her sexual dilemma.

To begin with, neither the tacit erotic connotation of the swing's rhythm, nor its orgasmic objective for both mother and daughter, can be denied; as such the swing's rhythm is a clear signifier of their solitary—yet public—masturbatory pursuit, a practice frowned upon by convention, hence culturally devalorised. The phrasing of the following quotation can be interpreted as being mimetic of swinging or slow rhythmic masturbation:

> *Jeanne adored swinging . . . the rush of wind against*
> *her face, the sensation of sudden flight, the continuous*
> *swaying to and fro, rhythmical as the beat of wings,*
> *thrilled her with exquisite pleasure, as if she were setting*
> *off into the clouds . . . [She] sat on the swing, radiant,*
> *an expression of rapt awe on her face, and her bare*
> *wrists quivering slightly with delight. (Zola, 1957:42,*
> *modified)*

Note that Zola specifically uses the word *jouissance*. The simple act of pushing Jeanne, as well as recollections of the past, trigger Hélène's arousal, and undoubtedly her secret desire is gratified in the rapture thus described: '. . . a sudden impetus would carry her off and she would sail down, her head thrown back, her eyelids closed, an ecstatic fugitive, dizzy with the fierce rapture of soaring and sinking' (Zola, 1957:44, modified). Again, that revealing word *jouissance* reappears.

The sexual tempo is also accentuated by orchestrated repetition. Evidently, sexual activity—especially of the above nature and devoid of procreative focus—usually associated with inferior instincts, even with sin, because of its ephemeral, terrestrial and physical nature, hence spatially with depth, is ironically also associated here—through symbolic inversion—with height, the realm of spiritual perfection, transcendence, ecstasy. The swing then, like the window, is an ambiguous signifier. Even light imagery, in the form of a golden aura denoting fire, emphasises the voluptuousness of Hélène's flight and here connotes physical passion instead of mystical and spiritual sublimation.

However, catamorphic signifiers lurking unobtrusively in the background enable the alert reader to predict a catastrophe. Hélène's literal fall, announcing her figurative moral one, is firstly prefigured in Jeanne's own recollected fall on a previous occasion. Hélène also experiences giddy spells on the swing. The calamitous connotation of this signifier—vertigo—which I have explored in other novels of the series (Rochecouste, 1979, 1988), again signals disaster, especially when reinforced by 'attitudinal markers', namely the reactivated hairstyle and vestmental codes[11] whose catamorphic connotations I referred to earlier.

Once all these combined catamorphic connotations reach their crescendo, Hélène's literal fall from the swing hardly comes as a surprise: it abruptly negates the implicit positively valorised anamorphic symbolism of this signifier. Flying, which connotes the myth of Icarus, could have warned us of this outcome.

The dangers of 'bovarysme' are thus clearly illustrated. And since it is Henri's arrival on the scene which prompts her to jump from the swing, his role as agent of her moral Fall becomes more apparent.

Hélène's self-inflicted pain and the sprain which ensues, form part of the ritual of mutilation in the unfolding initiatory scenario. Similarly, her ability to pick herself up with superhuman courage despite her pain, anticipates the outcome of the novel: her paradoxically sublimating yet damning return to her virtuous comatose state, her psychological death and spiritual rebirth.[12]

Only after Hélène's Fall from the swing—the fallen angel—can the full irony of the following sentence, with its religious overtones, be appreciated: '[She] seemed . . . like a saint with a halo of gold flying up to Paradise' (Zola, 1957:44).

I now come to my third and last example of semiotic polarity, le Passage des Eaux. Like the window and the swing, it connects the two axes of verticality, height and depth, and its symbolism is again ambiguous.

The very notion of 'passage' implied in this symbolic name associates it with the rites of passage referred to earlier, and the connotation of movement and change related to initiatory ordeals that it evokes makes it a dominant motif; it is therefore not surprising that it is described in minute topographical detail.

For example, one of its striking features, its seven flights of steep stairs, provides an important lead. The number 7 symbolises completion and/or perfection, and is therefore particularly relevant in the present context. Owing to their verticality, staircases are classic symbols of ascent, of the search for knowledge and hence of transcendence and are therefore anamorphic, but negatively they are also symbols of descent, of regression and hence potentially catamorphic.

Aspects of initiatory scenarios can be clearly detected in Hélène's hazardous trips up and down le Passage des Eaux: for instance, the novice's act of rupture in the attempt to break away from a present mode of existence which would positively valorise the passage. However, here Zola again appears to devalorise all this positive symbolism and more particularly the ascensional symbolism, for, instead of depicting Hélène moving UP from one plane to another, from the profane to the sacred, he emphasises her stepping DOWN, thereby indicating that she is going *down* the spiritual hierarchy and abandoning her moral rectitude.

On the other hand, this stage of her descent could also be interpreted as the descent to Hell, a major part of initiatory rites—always positively valorised—which ensures the symbolic death of the novice before symbolic rebirth. Eliade wrote: 'initiatory death is often symbolized . . . by cosmic night, by the telluric womb . . . images [which] express regression to a performed state . . . rather than total annihilation' (Beane and Doty, 1975:166). In this context, Hélène's descent could be regarded as the journey to a prenatal state or return to the womb, in which case an analogy could be drawn between le Passage des Eaux and the birth canal; I will explore this gynaecological link shortly.

A second equally important lead is the aquatic feature of this symbolic passage. Durand (1969:103–4) has shown how water can be doubly valorised: positively, as in the case of clear, pure, running waters like those of fountains or, negatively, as in the case of dark and gloomy mires or marshes. In the latter instance, such deep and still waters appear hostile and inauspicious owing to their treacherous capacity to flood and swamp, that is, to swallow and destroy—characteristics which associate them with what Bachelard (1964 [1942]: chs. II, III) calls 'the symbolic substance of death' (my translation). Hence, this ambiguous aquatic association matches the ambiguity of the stairs. But, because Hélène is depicted going down the passage and because of the return to the womb posited, the reader's imagination is directed towards two schemes: that termed 'avalage' or 'swallowing' by Durand (1969:233–34, 243–44, 256, 267), and that of descent again. Both evoke chthonian depths and consequently nocturnal realms; our cultural code could further expand this chain of connotations to include a negative 'evil-sin-hell' syntagm.

There can be no doubt then, as to the doubly catamorphic, though ambiguous, resonance of this carefully chosen name. Through it, le Passage des Eaux connecting Passy and Paris becomes the metaphorical and ambiguous gateway either to damnation or to salvation. This polarity automatically evokes the female sexual stereotype whore/saint, witch/angel, mistress/wife.

Figure 6

SIGN			
ACTANT	SIGNIFIER	SIGNIFIED	SIGNIFICATION
Le passage des Eaux	le passage des Eaux, un étrange *escalier étranglé* entre les murs des jardins voisins, une *ruelle escarpée* qui *descend* sur le quai, des *hauteurs* de Passy. *Au bas* de cette *pente*" (p. 73).[13]	threshold connecting link bridge gateway labyrinth	virtue = salvation ↑ | temptation ↓ sin = damnation

As can be seen, then, le Passage des Eaux is by no means an ordinary, straightforward stairway; it appears—on the surface—to have many attractive attributes, but paradoxically its labyrinthine aspects are equally prominent:

> She had, in particular, taken a strange liking to the
> Passage des Eaux. She enjoyed the coolness and the
> silence of this steep alley, the unvarying cleanness of
> its pavement, washed on rainy days by a rushing torrent
> from the heights. She had a queer feeling when she
> stood at the top and looked down the steep slope of the
> passage, which was usually deserted . . . Then she
> would venture down it . . . and carefully make her way
> down the seven flights of broad steps, alongside which,
> taking up half the width of the narrow passage, ran the
> pebbly bed of a stream. To right and left stood garden
> walls, bulging with age, and mouldering away with grey
> leprous patches. There were overhanging trees with
> drooping foliage, and a great cloak of ivy outspread;
> and all this verdure, disclosing only blue glimpses of
> sky, shed a dim, quiet, greenish light. Half-way down she
> would pause for breath, staring curiously at the street
> lamp that hung there, listening to laughter in the
> gardens . . . Sometimes an old woman would climb up
> the stairs, clutching the black gleaming iron rail . . . But
> more often she was alone, and she delighted in this
> quiet shady stairway, like a hollow lane through a forest.
> Once at the bottom she would look back, and the sight
> of the steep slope down which she had ventured always
> gave her a little shiver of fright. (Zola, 1957:33)

The extract invites two dominant interpretations. First, the iconicity of topographical anatomy can easily be detected, the passage being full of vulva imagery.[13] Indeed, neither the male writer's nor the female actant's erotic attention, focused on the zone of entry, ought to be underestimated. Hélène's journey through the passage is clearly analogous to the exploration and discovery of her own physical sexuality: she is obviously mesmerised by the trap or threshold of the sexual aperture. The analysis of concrete spatial referents shows a constant metaphorical transposition. The steep alley (narrow passage/hollow lane) with its surrounding overgrowth and rushing torrent are powerfully evocative of female sexuality and the various fluids associated with it. Even the reference to the colour green through the verdure, greenish light and bushes echoes Durand's (1969:250–51) equation of that colour to 'the maternal cavity'. Thus, gynaecological correlations are implicit throughout.

Second, a basic paradigm: virtue/sin, usually culturally linked with repulsion/attraction, resistance/surrender, emerges clearly from the analysis in Figure 7 entitled 'Passage des Eaux',[14] and reinforces the ambiguity of this labyrinthine refuge, making it difficult to determine at this early stage which semantic set predominates. Seen in an actantial context, the anthropomorphic characteristics of some of the spatial components expose the latter to be pseudo-'helpers': the walls, trees, ivy and foliage pretend to offer safe and attractive shelter, but the clear catamorphic impression of engulfment they convey indicates that they are in fact treacherous, that they are seducing Hélène and leading her into a trap; as such they are definite 'opponents' in the traditional sense of middle-class morality. So far, the 'pebbly bed of a stream' does not hold the promise of a bed of roses.

An analysis of the second description of Hélène going down le Passage des Eaux helps to disambiguate the metaphorical significance of the passage.

> Outside it was still thawing. The causeway was deep in
> mud ... The sky was grey, and from the pavement a
> mist was rising. The road lay dimly before her,
> deserted and uninviting, though the hour was yet early,
> the few gas-lamps looking in the damp haze like
> yellow spots. She quickened her steps, keeping close to
> the houses and shrinking from sight as though she
> were on the way to keep an assignation. But as she
> turned hastily into the Passage des Eaux, she halted
> beneath the archway, her heart giving way to genuine
> terror. The passage opened beneath her feet like some
> black gulf. The bottom was invisible; the only thing she
> could see in the black tunnel was the uncertain
> glimmer of the one lamp which lighted it. In the end her
> mind was made up; she grasped the iron railing to
> prevent her slipping. Feeling her way with the tip of her
> boot, she landed successively on the broad steps. The
> walls, right and left, grew closer, seemingly endless in
> the night, while the naked branches of the trees

*overhead cast vague shadows of gigantic arms with
shrivelled outstretched hands. She trembled as she
thought how one of the garden doors might open and a
man spring upon her. There were no passers-by, and
she stepped down as quickly as possible. Suddenly from
out the darkness issued a shadow; the shadow coughed
and she was frozen with fear; but it was only an old
woman creeping up with difficulty. Once more
reassured, she lifted up with greater care her dress which
had been trailing in the mud. So thick was the coating
of mud on the steps that her boots were constantly
sticking fast. At the bottom she turned aside
instinctively. From the branches the rain-drops dripped
fast into the passage, and the lamp glimmered like
that of some miner, hooked to the side of a pit down the
wall of which water was oozing dangerously (Zola,
1895:214).*

The second extract contains many important changes and
variations; these constitute semiotic elements which have a
distinct signifying function. The steep alley has lost its previous
appeal; Hélène's fondness for it has been replaced by an obvious
malaise. Her earlier 'strange sensation' and 'slight fear' have now
turned into a 'real fright'; the 'patches of blue sky' have
deteriorated to 'grey'; she is frozen with terror by an unidentifia-
ble shadow emerging from the darkness. Anthropomorphisation
as well as a powerful connotative iconicity now make the
passage, walls and trees definitely ghoulish and menacing,
confirming their actantial roles as opponents.

Instead of the previous purifying images of the clear paving
stone washed by rain, and the positively valorised running
waters of the stream, there are now images of decomposition and
filth—a liquefying process which connotes defilement, corruption and contamination; Hélène's stained frock symbolically
marks the beginning of her downfall (see Fig.7).

The soft and discreet greenish light that had filtered through
before and given the shaded stairs a quasi-religious charm has
vanished. Now, only the flickering glow of the streetlamp lights
the narrow passageway which appears like dark entrails or a
dangerous mine shaft. These two powerful second-level icons
reinforce the earlier association of the passage with the birth
canal. In addition, the hollow imagery of the homologous and
iconic 'black hole' and 'pit' evoke the womb. As Borie (1971:178)

Schema Number 3: Passage Des Eaux

MODES OF PERCEPTION (REAL/ METAPHORIC)	SIGN		SIGNIFICATION	CONVERGENCE OF SIGNIFIEDS	OPPOSITION OF SIGNIFIEDS
	SIGNIFIER	SIGNIFIED			
THERMIC AUDITORY VISUAL	fraîcheur silence pavé [...] propre [...] lavait coins bleus de ciel jour verdâtre très doux et très discret c'était un grand charme que cet escalier recueilli et ombragé	cleansing calmness intimacy safety	purification refuge shrine grotto		
VEGETAL	jardins arbres branches feuillage lierre verdures (jour) verdâtre forêts	garden bower	Eden freedom	VIRTUE	
ANAMORPHIC and URANIAN	hauteurs voûte d'en haut ciel	height	superiority strength inaccessibility		
KINETIC	montait levait les yeux	ascent	transcendence		
CHTHONIAN and CATAMORPHIC	ruelle escarpée pente raide passage étages larges marches étroit couloir descente escalier chemin creux pente si raide s'enforcer descendait jetait dégringolaient sous en bas	steep slope narrow path labyrinth descent depth	Underworld FALL inferiority failure		
CONTACTUAL	désert, connu à peine elle restait seule	seclusion solitude	alienation nothingness		
CLOSURE	murs portes [...] jamais ouvertes muraille	enclosed space	imprisonment	SIN	
SENSORY and KINETIC	elle avait [...] une étrange sensation se hasardait à petits pas elle s'arrêtait pour souffler s'aidant de la rampe s'appuyait sur son ombrelle comme une canne se risquer légère peur escarpée raide si raide	fear danger tribulation steepness	risk		
AQUATIC	pluie torrent coulant pleuvaient	flowing /falling waters	breaking of waters Valley of tears		
VISUAL	murs [...] mangés d'une lèpre grise	stain decay	defilement destruction		

says, 'the feminine body evidently defines itself through its hollowness, it is womb, envelope, container' (my translation).

In view of these gynaecological associations, the thawing snow and the 'flood of mud' are analogous to menstruation and the breaking of the waters. Such violent aquatic eruption with its threat of inundation can only be negatively valorised; given all these negative elements, the total change of tone in the second description of le Passage des Eaux can also be interpreted as a combination of post-orgasmic lassitude, masturbatory guilt and menstrual fear. Finally, the suggestive adverb upon which the extract ends—*dangerously*—is charged with evil omen.

This brief comparison clearly shows the prevalence of negative valorisations in the second extract, thereby confirming the catamorphic significance of the Passage des Eaux and exposing the earlier misleading and ironic valorisation of the anamorphic. This devalorisation process persists with an increasing emphasis on catamorphic aquatic imagery during Hélène's third frantic trip down the passage:

> *When she turned down into the Passage des Eaux, she hesitated for a second. The stairway had turned into a torrent, the gutters of the Rue Raynouard had overflowed and were pouring down. Foam was splashing over the steps, in a narrow passage, while patches of rain-washed pavement gleamed; a wan burst of light falling from the grey sky between the black branches of the trees whitened her way. Barely lifting her skirts, she hurried down. The water reached her ankles, her light thin slippers nearly came off in the puddles. (Zola, 1957:188)*

Furthermore, instead of the anticipated incubating womb with its positive characteristics, at the end of her trip down le Passage des Eaux the novice is confronted with the sordid 'pink room'—the iconic womb at the end of the birth canal—within a repulsive and dilapidated house. Thus, woman, the 'avaleuse' or 'swallower' par excellence, ambivalently finds herself 'avalée', or 'swallowed'.[15]

Needless to say, the climax of this negative initiation is punctuated from beginning to end by the catamorphic rain, which prompts Borie (1971:215) to term the love scene 'cesspit copulation' (my translation). Given such valorisation, it is not surprising that Hélène *fails* her initiation, despite the consummation of her love affair. This is reflected by the fiasco of her sexual awakening which is thus expressed: 'She shivered with a pleasure she had not yet known. Memories returned to her; her senses were aroused too late, leaving her with a tremendous unsatisfied desire' (Zola, 1895:270, 1957:218 modified). As Schor (1976:188) points out, 'desire can only be experienced after the event' (my translation).

Biblically, the Fall is the prerequisite to knowledge, but ironically, despite her Fall, Hélène's ignorance remains. When she eventually decides to become a wife again, rather than a mistress, she denies herself her individuality and the freedom and equality which widowhood placed within her reach; in so doing, she expresses to what extent she is the product of social and cultural constructs.

The manner in which her search for sexual identity is constructed can be seen as constituting a discourse. Within that discourse the narrative structures available to her remain limited. For a brief moment she is the subject in her own narrative quest, but in the final analysis, she remains the object of desire, the prize to be won. This discourse reflects Zola's understanding of female psychology and is a representation of the victimisation of women through sexual and patriarchal ideologies. My semiotic analysis of the catamorphic structures in *Une Page d'Amour* exposes the construction of woman as sufferer, unable to fulfil her drives and her femininity because of social repression.

To conclude, then, it can be seen that space and its constituents, especially the sexualisation of the urban landscape, are indeed key textual signifiers subtly contributing to the representation of the feminine which is intimately linked with the theme of the Fall. The malleability of the signs explored confirms that Zola's ironic valorisation and subsequent devalorisation—particularly of space—is a major contributing factor to such representation. I hope that my method and decoding of the text has brought to light some aspects of the nature and implications of gender bias in communication, by exposing some of the ideologies present in prose narrative.

7　Deconstructions of masculinity and femininity in the films of Marguerite Duras

Michelle Royer

I N 1975, when Hélène Cixous wrote 'Sorties' in *La jeune née* (1975:172), she began her text by the questioning of what is at stake in this chapter. She wrote:

Where is she?

Activity/passivity
Sun/moon
Culture/nature
Day/night
Father/mother
reason/feeling
Intelligible/sensitive
Logos/Pathos

$$\frac{Man}{Woman}$$

In that text, H. Cixous exposes the dichotomic system of binary oppositions as the basis of 'phallo-logocentrism'. Between the two terms of the couple there exists a relationship in which the masculine paradigm dominates 'the other'. The subordination of

the feminine to the masculine is also what is signified by the bar
of separation.

The question of the place of woman outside that system is
clearly formulated by Shoshana Felman when she asks:

> *How can the woman be thought about outside of the
> Masculine/Feminine framework, other than as opposed
> to man, without being subordinated to a primordial
> masculine model? How can madness, in a similar way,
> be conceived of outside its dichotomous oppositions to
> sanity, without being subjugated to reason? How can
> difference as such be thought out as non-subordinate
> to identity? In other words, how can thought break away
> from the logic of polar opposition?*[1]

How can one escape dichotomic thinking? Marguerite Duras
(1981:175) suggests the following strategy: 'Reverse everything.
Make women the point of departure in judging, make darkness
the point of departure in judging what men call light, make
obscurity the point of departure in judging what men call clarity.'
'When we have a male in front of us, we could ask: does he have
some female in him? And that could be the main point.'

When I decided to centre this chapter on one film, *India Song*, I
encountered my first problem. How can one centre an analysis
when the object of the study is scattered over different texts,
films, plays? In 1973, Marguerite Duras published what she
called the 'text-film-play': *India Song*. The film I propose to speak
about was made in 1975 and bears a lot of similarities with and
differences from the 1973 publication. It is placed in the vast
intertextual network of Marguerite Duras' production. Characters like the beggar, the Vice-Consul, Lol. V. Stein are in-
terspersed throughout several texts. To add to the 'confusion',
Marguerite Duras re-used the sound track of *India Song* to make
a new film in 1976, called 'Son nom de Venise dans Calcutta
Desert', but with a new visual track. The recycling of films is
common practice for Marguerite Duras who, in her film
L'Homme Atlantique made use of the remnants of *Agatha* to
make her visual track. The combination of a new soundtrack
with familiar images produces a film looking uncannily the same
but in fact different. The use of these deconstruction strategies is
certainly very uncommon and contributes to producing a cinema
which is subversive not only of conventional film techniques but
also of the whole 'economy' of film-making.

Now that I have acknowledged that *India Song* has a place in the long self-deconstructive activity of Marguerite Duras' works, I would like to examine the deconstructive process functioning in what is inevitably a somewhat arbitrarily selected unit of this complex intertextual history: the *India Song* film.

India Song does not give any place to 'the primordial masculine model' and the set of values attached to it. M. Duras wants to rid herself of everything she learnt from men: rules, theories, techniques, conventions. By doing so she invalidates the masculine side of the dichotomy with its logical thinking and its pretension to truth and re-evaluates the feminine side and paradigm: silence, madness, passivity, negativity, multiplicity, etc... Marguerite Duras undertakes the undoing of the dichotomic system of binary oppositions structuring the phallocentric order by repositioning the oppressed element of the dichotomy and by unsettling the bar of separation. Starting from the place where the feminine is traditionally assigned she goes on exploring it.

India Song tells the story of the last months of Anne-Marie Stretter's life and of her love affair with Michael Richardson. The story takes place in India in the 1930s, during the monsoon, and is told by voices whose faces stay invisible throughout the film. They do not remember the story perfectly, they hesitate, contradict themselves and one another and present a fragmented, non-chronological account of what they think might have happened. Another story is also told, that of the hunger, leprosy and misery of Calcutta. It is told by two characters: a beggar woman off-screen who is never seen but whose voice haunts the film and the Vice-Consul who is heard and seen and who is in love with Anne-Marie Stretter.

This analysis revolves around three characters: the beggar woman, Anne-Marie Stretter, and the Vice-Consul; and around one formal characteristic of the film: the disjunction of the soundtrack and the visual track. The roles given to the female characters play an important part in the process of the deconstruction of the masculine/feminine dichotomy. The female point of view is established as the reference point to engage an interplay of similarities and differences between feminine and masculine. At a technical level, *India Song* presents a similar strategy. In the conventional film, according to Stephen Heath (1981:201), 'The image is all powerful and the sound track is a supplement'. Christian Metz, in his book *The Imaginary Signifier* (1977) confirms this by drawing an analogy between the film and the mirror stage, thus considering the film as primarily a visual art at the expense of the soundtrack whose function is disparaged. *India Song* reverses this trend by giving the soundtrack a privileged role in the narration. Image and sound are never synchronised and maintain a gap as well as a relationship of identity and differences in which each track keeps a relative independence. This independence of the sound exposes the inability of psychoanalytic film theory to deal with the complete film as image and sound, and the necessity for film criticism to shift the emphasis from looking to hearing. Stephen Heath (1981:121) acknowledges that Lacan had already 'stressed hearing, or more exactly invocatory drive, as closest to the experience of the unconscious', but more research still needs to be done in this area.

The film opens (shot 2) with the voice of the beggar woman singing in an oriental language. The song stops and the voice starts laughing, then talks in the same oriental language. The communicative function of the language is rendered ineffective, at least for the French ear, but its materiality is emphasised. The sonorities, the rhythm, the intonation, the pitch, what Roland Barthes called the 'grain of the voice', are all we hear from the beggar and they become the distinctive traits by which this woman is identified in the rest of film. She stays a disembodied voice throughout and comes back repeatedly, haunting the sound track and provoking the same eerie feeling. The beggar expresses in the language what Hélène Cixous considers the most important: 'the vocal, the musical, the language at its most archaic and at the same time at its most wrought level' (1977:488) Cixous believes woman's writing never stops echoing the maternal voice, the first song, the first music, the voice of Love, deeply anchored and preserved within herself. In many of Duras' films, the voice is used in a similar way. For example, in *Le Navire Night* the two lovers know each other only by speaking on the phone: they never see each other, and the voice has a very erotic function.

From the beginning and throughout the film, the beggar's voice not only unveils the 'other' of language but also triggers the narration. In the second shot and following the beggar, two female voices begin to tell her story while on the screen the sun is slowly disappearing. The narrators reveal that the beggar is mad, of uncertain origin, has abandoned her children and is now sterile. She is a lost soul, completely dispossessed and wandering through Asia, aimlessly. We can only describe her in negative terms: she is the lack. The beggar woman assumes a totally negative function regarding social order: as a beggar, she is out of the system of exchange, she has no social status. She is complete-ly on the negative side of the dichotomy as described by Cixous; she has no definite origin, is no longer a mother nor a daughter, she is even sterile and insane. She assumes with perfection what Julia Kristeva (1981) believes is the function of women: 'If women have a role to play . . . it is only in assuming a negative function: reject everything finite, definite, structured, loaded with mean-ing in the existing order.' By never appearing on the screen, she also assumes a negative function regarding film as a visual art.

In shot 3, the stories of the beggar woman and of Anne-Marie Stretter begin to be woven together: as a way of introducing Anne-Marie Stretter, one of the voices says: 'they were together in Calcutta'. The beggar who had taken up a main role in the nar-ration is now relegated to a secondary position as the other by the second voice who asks, for precision, 'the white girl and the other?'. Beggar, colonised and a woman, she combines every-thing that is repressed, dominated, negative in a colonial patriar-chal society. Essentially a voice, she is also on the side of what is belittled in the traditional film: the soundtrack. Anne-Marie Stretter, as the wife of the Ambassador and as a colonial, has two things in common with the beggar: she is a woman in exile, and has followed the same itinerary through Asia.

Simultaneously the visual track shows the interior of a room with a piano. On it, a photograph of a woman dressed in black and white. An Indian waiter comes in and brings a bunch of flowers. At first, there seems to be a complete disjunction between the soundtrack and the visual track. Further consider-ations suggest an interplay of differences and similarities rather than a total separation. Because the characters were first men-tioned by the voices, the soundtrack becomes the point of reference from which to compare what can be seen on the screen. This situation leads the spectator to consider the soundtrack as having a high status in relation to the truth of the story although the truth is never unique or singular when told by two hesitant narrators.

Similarities begin with the entry of the waiter and the connotations attached to his costume (he is dressed in white Hindu clothing). But the Indian characteristic is displaced from feminine (the beggar) to masculine (the waiter). The rep-resentation of a male to signify woman can be very disconcerting although the dominated status of femininity is kept by the fact that the man is a waiter and an Indian. The Indian waiter stands for repression and domination, but femininity is so strongly repressed that it is obliterated, unrepresentable; it is there only as absent. If the visual track fails to represent woman, it is able to show a photograph of a young woman, now dead, which we have identified as the late Anne-Marie Stretter.

Anne-Marie Stretter is seen for the first time quite late in the film in shot 9, ten minutes after the beginning of the film. In shot 5, a slow pan lingers on her clothes and jewellery, traditional signs of her gender, while the voices talk about the party, and the love and desire between Anne-Marie Stretter and Michael Richardson. When later we see a woman dancing with a man, we identify them as this couple. The images are again understood in relation to voices heard earlier and not the other way around. In most of the shots the characters are seen reflected in mirrors. This certainly bears some resemblance to the myth of Narcissus and Echo, but contrary to a common use of the myth, this time Echo recovers her place, once lost in this phallocentred system.

India Song associates the following terms: femininity, colonisation, poverty, blackness, as what is repressed, to the extent of obliteration, of unrepresentability. The visual track shows luxurious decors, actors dressed in party clothes, bright lights and a general feeling of wealth. Poverty stays off-screen, as does blackness. The only sign of colonisation in that sumptuous house is the presence of the waiter dressed in white. All that is repressed is talked about by narrative voices, to which I would like to return now in more detail.

For the first 28 shots, these women's voices tell the story of the past of Anne-Marie Stretter, Michael Richardson, the beggar and the Vice-Consul by following their own random association, the mechanisms of their memories. They contradict each other, their own statements and the images in the visual track. The notion of truth based on coherence quickly becomes irrelevant. The truth of the story seems to be a collage of contradictory episodes, a patchwork of uncertainties, of half-sewn fragments of texts at times leaving gaps opened.

The story told by the soundtrack is punctuated by music, background noises and numerous long silences. These pauses contribute to creating the ragged aspect of the story and at the same time transgress another taboo in film-making, but this time a taboo of the soundtrack: the lack of sound. Silence is allowed in conventional films only in very strategic moments, for example to bring suspense. In *India Song* it is there to be heard as silence. Silence is there for what cannot be expressed. Like the 'black screen' used in another film by Marguerite Duras, *L'Homme*

Atlantique, it signifies what is repressed to the point of complete obliteration. Silence has always been one of the most subversive strategies used by Marguerite Duras. In *Nathalie Granger*, the silence of two women becomes terribly disruptive when a salesman desperately tries to sell them a washing machine. To his very wordy and lengthy speech, they offer their silence and their mute smiles. The salesman loses his confidence and stutters, unable to continue to play his game. According to Marguerite Duras (1981:175) silence is very relevant to women and to all oppressed people. Men should learn to be silent. She considers that it is a new mode of being to be fostered.

The language of the narration used by the voices is very unconventional: sentences are often elliptic and contain a great number of nouns for a very few verbs, thus creating a very stilted style. This intonation is often that of a question, with the voice rising at the end of the sentences, and the delivery is slow and/or hesitant. All these characteristics put into question the notion of truth as implying logic, confidence, unity, coherence. Again, the narration is on the negative side of the dichotomy.

The dialogues often have a poetic quality: associations between the words are provided by rhymes, alliterations, assonances, metaphors, rather than with logically constructed sentences. I would like to illustrate that point with an example from two different shots. The voices say alternately: *Cette lumière/la mousson/cette poussière/Calcutta Central/Il y a comme une odeur de fleur/la lèpre/Où est-on?* (That light/The monsoon/The dust/Central Calcutta/Isn't there a smell of flowers?/Leprosy/Where are we?) The statement *il y a comme une odeur de fleur/la lèpre* has a demystifying function. Flower and woman are traditionally associated, but in this sentence *leprosy* comes in to break the expectation, although the stereotype is used to create the relationship between the three elements: Flower Woman Leprosy. Later in this paper we will see how leprosy is closely associated with Anne-Marie Stretter. These dialogues show noun phrases, rhymes (*lumière/poussière, odeur/fleur*) which create a feeling of stillness. The play on sounds, on the intonation and rhythm, the disruption of the syntax, the multiplicity of meanings emphasise what Julia Kristeva (1977) calls 'the archaic dimension of language, the semiotic'.

The semiotic relates to the 'maternal' in Kristevan theory. As explained by Jane Gallop in *Feminism and Psychoanalysis* (1982), 'the semiotic is a more immediate expression of the drives and is linked to the bodily contact with the mother before the paternal order of language comes to separate subject from mother'. It is 'given freer play in works of "art": it is the poetic dimension of language'. The semiotic is seen as disruptive of the symbolic order as it 'sets the bodily rhythms of poetry against the linear structures and codified representations of the symbolic', (Kristeva, 1977:12). What *India Song* asks from spectators is very demanding, because it asks them to question all conventional behaviours. The spectators have to become attentive auditors, not only *voyeurs*, and have to listen 'otherwise'. Marguerite Duras leads the spectators into the space of woman, traditionally situated under the bar of the dichotomy masculine/feminine, and whose elements are: femininity-sound-track-voice-poetic language-silence-black-colonised-poverty.

But, later in the film, a male character, the Vice-Consul, topples over the spectator's imaginary bar of the dichotomy masculine/feminine into the void of the voices.

The Vice-Consul has a very special place in the film: in an act of madness, he shot at the lepers in Lahore and is now considered as a social outcast by his colleagues. Invited by Anne-Marie Stretter to a reception held at the Embassy (shot 24), his arrival is accompanied by the guests' comments: *elle aurait pu nous éviter cette présence. A Lahore personne ne le recevait* ('she should not have imposed this person upon us.' 'In Lahore, no-one received him'). During a conversation with Anne-Marie Stretter, at the party, he declares his love for her and shows that he is aware that other people consider him mad. He says (shot 52) *je parle faux/ma voix leur fait peur. De qui est-elle?* ('I sound false/my voice scares them. Whom does it come from?'). It is interesting to note that it is by the strangeness of his voice that he and others acknowledge his madness. In that sense, he is very similar to the beggar woman and to the female narrative voices.

The Vice-Consul sees Anne-Marie Stretter as part of himself and they both agree that 'they are the same'. They both have difficulties becoming accustomed to living in Calcutta. Like the Vice-Consul, Anne-Marie Stretter is often seen crying. Neither of them is able to cope with the separation from their country of origin which is for both of them the land of their mother, their motherland in a literal sense. The arrival in India meant their integration into the social order: for the Vice-Consul through his work at the Embassy and for Anne-Marie Stretter as the wife of the Ambassador. As one of the voices says (shot 21): 'she cannot bear the fences around her, the guards, the officials'. Neither of them is able to cope with the repressive institution of the Embassy.

Music is for Anne-Marie Stretter and the Vice-Consul very important. It reminds them of the time they were with their respective mothers in Europe. Anne-Marie Stretter, at the time called Anna-Maria Guardi, used to play the piano when she was in Venice with her mother. But when she married the Ambassador, she stopped. She says that, since then, (shot 39) 'a kind of suffering is attached to music'. The Vice-Consul also talks about his mother playing the piano when they were living in Neuilly. While listening to 'India Song' played on the piano, the Vice-Consul says (shot 35) *cette musique me donne envie d'aimer* ('this music gives me the desire to love'). Piano is a recurrent theme in Marguerite Duras' films: its music reminds of the mother and is often a metaphor of desire. In the film *Agatha*, music is one articulation point in the desire between mother–son, mother–daughter and brother–sister.

To express his love for Anne-Marie Stretter, the Vice-Consul uses maternal metaphors (shot 52): 'You are in me , I will take you with me and you will shoot at the lepers in Shalimar.' He seems to be unable to dissociate himself from her and from Lahore. He says (shot 52): 'Lahore, it is me.' Lahore is the symbol of his madness, and he is unwilling or unable to reject it. 'I shot at myself in Lahore without dying.' 'Others separate me from Lahore, I don't separate myself from it'. If we follow the association made by the Vice-Consul we come to think that there exists a series of equations between Vice-Consul-Lahore-madness-Anne-Marie Stretter. He is wishing to establish a kind of symbiosis with these elements and that is where his madness lies.

Madness seems to be the characteristic common to all of them, although Anne-Marie Stretter's madness is different. When she was young, in Venice, she used to play music to the extent of madness. She has always been mad, either because she was expressing too much of herself or because she was doing what she was supposed to do as the wife of the Ambassador, that is, nothing. Since her marriage with him, she exhibits signs of what has been designated as a typically feminine form of madness: a silencing of herself; hysteria. She does not show anything of it, and that is her madness. As one of the voices says, 'nothing can be seen' but 'she is imprisoned in a kind of suffering.' Anne-Marie Stretter's madness is also expressed metaphorically as (in shots

19 and 38) 'a leprosy of the heart'. Leprosy is a disease which is often mentioned in *India Song*. It is a good example of the way Marguerite Duras breaks a word meaning into a constellation of signifiers. Leprosy is a disease affecting a lot of Indians, therefore the repetition of the word by the voices and sentences such as 'lepers burst like dust bags' while the visual track is showing the luxurious decor of the Embassy has the strength of a political statement. It is also used as a metaphor for the shutting off of women's feelings in order to fit in the existing establishment. The disease affects the nervous system, it disturbs sensations and destroys feelings. Suffering from it consists in a general, gradual deterioriation into insensitivity, anaesthesia. It is also a contagious disease. Anne-Marie Stretter appears to have caught it at the Embassy. As one of the voices says: *les cercles fermes aux Indes, ça me fait toujours penser à la lepre* ('closed circles in India always remind me of leprosy'). Luce Irigaray (1985b) explains hysteria by the repression of female desire which is, according to her, common to all women. I would like to make this reference parallel with a quotation from Marguerite Duras: 'All women are neurotic in my opinion'; 'much female behaviour that one finds normal would be considered as neurotic if exhibited in males'. (1981:176).

Anne-Marie Stretter and the beggar suffer from a negative self-directed sort of madness. The Vice-Consul directs his actions more outwardly, and acts more voluntarily, by shooting at the beggars in Lahore. But he says he would like to catch leprosy to be like a woman, to stop his suffering. Through madness, the Vice-Consul comes nearer the women's world without being totally in it. His final attempt to reach the feminine will be in his decision to cry in the middle of the reception at the Embassy. This act will also project him outside the fences of the park of the Embassy, into the world of the lepers, of the outcasts.

In a major sequence lasting 25 minutes and including one shot of ten minutes, we hear the Vice-Consul's repeated cry. He also calls, 'An-na, Ma-ria Guardi'. On the screen, Anne-Marie Stretter and Michael Richardson are seen, standing up, immobile, silent. The disjunction between the soundtrack and the visual track accentuates the intensity of the cry and its effect, while the silence of the image is emphasised. As explained by Anne-Marie Stretter, Anna-Maria Guardi is her maiden name (shot 39): 'my father was French, my mother was from Venice, I had kept her name.' So Guardi is also her mother's and grandmother's name, the name of the female line of the family, and the father's patronymic stays unknown. The genealogy of women-mothers is kept functioning through the transmission of the name-of-the-mother, and as expressed by Luce Irigaray: 'By trying to re-establish a genealogy of women-mothers, we are calling into question the whole patriarchal order.'[2] Without the name of the father, the mother's morality is always in doubt and the father's paternity can always be contested. It is interesting to note that, in French, the sonorities of Guardi are associated with those of 'garder', to keep, although in Italian, it means to look (re-garder). But what is there to keep or look after?

When Anna-Maria Guardi marries the Ambassador, her whole name is changed: she becomes Anne-Marie Stretter. In this transaction, not only her mother's name is obliterated, but another transformation also takes place, Anna-Maria becomes Anne-Marie. The *a* becomes *e*. In French the two vowels are feminine gender marks, but the *a* is heard whereas the *e* is silent. Is that the sign for the reduction to silence of the feminine? In French *marie* also means 'to marry' and Maria is the past tense, 'married'. The name Anne-Maria Guardi tells us not only that the female line is preserved but the word *maria* (i.e. the preterite) (in English, 'married') reveals the desire between the mother and the daughter—opening a new possible field of exploration of the 'feminine' in the subversion of the mother–daughter incest taboo.

When she marries the Ambassador, the symbiotic relationship between the mother and the daughter is replaced by the marriage institution. Anna-Maria Guardi has adopted 'the name-of-the-father' and has entered what Lacan calls 'the symbolic order', under the name of the Husband. It is interesting to note that the sonorities of 'Stretter' are very hard in French because of the *t* and the *r*, and that in German, Stretter means to quarrel/argue. When the Vice-Consul cries out 'Anna-Maria Guardi', he also adds, *gardez-moi* (keep me with you) which reinforces the association made with *garder*, to keep contained in Guardi, and reverses the mother–child relationship he has expressed earlier when he said to Anne-Marie Stretter, 'You are in me'.

The Vice-Consul is calling the feminine within himself and in Anne-Marie Stretter. As one of the voices says, *il crie son nom de Venise dans Calcutta desert*, that is, he *calls* Anna-Maria Guardi, in Anne-Marie Stretter. He is *calling* the feminine which had been silenced by patriarchal order, and of which the names are the metaphors. A previous shot had revealed that obliteration of the feminine, when one of the narrative voices was reading, very slowly, detaching each syllable, the names on Anne-Marie Stretter's grave, 'Anne-Marie Stretter written on the grave, Anna-Maria Guardi erased'. It is read so as to make us hear otherwise. On the screen, the Vice-Consul is shown with tears running down his cheeks.

The dramatic cry of the Vice-Consul is also a disruptive act for the phallocratic order represented here by the reception at the Embassy. It is an emotional act out of keeping with his social position. Although it does create a scandal, one of the guests admits, 'don't you think, we could all cry'? Maybe they could all cry, but it would be at the risk of being excluded from the existing order. To illustrate that, on the screen, the image shows the Vice-Consul walking in the streets of Calcutta. It is the first time in the film apart from the opening shot, when we see outside the fences of the park of the Embassy. The Vice-Consul is now projected into the world of the lepers, of the poor, of the outcasts, of the mad, of the other.

This sequence finalises the breakdown of the dichotomy masculine/feminine by showing the Vice-Consul's search for the feminine. At this point, it seems to me that Marguerite Duras is really 'putting into practice' the question quoted earlier in this chapter: 'when we have a male in front of us, we could ask does he have some female in him?'

In this chapter I have shown how, by repositioning the oppressed element of the masculine/feminine dichotomy as the point of departure of her film, Marguerite Duras deconstructs the dichotomic system. The feminine with its paradigm silence, madness, colonised, blackness, outcasts, becomes the reference point for the narration and its characters. But the feminine is not essentially tied up with gender and the Vice-Consul's cry finishes undoing the dichotomy. Marguerite Duras does not simply reverse the phallocentric system, she shows that the opposition of the two terms is an illusion since in men the feminine can also be present. In the film *India Song* the strategies at work echo those suggested by Luce Irigaray for a redefinition of the language that would leave space for the feminine: 'There would no longer be either a right side or a wrong side of discourse or even of texts, but each passing from one to the other would make audible and comprehensible even what resists the recto-verso structure that supports commonsense.' (quoted in Johnson, 1981).

And what *India Song* makes audible is the name of the mother and her voice.

8 Cross-dressing in fiction: literary history and the cultural construction of sexuality

Virginia Blain

THE TITLE of this chapter plays on the titles of three texts, all novels from the 1890s: *The Woman Who Did* and *The Woman Who Didn't*, both published by John Lane and Company, in 1895, and *Six Chapters of a Man's Life*, published by the Walter Scott Publishing Company, Ltd in 1904 (but probably written earlier). All three form part of that turn-of-the-centruy literary debate perceived by literary historians as a debate about the phenomenon of the 'New Woman'. The publishers' names are significant because, as Kay Daniels first pointed out (1972—73:7), novels dealing with this topic in explicitly sexual terms were not accepted by the respectable publishing houses, who may none the less have come to regret their decisions in the face of the outstanding popular success of these 'immoral' texts.

The question of the representation of women and the modes of femininity attributed to them in fiction is an important issue at present in literary criticism. These three novels, published either just before or just after the end of the Queen Victoria's reign, raise certain questions which centre on the then controversial topic of emancipated woman—or the New Woman, as this construction was dubbed—and its relation to late Victorian representations of femininity. Was femininity seen as inimical to a New Woman? Was it to be suppressed, or redefined, in discourses representing her? Was the New Woman to be held responsible for 'free love'? Was maternity to remain an essential ingredient of femininity? Was the New Woman to be rewritten as masculine? *Is the New Woman really a Man?*

This last question, often posed at the time, is a key one, as it reveals a threat to masculinity disguised behind the apparent threat to femininity implied by redefinitions and redescriptions of women. I am going to argue in this chapter that women can be described as representing traits both feminine and masculine (as, indeed, can men). I will also assume that masculinity and femininity are not simply terms of a binary opposition, but instead represent a socially constructed hierarchy. That is, not only are masculinity and femininity defined as polar opposites whose (ideal) features contain mutually exclusive character-istics, but in addition, masculinity has arrogated to itself the right to judge and define the 'proper' characteristics of femininity. However, while I claim that both sexes have access to masculine and feminine characteristics, it is important to recognise that each sex takes on these attributes in different ways, with very different results. Any assumption of masculine characteristics by women—or representation of masculinity as part of a female character in a novel—still asks to be be read differently from the representation of men's masculinity, as Gatens (1983) has argued. Any move by women to take on any of the characteristics of masculinity (like muscular strength, or force of intellect) calls out in men and women alike a fear of their potency that can only be appeased by a reabsorption of women into that subordinate feminine category. Hence the fear of the emasculating potential of the New Woman that lies behind the contemporary Victorian concerns about a perceived link between female emancipation and cultural decadence, documented by Linda Dowling (1979:447).

In conjunction with an examination of some specifically located late Victorian notions of femininity and masculinity, I want also to bring into account the role played by contemporary reviewers and subsequent literary critics in the construction and validation of literary history itself. In particular, I want to question the validity of assigning a key place in literary history to just one of these texts, Grant Allen's *The Woman Who Did*, while ignoring the significance of the others.

Grounds given by literary historians for the place of Allen's text—its importance as an index of popular interest in questions of female emancipation and 'free love', rather than any intrinsic literary merit (Fernando, 1977:132; Cunningham, 1978:62)—are convincing enough. It was certainly popular, running through 21 editions in its first year and netting its author £1000 per annum in royalties (Fernando, 1977:131; Cunningham, 1978:63). But the other two texts also have strong claims to the same kind of position in literary history: *The Woman Who Didn't* as the most directly feminist response to *The Woman Who Did*, challenging many of the assumptions about female sexuality put forward in that text; and *Six Chapters* as an important development of the same debate, equally 'popular' in terms of sales (my undated but still early copy is the forty-first edition). I want now to look at each of these texts in more detail.

What Allen's 'Woman Who Did' *did*, of course, was to live with a man without marrying him, on the grounds that marriage law was inequitable and went against her feminist principles. Thus this novel symmetrically reverses conventional morality, making marriage the immoral, and free love the moral choice. Herminia receives her lover's marriage proposal 'with a flush of shame and horror'; as Cunningham puts it: 'the exact equivalent of the conventionally pure woman's reaction to a proposal for an adulterous relationship' (p. 61). By the end of the book, however, having done what she did, and stuck to her principles, despite suffering her lover's untimely death and the hardships of single motherhood, Herminia is faced with her daughter's rejection of her. This much-cherished daughter, for whom she has suffered and in whom she invests all her hopes for the freeing of half the human race from aeons of slavery, ends by despising her mother's martyrdom and determinedly avoiding it herself by getting married as fast as possible. Our heroine then takes prussic acid in the name of truth: 'Not for nothing', we read, 'does blind fate vouchsafe such martyrs to humanity. From their graves shall spring glorious the church of the future.' (Allen, 1895:240)

The male author of *The Woman Who Did* proclaimed himself an ardent supporter of modern woman's fight for freedom. Naturally enough many modern women didn't agree with his reading of What the New Woman Wants. Millicent Garrett Fawcett, the leader of the constitutional suffrage movement in England, reviewed the book with a cruel wit, dwelling ironically on its many absurdities. The final death scene, for instance, is described prettily in the novel in terms of the donning of appropriate dress and flowers by the heroine intending suicide:

'In her bosom she fastened two innocent white roses ... arranging them with studious care very daintily before her mirror. She was always a woman.' 'A woman' here *is* femininity, and femininity itself almost becomes a euphemism for the ultimate passivity of death. After drinking her prussic acid, Herminia arranges herself fetchingly on her deathbed 'and waited for the only friend she had left in the world, with hands folded on her breast, like some saint of the middle ages'. (Allen, 1895:240) Any solemnity is disposed of in Fawcett's acerbic description:

> *My experience of prussic acid is very limited; but I once knew a cat who took it, and if its effects are equally rapid on human beings, Herminia would have done well to lie down on her bed, arrange the folds of her drapery and compose herself into a saintlike attitude, before she drank the poison. The cat's 'only friend left in the world' did not keep her waiting a single second. She had no time even to strike an attitude. (Fawcett, 1895:629)*

Herminia is not a mortal being as she dies: however, she *is* feminine. Fawcett objects to the book's presumption to speak for women and for feminism, while in fact doing their cause an enormous disservice by linking feminism with precisely the doctrine most calculated to turn public opinion against the idea of women's emancipation—the doctrine of 'free love'. She also objects to its representation of women as beings locked into a male-devised femininity which still insists on their ultimate passivity while exalting their moral purity and prating about new freedoms—another version of the old Victorian double standard, in fact. But for Grant Allen and his ilk, a New Woman would be inconceivable *as* woman if she lost her femininity. Since femininity constitutes the grounds of masculine desire, a divorce between women and femininity is unthinkable.

Fawcett was not alone in her objections to this novel, though others were made on different grounds. A reviewer in *The Critic* points out that although '"Free Love" is [Allen's motto]—yet the book is dedicated to his dear wife', while *The Bookman* objected, more predictably, that 'his glorification of the mere brute instinct of mating is senseless and shallow'. In the *Academy*, however, Allen found a supporter in the shape of a reviewer called Percy Addleshaw, who claims, 'there is not a sensual thought or suggestion throughout the whole volume', and ends by assuring us, perhaps somewhat ambiguously, that 'there is no doubt that his story was worth telling, and that it is swiftly told'. Another reviewer comments that the aim of the book unconsciously subverts itself: 'From a plea for free love, the tale is changed into a powerful argument for the rights of children' (*The Critic*). Meanwhile, *Punch* parodied Herminia's eternal cry 'the truth had made women free' into: 'the terewth had made them free and easy'; while a rash of suggestions for sequels included: *The Woman Who Couldn't* and *The Woman Who Would If She Could*—and other such predictable jokes.

Several fictional ripostes to Allen's book were in fact published in the same year—1895—and all written by women. *The Man Who Didn't*, dedicated 'to Married Men' by Mrs Lovett Cameron, is a short rather insignificant comedy proposing that children should be maintained by the nation. More elaborate is the argument put forward by Adeline Kingscote, under the male pseudonym 'Lucas Cleeve', in *The Woman Who Wouldn't*. Here the Herminia-figure (renamed Opalia) addresses the question avoided or elided in Allen's book: that of asymmetry, or unequal power balance in any male—female sexual relationship. Opalia says: 'I read a book once in which the heroine would not go through the form of marriage in church for fear she should lose her liberty, yet every action of her life showed that her liberty had gone, whether she defied the conventional laws of society or not'. (p.11) This is clearly a critical reference to Herminia in *The Woman Who Did*. Opalia recognises that there is no such thing as 'free' love between unequal parties, and so she resolves to do the opposite of Herminia, in effect, by agreeing to a companionate marriage with the friendship and intellectual companionship for which he *says* he is asking, and refusing the bestiality of sex. In the end, however, she comes to see that women are forced to 'succumb' to sex in order to keep their men, so she becomes submissive and is rewarded with a child, whom, fortunately or unfortunately, we *don't* see grow up to reject her.

Clearly a big stumbling block for the representation of the New Woman was her maternal function. Could a woman be represented as feminine if this function were not somehow accommodated? Allen's book had laid its emphasis on motherhood as a compulsory part of the representation of femininity: 'Every woman should naturally live her whole life, to fulfil her whole functions; and that she could do only by becoming a mother, accepting the orbit for which nature designed her.' (p.73) Nature always has a lot to answer for in these arguments. A concept of female eroticism divorced from notions involving maternity is a long way off in a text like Allen's, and, presumably, in a society which popularised such a text. In fact this society's chief fear was of the *femme fatale*—the Belle Dame Sans Merci—and it is precisely this image which emerges in the second of my three texts.

The most interesting of the now-forgotten fictional ripostes to *The Woman Who Did*, this is precisely the one which defuses the issue of motherhood by making it irrelevant. This is the novel called *The Woman Who Didn't*, written by Vivian Cory, who took the rather extraordinary pseudonym 'Victoria Crosse'. *The Woman Who Didn't* was her first full-length publication, and it was published by John Lane in a volume uniform with Grant Allen's novel, even down to a matching title page, thus giving the impression of being the 'authorised' sequel to Allen's book.

Here the man falls in love on board ship with a woman called Eurydice, but the passion between them is never consummated.

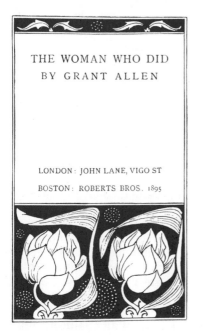
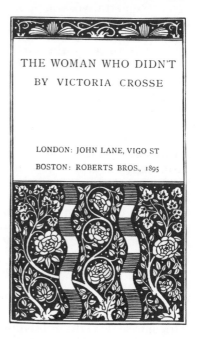

Title pages of *The Woman Who Did* by Grant Allen and *The Woman Who Didn't* by *Victoria Crosse*, published by John Lane in 1895. The similarity of design is clearly intentional.

She is married to another, and though her husband fills his time with other women, leaving her entirely to her own devices (only his portmanteau appears in the novel, not his person) she is tempted neither to divorce nor to cuckold him, having made up her mind, as she says, that matrimony is a holy tie, however faulty individual cases may appear. Yet the whole novel is sustained by an unresolved sexual tension which is only ended by the lover's departure back to the East. This lover is also the narrator, and so the tension can be ascribed primarily to him, which allows Eurydice to remain more ambiguous, shifting roles between *femme fatale* and preacher of duty. Clearly enough, on one reading, she enjoys power and has consciously conceived a way to achieve it. Yet the masculine subject-position taken up by a text signed by a woman adds an unusual dimension of dramatic irony to the reader's experience of the text. Eurydice's own sense of irony about the masculine will to power is apparent. Her first speech, which instantly draws the narrator's attention, in fact opens the narrative, which begins:

> '*But why not pay them? We may just as well now as when we reach the ship.*'
> *The words came in a clear, cultivated woman's voice through the foggy duskiness of an Egyptian night, from the farther end of the boat, which swayed slightly from side to side on the smoothly heaving water.* (Crosse, 1895:1)

It turns out that the other British passengers are causing delay by insultingly refusing to pay the deferential African boatmen until they have been conveyed out to their ship, with the dishonourable intention of not paying at all, and the narrator-hero is fascinated by the self-possession of a woman who will address a whole boatload of racist fellow countrymen with supercilious scepticism and shame them into paying; as indeed she does, by going on to say: '"I should pay now; if you mean to at all"'. (p.3)

What is set up in such an opening is the woman's exposure of a racist power nexus, which is subsequently transformed by its context into a metaphor for the exposure of sexism. Just as Eurydice disrupts the racist hierarchisation of British and Africans, so does the subsequent text attempt an analogous disruption of the masculine/feminine hierarchy by representing the woman as 'in control' of the man's sexuality; but it is a disruption that ends here merely in negation. Clearly sexual intercourse is not to be had on terms other than those posited by such a hierarchy. Reviewers appear to have been universally dissatisfied with the book, the *Saturday Review* finding it 'instinct with vulgarity from cover to cover', but having 'no doubt it will be extensively read by the nasty-minded pure' (21 September 1895). The *Athenaeum* found the tone disagreeable: 'her book positively reeks of whiskeys and sodas and of physical passion. Even the treatment of the heroine's purity becomes offensive by a sort of nauseous insistence on it; and altogether, if any advocate is needed for the sanctity of the marriage tie, Victoria Crosse certainly does not supply the place.' (14 September 1895)

Of course we can read these objections as springing at least in part from a resentment of an authorial 'she' taking on a male preserve of whiskeys and sodas and physical passion (even with the safeguard of a male narrator). But it is undeniable that the book does not add up to a good argument for retaining the sanctity of the marriage tie, just as it does not, despite its cheeky reversals of Grant Allen's story, effect any real transgression of the dominance of masculinity and the submissiveness of femininity. Playing the role of a Eurydice, a version of the *femme fatale*, still confirms femininity as no more than a projection of masculine desire. As a reviewer in *The Critic* (25 July 1896) remarked, rather patronisingly but with some justice, 'it would take a stronger antagonist to dislodge [Grant Allen]' despite the courage shown, as he puts it, by 'the young lady who writes under the name of Victoria Crosse [who] may or may not have chosen her *nom de guerre* with the idea of claiming distinguished gallantry in the face of the enemy'. Queen Victoria had instituted this highest of military awards in 1856, probably to lift flagging military spirits after the Crimean War. To take such a revered symbol of Britain's imperial power as a mere sobriquet was certainly a provocative gesture.

In 1903, two years after the Queen's death and seven years after the appearance of her own first novel, Victoria Crosse published *Six Chapters of a Man's Life*, which is the third and last novel I shall deal with here, and which is much more daring in its approach to sexual questions. Oddly enough, there is evidence to show that this book too may have been written in 1895. One of its less outrageous chapters appeared in *The Yellow Book* in that year, under the title 'Theodora: A Fragment'. Since Victoria Crosse had a penchant for meaningful names, I might mention that Theodora was the scandalous wife of the Roman emperor Justinian, who changed the law in order to be able to marry her, as she had been an actress and a prostitute. He then divided his power with her in an unprecedented act of good faith, and of course, according to Gibbon she abused it. (There is an ironic textual reference to Gibbon's Theodora.) Whether the rest of the text was too daring to achieve publication until its author's name was well established by her intervening publications we cannot know. By 1903 the author, or her publisher, had dropped the *e* from the end of the Cross: was this in order to take up more defiantly still such an ironically adopted pseudonym of masculine valour? Or was it to suggest more immediately another connotation of the word Cross; not heroism or martyrdom, not anger or angles, but an idea contained in the verb 'to cross', and released more easily without the substantive weight of that final e? Cross-dressing, perhaps? I am thinking here specifically of the implications of a male narrator's position when taken up by a writer who signs herself as female; who adopts not a *male* pseudonym (like Lucas Cleeve or George Eliot) but a *female* one. However much the name Victoria Cross plays on concepts of masculine militarism and masculine honour, it is none the less a woman's name—to say nothing of a queen's.

In any case, what I would like to suggest in my discussion of *Six Chapters* is the possibility that this particular text contains a more radical disruption of the hierarchical structure of masculinity/femininity than any of those encompassed by the seemingly so daring linkages of the New Woman and free love in the mid-1890s. This is a disruption that I would certainly wish to link back to 1895, a vintage year, of course, for sensations in literary circles, when we remember not only women who Did or Didn't, but also the furore created by the publication of *Jude the Obscure* on the one hand and the scandal of Oscar Wilde's trial on the other. Indeed it is possible that the latter event rather than the former would be found to provide a more crucial link in my theme of crossing, whether it be confined to textual cross-dressing or extended to other forms of travesty and transgression. And it was Wilde, after all, who is credited with the remark: 'If one could only marry Thomas Hardy to Victoria Cross he might gain something of real passion' (Stokes 1928:75).

Six Chapters of a Man's Life has a simple enough plot, made complex by the kind of sexual ambiguities it articulates. It is a text which would add weight to Shoshana Felman's thesis about Balzac's *Girl with the Golden Eyes*, in which she poses the question: 'are not sex roles but travesties of the ambiguous complexity of real sexuality, of real sexual difference?' (1981:28). *Six Chapters* is a novel written by a woman from a man's point of view about a man who falls in love with a woman who looks like a man . . .

As in *The Woman Who Didn't*, the narrator here is also the hero of the story. Called Cecil (still an ambiguously gendered name in the nineteenth century), he is represented as a man of the world; young, handsome, knowing and cynical, with a good deal of sexual experience and no very good opinion of women, whom he regards quite naturally as his intellectual inferiors. Thus far, very conventional. Then, he meets Theodora, introduced to him at a party by a friend who assures him he will like her, notwithstanding her moustache. In fact, the moustache becomes the sign by which he expects to identify her as he awaits her entrance into the room:

> I knew I must recognise Theodora by her peculiarity, and I scanned the upper lip of all the girls who passed, but without result. I was beginning to think she could not be in the room, when my eyes were suddenly attracted, for no reason that I was conscious of, from the ring of dancers passing round the room to some in the centre. And there, coming down the middle of the room, under the full flood of light, was the face I was looking for. My attention was so riveted upon the face that I was not conscious of what figure belonged to it, nor did I see the shoulders that bore it. It might have been floating down towards me on the stream of light. What a face it was, too! White, so that it looked blanched under the pale, changeful electric light, and lent a curious lustre by its gleaming, brilliant, swimming eyes. The mouth was a delicate curve of the brightest scarlet, and above, on the upper lip, was the sign I looked for, a narrow, glossy, black line. It was a handsome face of course, but that alone would not have excited my particular attention. One sees so many handsome faces. But such a tremendous force of intellect sat on the brow . . . such a curious fire shone in the scintillating eyes, and such a peculiar half-male character invested the whole countenance, that I felt violently attracted to it merely from its peculiarity.
> (Cross, 1903:12–14)

Apart from these mannish traits, her body is utterly feminine, not in terms of voluptuousness but a kind of strange bonelessness, so that even grasping her hand is to sink into her flesh:

> *It was a very curious hand, so extremely soft that as*
> *my fingers closed tighter and tighter over it, it seemed to*
> *yield and yield and collapse more and more like a*
> *piece of velvet within one's grasp. (p.29)*

What is going on? Is it a projection of epicene fantasy for pornographic effect? Or might it be a serious social critique of the fixity of sexual desire in those value-laden representations which never transgress the man-made barriers of masculinity and femininity? Let us go on.

After talking with Theodora about religion and morality, and discovering that she shares with him the socially unacceptable view that both are things of fashion which vary directly with the latitude, it appears to be but a step to the question of a sexual liaison. But there is a barrier for Cecil. He discovers that Theodora is an heiress who will lose her fortune if she either marries or forms an illegal union with a man (that is, if she Does or if she Doesn't). This is already an interesting change in the power dynamic from the earlier novel, since it removes the red herring of placing the institution of marriage as the basis of the sexual hierarchisation of power, and focuses directly onto the hierarchisation implicit in all representation of masculinity and femininity in terms of sexual desire.

The economic barrier to the characters' union threatens to become a deadlock, as Cecil decides he does not want the responsibility either of a disinherited wife in England or of a female companion on his travels back to his archaeological work in the East. He decides to forgo passion and keep his freedom. However, just as he is about to depart on the boat train, Theodora arrives at his lodgings and asks to accompany him. She is dressed as a man, or rather, 'some handsome boy of nineteen or twenty' (p.121), and in this guise, Cecil finds her irresistible. He has already told us that he 'disliked in a mild, theoretical way, women in the general term. I had an aversion, slight and faint it is true, but still an aversion, to everything suggestively feminine . . . ' (p.78). Her action, in coming to seek him out in the face of his previous cold suppression of his desire for her, is decidedly unfeminine, yet again this action is rendered ambiguous by its representation of recklessness as a kind of will-lessness:

> *It was her sudden, complete abandonment of self, the*
> *entire throwing away of her own will, the apparent*
> *absolute merging of all volition into another's, that*
> *must have always set ablaze all the manhood of a man*
> *who loved her. (p.118)*

Masculinity is here blurred with femininity, which in turn becomes the projection of a passive (masculine) desire that masculinity cannot tolerate within itself. At this point we might possibly feel tempted to read the text as a disguised representation of male homosexual desire masking a disavowed lesbian desire. But I think such a reading would be reductive if it failed to point out the ways in which such categories are in themselves man-made. This text is transgressive not because it represents erotic desires in terms of role-playing characters, but because in doing so it disturbs the rigid boundaries polarising the two sexes and opens up the socially constructed hierarchisation of sexuality to a new form of critique which I will now attempt to demonstrate.

The sense of this critique emerges slowly as one reads the text. Theodora becomes Theodore, a charming young man, for the other passengers on the boat to the East; and other young female passengers flirt with him/her. Cecil's possessive jealousy is aroused no less by this same-sex flirtation than it had been earlier, in a hotel in Marseilles, when he discovers Theodore playing cards in another man's bedroom. There is no safety in such mirrored intensities of role-playing. Safety for what? The answer this text throws up is: masculine power when deprived of feminine submissiveness. While Theodora's role-playing remains under Cecil's control, there is no problem, only heightened pleasure for him. For instance, as he says about playing billiards with her (a game in which she excels): 'If I won, I had the satisfaction of beating a better player than myself; if I lost, Theodora was my property, a part of myself . . . ' (p. 165) Elsewhere, the impulse to control is clearly represented as part of Cecil's masculine desire, and as the book progresses, we see Theodora cleverly playing on this desire to keep it at its height. The desire of femininity is, of course, masculine desire: the desire of masculine dominance for feminine submission. By the time we reach the climax, it is clear that there is no return to 'normality' possibly commensurate with the expanded desires conjured up by the rendering ambiguous of the woman's sex-role. And indeed, after an extraordinary crisis point is reached, the denouement comes.

Theodora's feminine 'purity' is about to be fatally compromised by her being held hostage to a violent and powerful stranger who wants sexual intercourse with her precisely because of her sexual ambiguity. At this point the text uncompromisingly reveals the compromised nature of masculine 'honour'. Cecil wants to shoot Theodora so that she will not be raped. She does not wish to be either raped or shot, but if forced to choose, would prefer the former. She pleads with Cecil not to kill her, but he, as he says, 'longed to destroy her now, as [he] had once longed to possess her' (p. 248). He then says to her:

> 'You value your life above your honour, then?'
> 'Infinitely,' she returned cynically, her face pale as that of a corpse already, and her eyes suddenly blazing with mockery and contempt.
> 'I do not, then,' I said in a low tone, my hand clasping tightly the revolver.
> 'I daresay!' answered Theodora, and the light scornful tone cut through my brain like a knife. 'My honour! A convenient term for the preservation to yourself and your own egotistical, jealous, tyrannical passion, of this flesh and blood.' (pp. 248–9).

Her refusal of a Lucretia's role throws into relief precisely those elements of masculinity that she has hitherto so assiduously fostered. Both characters have been trapped by the confines of the very sexual dichotomy they saw themselves as having transgressed. As she looks defiantly back down the gun barrel he points at her, it is what he terms the 'male' character of that look that drives him on in his desire to subjugate her. In possessing a 'her' who also comprises a 'him', he attains her femininity by subjugating her masculinity. As Shoshana Felman has remarked in a related context: 'the substitution of woman for man and of man for woman, the interchangeability and the reversibility of masculine and feminine manifests a discord which subverts the limits and compromises the coherence of each of the two principles' (1981:31).

Any idea of femininity as pure difference or as capable of autonomy is indeed suppressed in such a substitution. Yet if Gatens' argument is right, and masculinity in men reads differently from masculinity in women, Felman's position is problematised. In this text the suppression of femininity (rather than its simple substitution or replacement by masculinity) does not go unchallenged; masculinity is subverted from within by the 'cross-dressing' of the narrator, which takes the form of a continual play on notions of clear-cut sexual difference. By his constant foregrounding of femininity as a problem for masculinity, the narrator-hero necessarily spotlights his own masculinity. Yet simultaneously with the reader's attention being drawn in this way to his masculinity, comes the reader's awareness of its fictional nature: the story must ultimately purport to emanate not from a male subject (the narrator) but from a female subject, the book's signed author. In other words, the gap between the position of enunciation and the position of the narrator is used, in a sense, simultaneously to confuse and titillate the reader's expectations, and to destabilise the boundaries of both categories, highlighting not their difference but their ambiguous overlap.

Furthermore, this extraordinary novel, in its critique of masculinity, both implicit and overt, opens a way for the possibility of a new conception of feminine pleasure. One of the first and crucial steps towards this is the representation of a femininity independent of woman's maternal function (Theodora says: 'I should detest the man who made me a mother' (p. 163)). Such a separation of femininity from maternity would scarcely have been approved even by women as emancipated as Millicent Garrett Fawcett. Nonetheless it can be seen, I think, as a radical attempt to refocus the debate about the New Woman away from questions of functionality and towards questions of pleasure: a very different path from that laid out by Allen's pseudo-radical text. In this context, the name 'Victoria Cross' does take on a new connotation of an entirely subversive kind of female gallantry.

If literary historians avoid the task of contextualising popular landmarks like Allen's *The Woman Who Did*, then the very grounds upon which its minor canonisation rests are open to serious misreading. It was not the mere fact of its popularity, as critics like Cunningham and Fernando imply, that has led to its historical status: rather, it is the controversial nature of that 'popularity', which can only be interpreted in the light of the debate it bought into. The works of Victoria Cross(e) lay no more claim to 'literary' merit than Allen's book, but in popularity they were at least equal. Can it be that the questions they raise, in regard not only to Allen's book but also to their whole cultural ethos, have themselves been marginalised by the bias of literary historians? Questions, that is, of the ways in which these three novels problematise (with differing success) the polarisation and hierarchisation of masculinity and femininity, by exploring the ambiguous (and sometimes intolerable) crossing of sexual boundaries by the creation of figures (narrators and characters) who take on gender characteristics opposed to their sex. This is not simply a literary transsexualism, but blurs the presumed opposition between masculine and feminine and inverts the hierarchical privilege of masculinity.

9   Homosexualities: fiction, reading and moral training

Michael Hurley

Golden-haired boy on the edge of a street
In his tight blue jeans on his lonely beat.
Hush! Hush!
I'm rather afraid
Christopher Robin is looking for trade.

John Waller (1983:327)

A young fellow standing near a street lamp came into
its light, while approaching Michael modestly. His small
hands were manicured, his fine wrists and delicate
neck were blackish as with coaldust, but his hairless
face, with oval cheeks, was pink and powdered. His
eyes, large and timid, looked appealingly at Michael.
Michael brushed rudely past him. The boy retreated to
the fence once more to wait. Michael heard steps, the
boy coming after him, he thought, and he looked
back—only a tram conductor going home from the
depot.

Christina Stead (1934:245)

A ND SO, with the Waller text, a disrupted innocence: an innocence established through the repetition of familiar verse patterns, phrasing and naming; a genre of English whimsy celebrated, dispersed, rewritten. Desire is sexualised, specified. It is male, ambivalently masculine, softened from the harshness of manhood by being a boy's story, yet raunchified: a social organisation of desire particularised by 'beat' and 'trade', signifiers of availability, of importunity. As a hedonistic natural-isation of a metropolitan male homosexual voice, the register is knowing, divinable, already known to some. It is a rebellious naturalisation of identity, of sexuality.

And my second cameo: another boy, 'a young fellow'. Again importunate, but this time feminised. Unnatural, yet also a recognisable figure in a continuously moving series of more or less carefully particularised constructions of male (homo)sexu-ality. This time, in a demonstration of metonymic fluidity, the 'young fellow' is without torso or legs, a bust with arms: an aggregation of segmented, cosmetic detail (eyes, hands, wrists, face) and movement. Incapable of metamorphosis into a tram conductor, signifier of a decent masculinity, the boy preys ineffectually on the socially distressed yet assertive male, Michael. A second naturalisation of identities, of sexualities.

My concerns are with the discursive construction and textual deployments of sexualised identities; with the body as a site of conflicting desires socially organised and unified around the constructs 'gender' and 'sexuality'; with the textual organisation and disruption of (homo)sexualities. And while my pretexts and prefaces are male, the bodies of my discussion are female and male. I am following several unfinished lines of thought, around two different areas, first, the textuality of novels, and, second, homosexualities and their social construction: the discursive construction of homosexualities within fiction and readings of them from both inside and outside the literary academy.

Two working assumptions underlie what follows. The first is that fiction does not stand alone: the novel occupies a different social space according to how the 'social' itself is constructed at any given time (Weeks, 1985:178). In the late nineteenth century the popular novel is constructed as socially dangerous (Leavis, 1932; Williams, 1971; Jackson, 1981). For much of the twentieth century it is a device for moral training. The second assumption is that a major social function of English studies, as administered in secondary and tertiary education, is to produce a secular moral subject; an individual capable of 'intimate and infinite self-correction' (King, 1985:21). English studies is a moral technology, a series of social techniques, skills and trainings which produce and value a particular mode of subjectivity.

Terry Eagleton recently described it this way:

> *What Literature teaches is not so much this or that moral value . . . It teaches us rather to be—let me rehearse some of the cherished terms—sensitive, imaginative, responsive, sympathetic, creative, perceptive, reflective. Notice the resounding intransitivity of all these familiar shibboleths. The task of the moral technology of Literature is to produce an historically peculiar form of human subject who is sensitive, receptive, imaginative, and so on . . . about nothing in particular . . . Literature is that process in which the quality of the response is more significiant than the quality of the object . . . What's important is just the production of a specific form of subjectivity, about which we can say—quite intransitively—that it is sensitive, creative, imaginative and so on. (1985:3)*

Several objections might be made to Eagleton here. He universalises the institution of literature, underestimating the effects of exposure to a variety of criticisms, and their purchase in different schooling systems. It is quite clear to any participant observer of English studies that the 'sensitive' political choices made by literary liberal humanists, for example, in the texts chosen for study, in the readings of them that are circulated and approved, do not forclose *resistant* readings and practices. The justification for these choices may claim political neutrality, but secondary classrooms are not successful machines of total control. What is more, Eagleton's 'subjectivity' is as conceptually limited as the one he criticises (Greenfield 1984). Even if for polemical purposes, his positing of subjectivity as an effect of a limited range of critical practices is underdeveloped. This simplicity is compounded by the later unproblematical linking of them to a set of class interests (1985:5). He ignores, deliberately no doubt, the implications of his excursion into Foucauldian analysis, in particular the need for a more extensive theory which connects techniques of reading with technologies of self-formation.

As an opening manoeuvre in the development of such a theory, I want to turn instead to the work of Catherine Greenfield (1983) and Ian Hunter (1982, 1983, 1984a, 1984b). For reasons of time and space, I want to take for granted Hunter's claim that the literary sense is an 'artefact of a whole social technology; the point at which techniques of reading, disciplinary training and the requirements of modern sociality are focussed in the formation of a secular conscience' (1984a:132). If some version of this is the case, and there are other reasons for thinking so (Bennett, 1979, 1985), the field of literary studies has nothing intrinsically 'aesthetic' about it. Reading, rather than recovering an act of vision on the part of the writer, 'indicates the definite recognition-effects produced by the *iteration* of certain rules and practices' (1982:82). When institutionally formalised in critical practices, these rules create the literary as an object of study: reading trains 'people in a specific mode of textual consumption' (1982:88). This training is what produces in English departments Eagleton's morally sensitive critic whose primary occupation is the endless repetition of commentaries on selected pieces of writing. However, for Hunter, it is the training effect (the transmission of 'definite criteria of textual recognition') that matters here, rather than the sensitivity.

The possibility of non-literary readings of 'literary' texts indicates that literary commentary involves a specific training of readers. Whether literary or otherwise, different readings of texts indicate different trainings, not simply differences in subjective (private) points of view of a given text (1982:87). Understanding of a different reading comes when we understand the procedures used to produce that reading. The meanings generated do not come from the text itself as though one can check one's reading by the text to test the fit: 'One cannot first give it [the text], as it were, a quick neutral glance without reading it, and then judge later whether a reading fits it or not. That is to say one cannot justify the rules of reading by pointing to the text, because applying the rules of reading is *how* one points to it.' (1982:88)

Catherine Greenfield extends this notion of reading as a form of social training by pointing out that it is not

> *predicated upon a subject—it is not conceived as the relation between a subject, or a reader, and a text. Therefore a 'readership' is not defined as the space of a reader qua subject of knowledge (or subject of language as Signifier in the psychoanalytic*

'subversion'), but as a space occupied by available and
discontinuous, heterogeneous discursive forms. The
reader is the bearer of these discursive forms according
to various and changing institutional trainings which
confer special competencies. (Greenfield 1983:133)

For my purposes here I will employ the notion of 'reading
formations' to designate ensembles of these 'discontinuous,
heterogeneous discursive forms'. Among these forms we can
include not only the various 'literary' reading practices, but also
their objects of analysis. That is, reading formations are sets 'of
discursive and inter-textual determinations which organise and
animate the practice of reading, connecting texts and readers as
reading subjects of particular types and texts as objects-to-be-
read in particular ways' (Bennett, 1984:7).

Granted my two working assumptions, that the novel is part of
an institutional process of moral training and that it functions to
produce moral subjects, it follows that not all literature is
deemed suitable for use in the formation of those moral subjects.
Because the articulation of rhetorical and moral criticism varies
considerably at different times it is not easy to predict what texts
and readings will appear in syllabi nor at what stage in the
certification process (Hunter, 1983:237). And there is considerable variation according to institutional site. I'm thinking here of
the discrimination against popular genres, whether written or
visual, found within the Leavisite and New Critical legacies and
the virtual exclusion of sexual fiction from canons and syllabi
unless that fiction is incorporable as somehow morally
exemplary.

So, for example, one finds competing canons in the literary and
extra-literary institutions. Not surprisingly, these canons valorise different texts, though there is some crossover at the
popular and contemporary levels. However, in any literary
variation of the canon of Australian literature, there is both a
paucity and a regularity of texts that have explicit homosexual
discourses inscribed in their readings. All the most likely
contenders come from recent Australian fiction and only two are
likely for immediate university canonisation: Jolley's *Miss
Peabody's Inheritance* and White's *The Twyborn Affair*.

When I raise the question of homosexuality and Australian
fiction, critics draw my attention to motifs, minor themes, casual
references, incidents and characters in any number of novels. A

partial list includes: Kingsley's *Geoffrey Hamlyn*, Clarke's *For the Term of His Natural Life*, Praed's *Affinities*, *Fugitive Anne* and possibly *The Scourge Stick*, Richardson's *Maurice Guest*, Stead's *Seven Poor Men of Sydney*, Tennant's *Foveaux*, McKenzie's *The Young Desire It*, almost every Boyd novel, White's *Riders in the Chariot*, Harrower's *The Watch Tower*, Jessica Anderson's *An Ordinary Lunacy* and *Tirra Lirra by the River*, Malouf's *Johnno* and *Harland's Half Acre*, Moorhouse's stories, Farmer's *Alone*, Jolley's *Palomino*. There are more, and the last three complicate the issue nicely in terms of any attempted construction of a canon of lesbian and gay fiction that makes assumptions about the writers' (homo)sexuality.

There is another more informally institutionalised list which gives greater weight to matters gay, excessive, different. It includes Neville Jackson's *No End to the Way*, Robert Adamson and Bruce Hanford's *Zimmers Essay*, Rae Desmond Jones' *Walking the Line*, Elizabeth Riley's *All That False Instruction*, Lee Cataldi's *Invitation to a Marxist Lesbian Party*, Gary Dunne's *If Blood Should Stain the Lino*, the two inVersions collections, Barry Nonweiler's *That Other Realm of Freedom*, the 40-plus contributors to *Edge City on Two Different Plans*, Emily George's novels, a myriad of stories and poems by Jeremy Fisher, Susan Hampton, Pam Brown, Javant Biarujia, Margaret Bradstock, Louise Wakefield, Ian Birks, Jan MacKemmish, Finola Moorhead, Sasha Soldatow, Roger Raftery's *The Pink Triangle*, Simon Payne's *The Beat*, Barry Hughes' *The Martini-Henry Modification*, Karel Florsheim's *Else Halberstadt*, and Ross Davy's *Kenzo*. Most of these texts come from and are valorised only in explicitly Australian gay male and lesbian reading formations. To put it another way: 'Different reading formations . . . produce their own texts, their own readers and their own contexts.' (Bennett, 1984:8). While these texts and authors have sometimes received mainstream press reviews, with few exceptions they do not emerge as objects for discussion in the literary journals and are not incorporated into the moral training that is literary studies. Who speaks, where and when? Who is able to listen?

Notice what gets constructed as homosexual in the first list I mentioned: male same-sex friendship in Kingsley and Malouf, same-sex paedophilia and sodomy as rape in Clark, unwillingness on the part of a male character to fix consistently on a sex object of either gender in Richardson; male use of cosmetics, a high vocal register, and effusiveness in Stead and Tennant; artistic interests among men in Tennant and Anderson; cross-dressing in Stead (for men) and for women in Langley; same-sex teacher–student relationships in McKenzie; misogyny in Harrower and Anderson; emotional sensitivity in Anderson and grotesquerie in Hanrahan.

Such lists make it patently obvious that what is involved here is the condensing of questions of sex and gender, homosociality, homosexual desire, paedophilia, homosexual behaviour and homosexual identity into discrete, single, essentialist images of 'the' male and female homosexual (Plummer, 1981; Gatens, 1983; Sedgwick, 1985).

At this juncture we do well to return to Foucault:

> We must not forget that the psychological, psychiatric, medical category of homosexuality was constituted from the moment it was characterised . . . less by a type of sexual relations than by a certain quality of sexual sensibility, a certain way of inverting the masculine and feminine in oneself. Homosexuality appeared as one of the forms of sexuality when it was transposed from the practice of sodomy onto a kind of interior androgeny, a hermaphroditism of the soul. The sodomite had been a temporary aberration; the homosexual was now a species. (Foucault, 1978:43)

Foucault is referring to male homosexuality, but while I do not wish to assume that the formation of sexed identities (masculine, feminine) and of sexualised identities (heterosexual, homosexual) are complementary, symmetrical processes, his point has a general methodological force when we think of how 'species' is often deployed in popularised pyschological discourses under the guise of common sense. Here a binary opposition of hetero- and homo-sexuality is made definitive of sexual truth. The social power of this opposition is such that 'homosexual' is often used to signify the social 'unity of interests between subjects otherwise categorised as perverse/sick/mad/queer/contagious and so on' (Watney, 1987). I began to indicate this with reference to what is constituted as homosexual in the first list above, where we begin to glimpse a second-order mythology of the homosexual as 'other', mostly odd, sometimes funny and/or mysterious, simultaneously 'sympathetic' and threatening; it doesn't take much of a twist to sense 'stranger danger'. In a more ironic, but not so disconnected twist, most often associated with liber-ationist politics, we also see a reverse process in attempts to distinguish a 'true' (= non-perverse, respectable) homosexuality within 'these thousand aberrant sexualities' (Foucault, 1978:44).

Before I turn to the analysis of readings of two texts, Rosa Praed's *Affinities* (1886) and Patrick White's *The Twyborn Affair* (1979), I want to say specifically that reading formations involve reading positions which are effects of the narrative process, its structures and discursive organisation in any given text. They generate, if you wish, the text's own preferred reading, the points at which narrative closure comes into play.

Affinities can be usefully discussed in terms of reading formations and positions. First, in an act of literary recuperation we can restore it to public discussions of the Praed *oeuvre* (Hurley, 1985), itself fragile but re-emerging (Summers, 1975; Modjeska, 1981; Sharkey, 1983; Sheridan, 1982). Second, this recuperation can position itself at some critical distance from the relatively dismissive radical nationalist reading formations (Byrne, 1896; Miller and McCartney, 1956; Green, 1966; Dutton 1976; Beilby and Hadgraft, 1979). It can do so initially by taking seriously the use of spiritualist and occult discourses in much of Praed's writing (Roderick, 1948). Within reading formations that articulate these themes in relation to issues of sex and gender and do not downgrade the genre of female romance (Praed, Tasma, Ada Cambridge) as distinct from the male (Clarke, Boldrewood) (Sheridan, 1982), we can open out the contexts in which Praed's writing is read. Finally, though with some difficulty, since it is out of print, we can read the text.

Affinities can be read as a disguised homosexual novel (Hurley, 1975), a potential gay 'Australian' novel of international significance. For if you accept that the construction of male homosexuality as a sexual identity only begins to emerge in the late nineteenth century as distinct from a set of previously loosely and confusingly linked sexual practices, and that female homosexuality emerges somewhat later (Weeks, 1977), then *Affinities* is a formative text. Very briefly, I read the novel this way: it is a romance which establishes a lineage connecting English aestheticism with French literary decadence. The heterosexual male hero is irrelevant except as a plot device and is formally supplanted by the male anti-hero, who is clearly modelled on Oscar Wilde. (It is important to remember that we are seeing constructed a pre-trial Oscar Wilde figure.) There are also two female protagonists. The first of these reminds one character irresistibly of George Sand, though she is unable to say why. The 'Wilde' and 'Sand' figures have had an affair, but she rejects his physical desire in favour of non-sexual comradeship. He cannot accept the rejection. She then establishes a comradely friendship with another woman, an 'innocent', who in turn marries the Wilde figure. Wilde 'corrupts' then murders her by telepathy, out of jealousy for the women's friendship and his rejection by Sand.

Within the romance genre the discourses of aestheticism, dandyism and decadence are used to construct a parody of the literary and social conventions of romantic love. This parody enunciates what I would call a 'camp' reading position which relies on a series of naughty 'underworld' codes available only to a select metropolitan readership (Weeks, 1977; Sontag, 1978; Britton, 1978; Booth, 1983; Dyer, 1986). The camp enunciation is then undercut by a feminist discourse which values female friendship over male lust. And at this level another reading position is installed that articulates questions of female friendship and lesbianism.

Issues of language and discursive formations now become central. The reading I have just given is an example of the assumption that the several codes or discourses involved described two *pre-existing* sexual identities, the male homosexual and the lesbian, who merely await a member of the cognoscenti to recognise them.

The main problems I see now with this procedure are first that the 'sensitive' recreation of the discourses of masculinity, femininity and sexuality 'found' by me in this reading of *Affinities* presumes a sexological taxonomy at odds with the reading positions established by the narrative. That taxonomy effectively postdates the discourses available to and mobilised in the novel. My point here is not so much one of narrowly insisting on historical accuracy but of suggesting that this whole arena is in dispute. The price of foregrounding those taxonomic discourses in the reading is insufficient attention to the alternative discourses circulating in the text. Any reading of the Wilde figure as homosexual installs a male homosexual subject; a subject that is an effect of the discourses which circulate in the *post-trial* figure of 'Wilde': a much 'queerer' subject (because far more socially determined medically, legally and by the media) than that visible in the 1880s. As Leigh Raymond suggests, the trials mobilised and extended elements of previously extant (homo)sexual discourses and the press condemned largely in moral terms rather than those of medical discourse.[1] Through its campness and feminism, *Affinities* iterates, like many popular nineteenth-century novels, a series of procedures for recognising sexual difference: procedures on the verge of being redeployed by other agencies to construct a new object of social regulation, the homosexual male.[2]

Among the costs of condensing multiple forms of sexual difference into a single basket ('homosexuality') is an acceptance of the categories mobilised in social policies of regulation, and a certain analytic confusion. Whatever else it may be, camp is not a form of official social regulation. 'Lily law' forbid: whether *naive* or deliberate, camp flouts administrated seriousness, literary or otherwise. The mechanisms for recognising 'the' male homosexual as a regulated social agent are not those which construct 'camp'. Both are quite precise. Where they frequently overlap, for my purposes here, is in particular textual forms: twentieth-century novels which deploy approved discourses of (homo)sexuality as well as those which parody those discourses. Nor can one just appropriate 'camp' as a category when discussing lesbian parody. Camp can be misogynistic as the 'Wilde' figure in *Affinities* partially suggests.

This may all seem a long way from conventional literary criticism, but locating with some technical precision the procedures whereby sexual difference is regulated in literary commentary has its difficulties. It requires simultaneously tracing the emergence of English studies in relation to the social regulation of sexuality, identifying the relevant reading and writing mechanisms and analysing how they are used. To quote Hunter once more:

> *The important point to keep in mind here is that, in the modern apparatus of character-reading, it is not only the fictional character that is formed, but also the moral character of the student . . . In particular, the modern apparatus of character-reading is distinguished by its utilisation of textual analysis in a systematic regime of moral training. At the level of the social policy, the apparatus of nineteenth century popular education is argued for precisely in terms of the need to combat [social deviance] by forming a sober, moral population via the new apparatus of popular education.* (Hunter, 1983:234)

The appearance of the post-trial 'Wilde' figure as demonic in the popular press, installed a new aspect in existing reading formations: the public was given a way of recognising male homosexuality. As a mode of perception, it involved particular deployments of the male body (voice, hands, stance), clothes, and social interests, a combination of specific aspects of 'camp' and the dandy as found in certain social circles which came under legal persecution and media scrutiny. These agencies, together with more specialised 'knowledges' of psychology and medicine, iterated particular rules for recognition of deviance.

Although contemporary urban male homosexuals have re-created a clear difference between a masculine gender identity and a homosexual sexual identity, paradoxically by an ironic merging of the two, this situation is not symmetrical with the sexual fluidity found in *Affinities*. The modern clone is in part a resistant response to the social deployments of the 'Wilde' figure as an effeminate pervert throughout the twentieth century (Marshall, 1981; Blachford, 1981). The 'masculine' homosexual often celebrates Wilde's reputation as a sodomite while refusing camp as a personal mode of expression. In *Affinities* there is no such social distinction between gender and sexuality. Rather the 'masculinity' of the male rural gentry is parodied and that of the metropolitan male 'decadent' is rejected eventually as 'brute' lust. Masculinity is relatively dispersed, less socially controlled than when organised primarily around questions of sexual identity. To ignore the social power of later more fixed significations is to accept and project a purportedly general, popular representation: 'Wilde'. And 'Wilde' is part of a social mobilisation of a viciously negative system of sexual regulation. This point becomes central when I later discuss a particular reading of White's *Twyborn Affair*.

Similarly, to accept a binary female friendship/lesbian opposition presumes a lesbianism constructed of the same characteristics as sexology and psychology postulate for the male: a combination of homosociality and same-sex genital sex, with the same confusions of cross-dressing and sexual desire. The presumption is that male and female bodies are inscribed in the same ways by sexual discourses which are mirror images of each other.

The semiotic organisation of discourses of difference in a novel such as *Affinities* requires that these matters be rethought. There, for example, male desire is constructed as lust irrespective of the gender of the desired. For the female, desire moves in and between discourses of marriage, extramarital friendship, bodily autonomy, spirituality, moral corruption and homosociality. With all their discontinuities these discourses are the signifiers of (sometimes sexual) differences, not (lesbian) sexual identity. The sublime of female desire is articulated in relation to the occult, an ineffable other. Male desire is a disease which corrupts friendship between the sexes and makes women ill.

Together these articulations of gender, sexuality and desire make the novel's preferred reading position dangerous. That position calls on a coterie knowledge, creating a specialised reading formation, which, when mobilised through distribution, enables a social celebration of difference, provides a rite of passage for the neophyte (the about to be identified/newly identifying male homosexual and the 'new' woman) and potentially constitutes resistance to the emerging mechanisms of social regulation. In this sense, *Affinities* not only predates most of the English sexologists but also pre-empts their claim to scientific and juridical authority. The reader constituted by that coterie knowledge is perforce a specialist in recognising particular codes and becomes part of a reading formation later marginalised in the literary academy. (One suspects this is more so in Australia where the histories of difference have been arguably more problematic than in England, but that's another matter.)

So the relationship of reading formations and reading positions is socially dynamic, nicely complicating questions of moral training. In terms of lesbianism this account needs further development in relation to the, until recently, dominant critical readings of *The Well of Loneliness* (Rule, 1975; Ruehl, 1982; Martinez, 1983; Brown and Whitlock, 1985). In earlier readings, as in some of the novel's own discursive mobilisations, the operative category of lesbianism is sexological: 'inversion'. The women are 'inverts', not properly female, and 'perverts', unhealthy and degenerate. The trial of *The Well* simultaneously conflates and creates (homo)sexual identity and female desire into a discursive construction for homosocial women in some ways parallel to that which emerged for men in the trial of Oscar Wilde. The result in terms of publicly circulated cultural artefacts was 'the' female homosexual. As Gillian Whitlock (1985:37) has argued in the case of *The Well of Loneliness*, 'most forms of self-identification and expression reflect a gendered heterosexual orientation that is policed by conventions within existing forms of language and art'. This double articulation of gender and sexuality has obvious implications for the assumptions with which I began.

English studies is a form of moral training with numerous

effects, including constituting moral subjects whose gender and desires remain rhetorically and morally male and heterosexual. That phallocentric constitution is achieved partly by the rules and procedures of literary readings that produce particular aesthetic effects (among others 'seriousness' which often excludes camp as an acceptable literary genre, except where it can be subsumed into satire), and partly by the simultaneous articulation of moral rules and procedures which construct 'the' homosexual as a 'Wilde', a 'Sand' or a 'Hall'. Obviously another study is needed to document how this occurs. In contrast some gay readings are far more pleasantly promiscuous and likely to claim any hint of difference as indicative of homosexuality (Wotherspoon, 1984). When faced with dominant assumptions of heterosexuality and sexually sanitised readings, this practice is quite understandable and frequently unavoidable.

The rhetorical use of 'Sand' and 'Wilde' should not necessarily be understood as assuming that, because an author's sexuality is known, one can automatically 'read off' the sexual dimension of the texts which circulate in their name. Apart from the obvious empirical and conceptual difficulties with intentional and contextual criticism, there is the issue of how authorship becomes imbricated in particular reading formations. This is especially the case with camp, gay male and lesbian readings in which naming takes on several different functions, one specialised version of which is to maintain competing, unauthorised literary canons. Such canons, however, do not function so much as policings of a purported excellence, but as points of cultural resistance. Sand/'Sand' and Hall/'Hall' are part of an international lesbian reading formation, central to the processes of lesbian self-identification. That formation, like camp, with which it has a problematic relation (Hurley, 1985), may be seen as another apparatus for moral training. Thankfully neither is under the control of the academy against which their reading practices may be mobilised. Ironically perhaps, part of my purpose in interrogating literary criticism is to expand the range of texts in its purview, thereby increasing the risk of the appropriation of those texts by reading practices which will attempt to destroy them in the name of literary standards or other moralities. This already occurs in the case of 'names' who have received recognition for other reasons.

How this matters in terms of differences in reading formations and the importance of taking reading position into account is clear when we look at the reception of *The Twyborn Affair* in *Quadrant* (Kramer, 1980).

In answer to the possible objection that reviews are not usually extended pieces of critical discussion, I would argue that they constitute a public form of training. Though there are differences between reviews and more formal criticism (Morris, n.d.), the conditions under which reviews are produced are conducive to highly condensed exemplary texts. In this review, White is described as dealing with 'reality and illusion, fragmentation and wholeness, discord and harmony ... some of the large abstractions' (p.66). The problem for the reviewer is that these opposing abstractions are not at the heart of the novel. Rather at its centre is the character E. and the question of sexual ambivalence. 'Ambivalence' is deployed here to a mean inability to maintain a single, fixed, sexual role and identity. Thus, in E., there is no 'wholeness of character': 'no theories about the fragmentation of personality, transsexual experience or Jungian symbolism can rescue *The Twyborn Affair* from its persistent preoccupation with surfaces and exteriors, its empty virtuosity' (p.67). Apart from the implication that one can discuss the field of moral character without any recourse to theory, the review suggests that 'virtuosity' is a purely technical matter separate from (semiotically 'empty') the matters under discussion. This is a total refusal to engage with the formal organisation of the novel and its role as a signifier in the articulation of difference.

Somewhat surprisingly, for a critic who presumably would assert that the meaning lies in a text itself rather than in the procedures used to read it, the final prescription is for a different, totally predictable, novel:

> As E. leads a submerged (actual?) life, so the novel has
> a submerged subject. It is the problem and mystery of
> family relationships, those subtle and for E. often
> painful connections between father, mother and son in
> which E. (as Eadith) seeks some explanation of 'the life
> she has chosen, or which had been chosen for her'.
> There is a real subject here, but in The Twyborn
> Affair it is not permitted to establish itself at the
> centre. The extravagant disguises, the fluctuations of
> tone between revulsion and jesting mockery are
> discordant and, finally evasive. If only, one feels, White
> could desert the circus animals
>
> > Those stilted boys, that burnished chariot,
> > Lion and woman and the Lord knows what

> and at last be satisfied as Yeats became, with his
> heart. Certainly The Twyborn Affair, *whatever its*
> *subject, comes nowhere near the heart of the matter.*
> *(p.66)*

I intend ignoring, with some difficulty, the gratuitous offensiveness and patrician sentimentality of these formulations.[3] In this particular passage the reviewer's metaphors are those of depth. The real theme ('submerged subject') of the novel is 'the problem and mystery of family relationships' as distinct from the narrative's emphasis on the character E. The reviewer initially sets up an opposition between the aesthetico-moral category 'character' and the subject (theme) of the novel. Character fails as a guide to the novel's meaning because E. has no 'wholeness'. The 'real' theme has to be recuperated by understanding that E., in his/her third and chronologically last manifestation as Eadith, is a unification and culmination of what has gone before in relation to father, mother and son. (What happened to Eudoxia?) Understood this way, 'there is a real subject here', one that the intratextual organisation of discourse refuses to centre.

Notice how what is at stake is not so much the moral character of E. but the moral character of the novel as a whole. We are still in the realm of moral introspection, but its object has shifted. The practice of paraphrase which reads the text for us is instructive (Williamson, 1985). First, familiar elements of literary analysis (character, subject) are used to suggest the displacement of the morally proper: the family. Second, this procedure is amplified by interpolating a transcendental morality: 'the heart', for goodness sake! Neither of these techniques is used reflexively, consequently the purported 'real subject' is naturalised as unproblematic. Heterosexuality and family life are quite simply the space on which 'circus animals' may be inscribed.

Now it is not the reliance on adjacent discourses ('family', 'sexual ambivalence') which is the problem here. That reliance, though not its uses, is unexceptionable. Nor is it necessarily the disguising of moral judgment as formalist description which grates: 'the *extravagant* disguises, the *fluctuations* of tone between revulsion and jesting mockery.' What is objectionable is the whole policing strategy of a moral anthropology which would prescribe who speaks, where from, what of, who may listen and how. Quite simply, one is not allowed to identify with or be like E: extravagant, mocking, jesting, of uncertain sexuality and gender. The review form has the advantage of not having to justify this process. As an apparatus of public training it can simply connect the authority of the literary sense with a mechanism for policing moral character.

The attempt to establish a common moral ground between criticism and reader in the 'heart' is a refusal to open for public discussion the implicit recognition that those matters are problematic. This refusal occurs not because families and sexuality are being installed in writing circulating in the name of Australia's nobel laureate, though earlier in the review careful references to White's autobiographical *Flaws in the Glass* are used to undermine his authority to speak 'well' on such matters. It occurs because of what the textual organisation of those discourses highlighted is doing: undermining the notion of a homogeneous, unified moral field which is the proper subject of Literature. The review tries to undermine the conditions of intelligibility of *The Twyborn Affair* by suggesting it evades its 'real' subject.

The text's preferred reading position requires that the characters circulating under the name E. be understood by readers who are prepared to shift across several combinations of gender and sexuality, none of which is fixed. There is no easy point of social identification, except perhaps that of fluidity itself. Consequently a reading which refuses to relativise heterosexuality is perforce hostile to the text. The narrative estranges particular notions of permanently stable sexual identities. Like E., the reader who identifies with the narrative flow is continuously relocated. This has the effect of formally giving the male and female, heterosexual and homosexual reader equal access to the text in terms of processes of identification. Access to this fantasy is heavily structured. The narrative distinguishes between desire organised in terms of sexual object choice and the changeability of identities which open from desire via shifting identifications, through the operation of fantasy. *The Twyborn Affair* refuses to confine the psychic negotiation of identity to socially prescribed categories.

The political calculation implicit in reading formations that refuse these strategies results not in a proscription of homosexualities as such, but of all forms of sexual variety. The discourses found in the *Quadrant* text compete with those of *The Twyborn Affair* for our acceptance. The reviewer's disgust is of a different kind from that elaborated so carefully at different points of the narrative. MacNeill discusses this question in relation to Eddie's rape by Prowse in Part Two: 'the humour, expressed even unto the minutiae of punctuation, the sardonic tone, reveal a disgust at history which so shaped circumstance and the act, as well as charging the writing with a disgust—much wider than a mere recoiling from homosexuality—that is probably the writer's own' (1984:8). That 'history' is what I have been addressing in part throughout this chapter. The discourses of Australian identity at stake here require more analysis. This issue is addressed at length in *The Twyborn Affair*. Also required is a discussion of how the category 'Australian' is used within literary theory and criticism in relation to these matters.

Once more we can see that the shifting object 'literature' is determined institutionally by an ensemble of moral, sexual and writing practices quite at variance with each other. An important consequence of this for criticism is that, in principle, all the documents of the competing discourses ought to be of equal pedagogic status. Any discussion of character formation ought to be able to refer to the adjacent fields on which it relies, otherwise it is doomed to repetition, the reproduction of the same. That, of course, is what some reading formations desire.

In practice, however, the bounds of existing training institutions, such as university English departments, require tactical manoeuvres that recognise the priority particular procedures give to the 'creative' as distinct from the non-fictional prose text. Any knowledge then of how selected fictional texts and their 'certified' readers deploy those adjacent discourses, and to what effect, has to be supplemented with an awareness of the specific writing practices involved. In the case of that problematic category 'homosexual' writing, little understanding of those practices comes from established criticism.

10 Soap opera as gender training: teenage girls and TV

Anne Cranny-Francis and Patricia Palmer Gillard

T EENAGE GIRLS in Australia watch a great deal of television
soap opera. It is a major topic of conversation both in and
out of school hours and it seems to be a major source of role
model behaviour for these girls. In this chapter we report some
recent research on girls' viewing habits, the kinds of programs
the girls favour and the reasons they give for doing so. We then
discuss some of the terms they use in their discussions and
attempt to denaturalise their meanings. We conclude with a
discussion of some recent work on soap opera as a women's
genre, with special reference to Tania Modleski's book, Loving
with a Vengeance.

Patricia Gillard: interviewing teenage girls about television

My interest in studying the significance of television in the lives
of teenage girls began when I was teaching at a girls' school. One
day, after showing segments of soap operas, I asked a class of
16-year-olds what the women all had in common. They were not
so good at playing the game 'guess what's in the teacher's mind'

so they answered frankly: 'they were all unhappy.' Yet these were the favourite programs of the girls in my class, their mothers and their older sisters. It was enough to make me start studying again, and move from teaching into research.

In 1980 I conducted a study of 34 teenage girls aged between thirteen and a half and fourteen and a half. The aim of the research was to understand how girls of this age defined their experience of television viewing: the meaning it had in relationships with friends and family and its significance to the way they thought about themselves in the present and in the future.

Television's significance to teenage girls

To the question, 'Do you watch television?' all the girls but one answered yes, and some went on to describe particular programs. All took it for granted that 'television' meant a succession of regularly appearing programs—the ones they watched. Without exception the girls stated that they knew at the beginning of the week what their viewing would be.

In order to discuss the programs most significant to teenage girls the interviewer focused on girls' favourite TV shows. The range of favourite programs for girls this age was found to be quite narrow, and consisted mainly of regularly appearing dramas, usually in series of serial form. Those mentioned most often were 'Restless Years', 'Young Doctors', 'Dallas', 'California Fever', 'MASH', 'Prisoner', 'Brady Bunch', and 'Eight is Enough'— in other words, what are known as soapies.

Individuals differed a great deal in the combinations of programs they liked, but the reasons they gave for loyalty to favourite programs were strikingly similar. Girls enjoyed programs which they felt were 'true to life', 'realistic', 'down to earth' and which usually concerned people their age and older.

Interviewer [I]: Why do you like 'Restless Years'?
Student [S]: It's about teenagers, how they struggle with their lives, what problems they have, how they can look at things. The things they do, what mischief they get into, stuff like that.

In the 'Restless Years', most of them, they're really natural. Especially the ones at home. They mostly sit around and think about what they'll be or do next. They're really kind of natural.

I: Why do you like 'Prisoner'?

S: Because it's sort of down to earth. Like some programs they have are sort of real ham-acted. You really can't believe things that you see. On 'Prisoner' everything's sort of plain and everything. Like you really get into it. You really get interested and involved in the characters that are in it.

I: Do you think you could ever be in a similar situation to some of the people in 'Prisoner'? I don't mean that they're in prison. I mean things that could happen to you.

S: I suppose so.

I: And what would you do?

S: I don't know, I'd probably follow their footsteps, and see what happened to those.

I: Why?

S: I don't know, because otherwise I wouldn't be able to work it out for myself. If I saw it I would probably, you know, go after them, because I'd know what they turned out like.

Girls generally disliked documentaries, the news and nature shows and thought that they were 'boring'. However, if girls felt that a program was real for them on a personal level, it received some acceptance.

Once accepted as being 'true to life', a high level of involvement by the girls followed. Closer attention to the description of favourite programs revealed different kinds of involvement, though all were concerned with the details of interpersonal interaction and its consequences. For example, girls watched the interaction between characters very closely and sometimes adopted gestures or behaviour as their own. However, apart from appropriating particular mannerisms, the girls found it difficult to describe themselves in relation to a single TV character, though this comparison process was a subject which interested them greatly and was a topic they discussed together.

S: My friends say I look like Marcia Brady. I am like her but I can't see it. I can't see myself looking like her.

I: Just appearance-wise they say?

S: No, personality and everything too.

173

More often the girls chose qualities from a number of characters which they then put into a composite image which they felt described themselves. Interestingly they sometimes chose qualities from male characters as part of their composite.

So, in constructing a self-representation in terms of television characters, a practice the girls enjoyed and which formed part of their peer group interaction, they were prepared to range over a variety of characters, female and male, and to attempt to give complexity and diversity to the finished product. However, when it came to using television characters to predict their own future, to represent themselves as adults, the picture was quite different. Diversity and complexity gave way to uniformity. The girls used a narrow range of qualities repeatedly to represent their future selves: they aspired to be friendly, understanding, and to live in a happy home, married and with children. The models for this future self-representation were provided by sisters, mothers and female, not male, television characters. And they did not find it difficult to find female television characters who exactly fitted their adult self-image; composites were no longer necessary.

In other words, teenage girls used the qualities of television characters discerningly to represent themselves in the present. They were prepared to pick and choose attributes from a number of characters, and from both sexes, to construct an adequately subtle and complex self-image. But when it came to representing their adult selves, the girls were apparently channelled into a narrow range of options which emphasised interpersonal skills: homemaker, mother. And they felt unable to appropriate qualities from male characters. At the same time the girls constantly emphasised that the reason they enjoyed their television programs was that they were realistic and down-to-earth, and that they provided a means by which to witness the consequences of specific forms of behaviour by women: 'If I saw it I would probably, you know, go after them, because I'd know what they turned out like.' The implication is that television characterisations provide them with a number of possible role models which they can witness in operation from the safety of their lounge rooms and from which they can make choices about their own future. In practice, however, this does not seem to happen: only one role model is seen as viable: mother and homemaker. One must question, therefore, how these programs and characterisations come to seem 'natural' and what is the role of that kind of process in the girls' acculturation.

Television and relationships with friends

The girls' definitions of TV's 'realism' and their active use of its content were made with friends, even though they watched TV at home with their families. They would discuss new programs with friends to decide whether they were the ones which their group would 'follow'. Once a program was adopted as a group favourite, it was discussed regularly and sometimes acted out within the group. It became clear during interviews that favourite television shows were often used by friends to express their own values and perhaps to reinforce each other's opinions. For example, during a group discussion with ten girls, all close friends because of their ethnic background, talk about the recent marriage of Kitty on 'The Sullivans' prompted many statements comparing love and relationships in the past and present:

> S: *Her wedding wasn't like weddings now, it was different. They looked like they were really, truly in love. It was more emotional—people really felt about it. Now, people just get married because everyone expects it.*

The girls accepted the fictional representation of the marriage as realistic for a particular time and place and compared it with their own experience of marriages, or with their understanding of contemporary marriage. They did not question the realism of the fictional representation in any way, and this surely has important implications for their use of television as a medium.

Some of the girls also play-acted scenes from television in their own groups. Acting-out roles was used to 'fill in' parts of the show which friends had missed, or to enjoy again the most dramatic parts of programs. Roles were sometimes assigned on the basis of physical resemblance or similar personality types and the aim was usually to act out TV events as faithfully as possible. From their demonstrations in the interviews many girls were excellent mimics. Although they derived enjoyment from the time when their performance broke down, acting out of programs was not intended as criticism or spoof, but as a faithful imitation of events on screen.

There was only one girl who thought TV was inadequate in its portrayal of women. She wanted a program which showed what happened when a woman was 'boss'.

> S: I wouldn't mind being a doctor or lawyer, something like that. Something where I tell people what to do . . .
>
> I: Would you like to see things like that on television?
>
> S: Yeah—It's more realistic.
>
> I: What do you mean?
>
> S: Like nowadays there's women's liberation and I think there should be more of that. So I'm up for women's lib. I like seeing more women being head and not men always—because it's always been men.
>
> I: What difference would it make to you?
>
> S: I'd pay more attention to it—because it's a woman being the boss.
>
> I: What if it is a woman, would you tend to try out what she does, [more so] than if it was a man?
>
> S: Yeah.
>
> I: Why's that?
>
> S: Because if it worked for her, being a woman, it might work for me. If it's a man it doesn't always work. They say that a man's stronger than a woman and all that. So if it works for her it probably might work for me.

This interview reinforces the points made earlier about the girl's use of TV characters as role models as well as pinpointing the problems faced by girls attempting to formulate a self-image which differs from those represented on television. This girl uses the 'realism' criterion to criticise the portrayal of women on television in traditional supportive roles. Since women are now active in the professions to which she is attracted, she would like to see female television characters in those roles. Her desire for these role models also reveals the impact of these characterisations on girls at a time when they are attempting to formulate their future, to make decisions (about school subjects, for example) which influence profoundly the rest of their lives. The girl in this interview repeats the view that girls can use the actions of television characters and their consequences to make decisions about their own lives. So she argues that she would follow what happens to a female character in a traditionally male role in order to see what happens because 'if it worked for her . . . it might work for me'. She adds a recognition that role-reversal does not necessarily work—that, if it worked for a male character, it doesn't always work for women—following this with a crude statement of patriarchal ideology: 'They say that a man's stronger . . . ' She then reiterates her point about role-modelling: 'So if it works for her it probably might work for me.' Her repetition of this point suggests that the characterisation of women on television is used quite explicitly in the decisions they make about their futures.

Many efforts are currently being made to increase the participation by girls in schooling and further education, and in lifetime vocational work. However, this participation is largely dependent on the possibilities girls see available to them, on their ability to formulate images of alternative futures and alternative selves. What this research on girls and television shows quite clearly is that teenage girls are profoundly affected by the representations of women they see on television in the programs that they themselves choose to watch and which form the basis of so much of their peer group interaction—soap operas. Furthermore, as argued earlier, television soap operas offer a narrow and distorted view of the identities available to adult women: they can be wives and mothers.

Anne Cranny-Francis: deconstructing soap opera

The Girls and Television report

It is useful to consider further some of the terms used by the girls in this study to talk about their favourite soap operas. What do they reveal about the girls' viewing practices? How they are being positioned by those texts? And what kinds of ideological assumptions are coded into that viewing position?

It was found that the girls did not like news or documentaries or current affairs programs, because they found them boring. One girl, Danielle, did express an interest in the Mike Willesee program:

S: *I like 'Willesee' because they have, you know, children, really people who are sick and they cope and all that. They have interesting things on. It's not just politics. They hardly ever have politics or anything like that on. It's just people who are crippled and how some people have healed and things like that.*

Not too many people would be surprised if the generic basis of the Willesee program was found to be closer to soap opera than current affairs, given its emphasis on the interpersonal. Danielle's description of the program might serve equally well to describe the girls' favourite programs, which included 'The Sullivans', 'Dallas', 'Prisoner', 'Restless Years'.

The highest praise the girls had for these programs was that they were 'realistic'; they were 'true to life' and 'down to earth'. Conversely the programs they did not like were 'boring' and 'unrealistic', with the words often being used as synonyms. What was this 'realism'? It could hardly be experiential in the literal sense. Very few of the girls interviewed would have had any contact with female prisons or the Dallas business world and none of them were alive during World War II. Only 'Restless Years', a program about a school, might directly reflect their own experience. Why then did they consistently use the term 'realistic' to describe programs whose settings were unknown to them?

In the report on her research Gillard notes:

> *Whatever the kinds of interests the girls described, the striking finding throughout the interviews was the association of 'realistic' with an ability to be involved with the situations and the people in a particular program. There was not one girl whose television viewing showed an undifferentiated enjoyment of a wide range of programs. Girls were very definite about favourite programs and their reasons for choosing them. However their definition of 'realistic' and 'true to life' was not that of an outsider making a judgement about 'the way life is', but was more an intuitive response to the authenticity of the characters and events portrayed.*

An alternative reading might be that the girls are learning the conventions of the soap opera genre, the genre characterised as 'women's television' (in the same way that romantic novels are characterised as 'women's fiction'). With a genre so heavily dependent on the portrayal of character and of interpersonal relationships, it is not surprising to find the adjective 'realistic' a major element of non-specialist critical opinion. It might be suggested that what the girls are concerned with is not so much

'realism' as 'consistency', that characters and events are consistent—not by reference to 'reality', but to the conventions of
the genre in which they are operating.

Gillard reports the response of the girls to having a favourite
character written out of a soapie: 'Sudden deaths, such as that of
Grace Sullivan, were not tolerated, and for one fifth of the girls
interviewed this particular event caused a change in program
preference. They switched permanently to another serial drama.'
The girls here show their novice status in the field of soapie
viewing. Sudden death of a character is a time-honoured means
of allowing actors to change jobs, and has become a convention of
the genre itself. However, at this stage in their viewing history,
the girls are still primarily concerned with consistency of
characterisation, which is an attribute of the narrative characteristic of soap opera. Characters do not disappear from narratives for no apparent reason; that tends to violate the
superficial cohesiveness of the narrative. If characterisation
becomes fragmentary (that is, if characters behave or are disposed of in a way which is not consistent with their previous
operation), or if events seem to follow no logical order, then the
narrative loses its function as an apparently realistic representation of causality.

The relationship between the temporal sequence of traditional
Western narrative and notions of causality has been widely
theorised. Roland Barthes, for example, noted: 'Everything suggests, indeed, that the mainspring of narrative is precisely the
confusion of consecution and consequence, what comes *after*
being read in narrative as what is *caused by*; in which case
narrative would be a systematic application of the logical fallacy
denounced by Scholasticism in the formula *post hoc, ergo propter
hoc . . .* ' (1977:94). Peter Brooks makes a similar point in *Reading
for the Plot*: 'Plot as it interests me is not a matter of typology or of
fixed structures, but rather a structuring operation peculiar to
those messages that are developed through temporal succession,
the instrumental logic of a specific mode of human understanding. Plot . . . is the logic and dynamic of narrative, and
narrative itself a form of understanding and explanation.'
(1984:10).

The significance of this practice is not only aesthetic, of course;
it is also political. Writing about narrative and the cinema,
Christopher Williams claimed: 'narrative militates against knowledge . . . because it attempts to conceal itself, to imply that this is

how the world is' (Masterman, 1983:6). And the way narrative does this is by concealing or obscuring the social, political, economic and historical determinants of social interactions, by concealing class difference, by concealing sexist practices, by fabricating an 'objective' or 'unbiased' viewpoint which is usually the viewpoint of the ideologically dominant class, that is, white, male, middle-class. Fredric Jameson in *The Political Unconscious*: 'We may suggest that . . . ideology is not something which informs or invests symbolic production; rather the aesthetic act is itself ideological, and the production of aesthetic or narrative form is to be seen as an ideological act in its own right, with the function of inventing imaginary or formal "solutions" to unresolvable social contradictions' (1981:79). By watching soap opera teenage girls are learning our society's narrative about our society. They do not see the material conditions of our society; they do not see (that is, they are not shown) class conflict in its historical, economic framework; they do not see (that is, they are not shown) sexism as an effect or function of a patriarchal social formation. In learning our society's narrative about itself these girls are learning not to question anomalies or injustices; they are learning not to see them. They are learning to accept ideological justifications for the 'way things are', justifications which use concepts such as 'human nature' and 'natural' to obscure the ideological *construction* of 'human nature' and the social by a particular socio-economic formation. And they are learning not to ask *why* things are the way they are, or whether there are alternatives.

This problem of alternatives is also a function of class, that of the girls themselves, and it would be interesting to address a number of issues not taken up in the *Girls and Television* report: how do viewing practices differ from class to class? do different classes assign more or less value to their television viewing? if different kinds of programs are favoured by different classes, do their ideological inputs differ significantly? (see, by comparison, the investigation of the ideology of women's work in mother—child interactions in Hasan (1986)) Whatever the answers to these questions, it is pertinent at the moment to devote continuing attention to the kind of program that current research by academics, television companies and market researchers identify as having a huge teenage following, and that is soap opera.

It was noted earlier that there are very few strong female characters in soap operas. It is worth adding that those who do exist are usually circumscribed in some crucial way. For example, 'Prisoner' was very important to some girls as it was seen as having strong women characters, principally Bea, whom the girls might emulate. Without going into a long discussion of what 'strong' might mean in relation to female characters, it is important to contextualise those characters and to realise that they are all *in jail*. If these characters are strong, might not their position within the narrative suggest that strong women are suppressed by society? They might be self-determining and independent but can only practise these attributes when safely removed from the rest of society. In jail their self-determination and independence is highly conditional and depends ultimately on the dictates of a patriarchal society and its representatives. Furthermore, it may be this very independence which got them into prison in the first place . . .

It should be remembered here that the girls repeatedly described the way they study the outcome of events in soap opera as a guide to their own behaviour:

S: *I often think back to the show I've watched and I relate with that character.*
I: *And what do you do as a result of that?*
S: *Well, I don't do anything about it, but I often think about it and if it's good what happened to them to fix it, I'll try and do the same, but if it's not, well I'll go about it my own way.*

The setting of 'Prisoner' might be considered here: why the series is set in a jail. Surely there are alternative settings available for an all-female soap opera, from an all-female magazine or publisher to a factory or sweat-shop to a convent. So why choose a prison in which to situate strong female characters? Is this the only setting in which they are tolerable? in which the narrative of bourgeois patriarchal society can situate them?

The other side of this strong female character issue is the problem of role models. The poverty of female role models with whom girls can identify at a time when they are making important career choices was noted earlier in the discussion of the *Girls and Television* report. There are not many female lawyers, scientists, plumbers, electricians, mechanics, or mathematicians on television. When they do appear, their profession is often treated in the same way as the man's shirt on Bo Derek, the laughable 'contradiction' serving to make the woman underneath more feminine, cute, sexy. The important feature, of course, is the woman underneath, the body, the physical femininity, not the professional person. So when Alexis is running the company in 'Dynasty', is she treated as a scheming executive who happens to be a woman, or as a scheming woman who happens to be an executive?

This treatment of the professional woman is not surprising, given the conservative (patriarchal bourgeois) ideology of the narrative. Since female assertiveness is considered an abnormal trait in a patriarchal society, it is not surprising that patriarchal narratives should assign this trait only to female characters who are evil and inevitably defeated in some way, or who are somehow restricted (Jackson, 1981:121). And since it is difficult to be any sort of professional without being assertive, it is again not surprising that there are so few professional female characters. The importation of such characters into contemporary narratives would be very difficult as there is no space for them, no role they can play; the narrative would then seem 'unrealistic', which, among teenage girls at least, is a mortal blow to its acceptability.

Of course space for such characters can be and has been negotiated in other ways (e.g. Billie in 'Lou Grant', the major female characters in 'Seeing Things', the female lawyers in 'L.A. Law', the main characters of 'Cagney and Lacey') but this is still the exception rather than the rule. As the *Girls and Television* report recommends, probably one of the best solutions here is to have teenage girls (and boys) not only construct female role models themselves, but also suggest reasons why those models do not appear in television soap operas, or just about any other kind of television program.

Again the invidious feature of the (soap opera) narrative is not so much what it shows (though that is often bad enough), but what it conceals, such as the career possibilities available to women and the self-determination women can choose to exercise (even when limited by economic circumstances). These exclusions and concealments are not only a feature of the entertainment of women (and men) who are already living out their choices, but also of young girls (and boys) whose choices have yet to be made. Not that these exclusions and concealments are always performed literally; there are professional women characters and strong female characters in television programs, including some soap operas, but we need to look closely at their roles in the narratives before we get too excited about that. The important point that arises from the *Girls and Television* research and the discussion of it is that the construction of femininity in television programs, including soap operas, with their notoriously conservative gender, class and race ideologies, is being used as a guide to the construction of femininity in society as a whole by teenage girls at a very vulnerable time in their lives, personally and professionally. Teenage girls are reading these ideologically constructed narratives as 'realistic' in an experiential sense, seeing their characterisations of women and their interactions as sufficiently 'realistic' to be a guide to behaviour in their own lives.

Soap opera as feminine culture

In *Loving with a Vengeance* Tania Modleski puts what seems to be an increasingly popular case for soapies, that they should be regarded as part of feminine culture and that we should, therefore, concentrate on the good in them.

It is uncontestable that soap operas are often fun. Chocolates are fun too. They taste good, but they produce acid in your mouth which rots your teeth; fat for your body which makes you unhealthy; and they ruin your skin, which makes you miserable. On a very few occasions they might also have a beneficial effect, a sugar boost, but with chocolates—as with soap operas—that is very rare. We cannot get rid of soap operas any more than chocolates, and we probably do not want to, but we should be aware of what they are about most of the time. The sugar producers' expensive reassurances that sugar is good for you seem extremely unconvincing; so is much of the recent feminist work suggesting that soap opera is a 'female' (as opposed to the patriarchally constructed 'feminine') genre. It is important to respond to this work for a number of reasons, but one of the most important must be that teenage girls specify soap operas as their favourite television programs.

Modleski argues that soap opera (sometimes identified as 'daytime television') is a 'caring', female-oriented, 'politically liberal' program genre. Writing of the aesthetics, and hence the politics, of soap opera Modleski says: 'It is scarcely an accident that this essentially nineteenth-century form continues to appeal strongly to women, whereas the classic (male) narrative film is, as Laura Mulvey points out, structured 'around a main controlling figure with whom the spectator can identify'. Soap operas continually insist on the insignificance of the individual life . . . ' (Modleski, 1982:91). A few pages later she adds: 'Marcia Kinder . . . suggests that the "open-ended, slow-paced, multi-climaxed" structure of soap opera is "in tune with patterns of female sexuality"' (Modleski, 1982:98). The problem with the latter quotation is that it tends to obscure the history of the soap opera genre, which must have as much to do with the nineteenth-century serial novel as it does with melodrama, Modleski's choice (Modleski, 1982:90). The serial novel was very popular in the nineteenth century, chiefly, of course, because of the prohibitively expensive price of books, and it was not limited to female readership. Without engaging in detail with the psychosexual interpretation it should be noted that soap opera, like the serial novel, was developed to meet the economic imperatives of a particular social formation. That its narrative has some attraction for its readership is hardly surprising, as that is a condition of its existence. If the rhythm Modleski via Kinder refers to has something to do with female sexuality, that is most likely a fortunate accident, since those rhythms correspond primarily to the demands of sponsors and television executives, about advertising and programming. As to the notion that soap operas insist on the insignificance of the individual, again there are problems. Even if 'Dallas', 'Dynasty', 'Falconcrest', 'Prisoner' and 'A Country Practice', all of which have prominent main characters, are not considered typical, this judgment does not seem valid. Most soapies feature a sequence of characters adopting the main role. It may not be quite the traditional (quest narrative) hero role, although at least one character is usually in this role most of the time—whether it is Victor Newman in 'The Young and the Restless' or Doctor Elliott of 'A Country Practice'. The point is that no *social context* is provided for these characters and their interactions. They are not social beings; they are disconnected individuals. Soap operas do, in fact, continually insist on the significance of the individual; what is insignificant for them is the social formation in which characters might be situated. In so doing they produce a series of traditional narratives, the premises or conclusions of which are continually revised to produce yet another narrative. In soap operas the only thing which is significant is the individual, represented in a series of contextless characters.

Elsewhere Modleski herself writes directly about the political consequences of soap opera viewing: 'Soap operas, contrary to many people's conception of them, are not conservative but liberal, and the mother [Modleski's construction of the ideal soap opera subject/spectator] is the liberal par excellence. By constantly presenting her with the many-sidedness of any question, by never reaching a permanent conclusion, soap operas undermine her capacity to form unambiguous judgements' (1982:93). As noted above, events in soap operas never reach a single, permanent, unambiguous conclusion; every apparent conclusion is the possible source of yet another complex narrative. Soap operas do, in a sense, reject closure, the closure associated with the construction of a particular meaning for the viewer which almost invariably encodes dominant ideological discourses. That is, the narrative is theorised as positioning the viewer to accept a particular set of ideological discourses as natural or valid, and her/his acceptance of those (usually conservative) discourses is signified by acceptance of the closure of the narrative at a particular point (DuPlessis, 1985:1–19). The viewer, thereby, accepts the causal sequence established in the narrative, which is premised on the acceptance of particular ideological discourses. The avoidance of closure by soap operas does not necessarily indicate any kind of political radicalism; viewers are not necessarily positioned to be liberal or open-minded. Instead soap operas reach a discontinuous series of permanent conclusions, each narrative in the ongoing series of interwoven narratives reaching its own conclusion. The conclusions change because the premises change, but this is less like liberalism than double-think. It is not that the viewer's understanding of her/his society is going to be enriched by these revisions, because social context, historical development, political economy have no place in soap opera narratives. It is simply that today $1 + 1 = 2$ and tomorrow $1 + 1 = 3$. And it is in this way that soap operas may well challenge our construction of the 'real', may reveal the construction itself. But they are not agents of liberalism in quite the sense Modleski suggests.

Another positive quality described by Modleski concerns the position of the villainess: 'If soap operas keep us caring about everyone; if they refuse to allow us to condemn most characters and actions until all the evidence is in (and, of course, it never is), there is one character whom we are allowed to hate unreservedly: the villainess, the negative image of the spectator's ideal self' (Modleski, 1982:94). Although much of the suffering on soap opera is presented as unavoidable, the surplus suffering is often the fault of a villainess who tries to 'make things happen and control events better than the subject/spectator can' (Modleski, 1982:94).

Modleski's first 'if' requires considerable scrutiny. Modleski's belief that soap operas encourage 'caring' is premised on the notion that soap operas never let the viewer condemn a character totally, because the evidence about each character is never fully gathered. As noted above, soap opera viewers do condemn characters, over and over again, judgment (viewing position) being modified by the current state of narrative double-think: the character we condemn this week may be next week's hero. So even if one accepts that a viewer can learn about causality from TV narratives in the literal way Modleski suggests, then these narratives still do not function as the bastion of liberal humanism.

More disturbing in this position, however, is the idea of the villainess whom we all hate. This soap opera villainess is a standard character in fiction. She is the woman who steps out of her socially (ideologically) acceptable role. Modleski's own language is revealing here. The villainess is one who 'tries to make things happen', that is, to be active, not passive as 'befits' a (patriarchally-constructed) woman. She tries to 'control events better than the subject/spectator can'. The ontology of this statement is very confusing. It seems rather that the villainess tries to control events better than the main, usually male, character can—which identifies the subject/spectator position with that of the main, usually male, character. Further, her evil is not so much that she is a negative of the spectator, but consists in her personification of the transgressive woman, the active, dominating, powerful woman. Her fictional characterisation is 'the bitch'. She is there to be bested, to be defeated, usually by a man, but sometimes by a woman in the role of patriarchal female (feminine) subject. Villainesses almost always use sex as a major weapon against their enemies, so that their own sexuality is fore-grounded: they are not villains who happen to be women, but women who happen to be villains. Their ideological function within the narrative is a highly conservative one: they represent and reinforce the sexist definition of women. With teenage girls as viewers this is obviously a disturbing function of soap opera narrative.

Finally consider Modleski's descriptions of the value of soap opera for women, first in relation to their enforced passivity: 'While soap operas thrive they present a continual reminder that women's anger is alive, if not well' (Modleski, 1982:98). Modleski here accounts for the popularity of the villainess, tracing it to her acting out of the female viewers' frustrated demands for power in a (patriarchal) society which defines them in terms of powerlessness and passivity. Modleski follows with this statement a couple of pages later: 'Daytime television plays a part in habituating women to distraction, interruption, and spasmodic toil . . . her duties are split among a variety of domestic and familial tasks, and her television programs keep her from desiring a focussed existence by involving her in the pleasures of a fragmented life' (Modleski, 1982:100–01). The second statement is extremely problematic, and again Modleski's own language highlights the problem areas. She describes soap opera as functioning as a behaviour modifier, 'habituating' women to their existence. This seems to imply that this 'fragmented life' is not particularly pleasurable; why else would women need to be habituated to it (and note the disposition of female viewers as receptive, passive puppets). This statement suggests that soap opera functions as a valium substitute. The other sentence in this statement contains an equally revealing verb: the female viewers' television programs 'keep her from desiring a focussed existence'; in other words, this function of soap opera is actively repressive. Soaps *prevent* women from even wanting a coherent existence, supposedly by replacing this desire with the pleasures of a fragmented, discontinuous lifestyle.

The whole statement seems profoundly evasive. If a pleasure is not desired, one usually does not have to be *kept* from it. And being involved in the pleasures of a fragmented life sounds a lot like learning to love your disease. The whole line of reasoning is profoundly disturbing. Perhaps there is some value in being deadened to what you (apparently) cannot have, but again that represents soap opera viewing as the same kind of behaviour modifier as gin or cocaine or valium. Perhaps soap opera viewing can be used to make unpleasant living conditions tolerable, but it does nothing to change those conditions. Worse, it reproduces and reinforces the ideology which produces the working conditions women find so difficult.

Even if mature women do use soap opera creatively to alleviate their difficult working conditions (for example, by using their knowledge of soap opera conventions to interact recreationally with the text), it is important to remember that these women do not constitute the entire audience; part of it consists of immature, less media-literate teenage girls. If soap operas operate as repressive mechanisms for women, are they not doing the same for these girls?

Modleski's statement about female anger might be read an entirely different way. Perhaps soap operas should remind us that women's oppression and dissatisfaction and frustration and pain are alive, requiring daily doses of soma television to suppress them. And one might ask whether viewing contains that anger, or prevents it ever being formulated. Are its (ideological) practices of mystification, concealment and naturalisation so effective that they deflect frustration and dissatisfaction into self-criticism and personal insecurity, so that anger never forms?

There is a need, as Modleski's arguments suggest, to re-evaluate conservative critiques of soap opera which position the largely female viewing audience as mindless puppets (though Modleski is susceptible to this criticism herself at times). Such work proceeds from the same ideological premises as much soap opera. However, it must nevertheless be recognised that soap opera has negative characteristics, many of which are concerned with the representation, and so definition, of femininity and masculinity in our society. These practices may be harmful enough in the lives of adult women, but in the lives of young girls about to make decisions about their appropriate future roles and careers, they may be disastrous.

The best remedy, as the *Girls and Television* report suggests, is to enhance the media literacy of girls (and boys) so that they themselves have the critical tools to deconstruct television narratives. They then have the option to accept or reject the viewing position constructed for them, a position often premised on an acceptance of sexist discourse. Adult women often achieve this level of literacy as a result of long-term viewing and their own experiential input; they are as adept at manipulating the conventions of the genre as the writers themselves. But teenage girls are not. As seen repeatedly in the research, they view these texts as 'realistic' and use them in constructing their own reality. Perhaps their fetishisation of the term suggests that already their own experience is leading them to detect contradictions, problems with these narratives and their relation to the social formation in which the viewing takes place. Often, however, the disturbance felt by teenage viewers is a consequence of their lack of familiarity with the genre conventions; in time all will be naturalised. Obviously the time to intervene in this process most usefully is at the stage when girls are making decisions about their future, not after those decisions have been made and the consequences are being lived through with the help of a behaviour modifier-cum-tranquilliser known as soap opera.

Soap opera may be a feminine genre in that it is produced within a patriarchal culture by largely male production teams for consumption by a largely female audience. Its attractiveness for this audience is excellent reason for its analysis by feminist critics. However, it is not reason to find soap operas necessarily good or valid in themselves. Their popularity with and use by teenage girls must make feminist critics particularly wary of adopting essentialist or liberal stances which position them to celebrate these texts simply on the basis of their consumption by women. The most useful role for feminist critics is to lead the way in the deconstruction of these texts, which give so much pleasure to women—not in order to destroy that pleasure, but to show women the assumptions, the ideology, on which it is based and so to give them the option of participating (or not) as active, interventionist viewers.

11 Gender, class and power: text, process and production in Strindberg's *Miss Julie*

Susan Yell

THIS CHAPTER sets out to explore some of the rich semiotic potential of a theatrical text as it unfolds in space and time, and to examine some of the ways in which gender-related paradigms are constructed and reconstructed in a particular text. The text in question, Strindberg's play *Miss Julie*, was staged as a workshop project through the collaboration of the English Department and the Theatre Studies Service Unit of the University of Sydney. All rehearsals and performances were fully documented, using audio and video taping as well as still photography. It must be stressed that this analysis is not concerned with critical, biographical or translation issues relating to the text as a literary work: it is an exploration of this particular text as it was constructed in the Seymour Centre, Sydney, April 1986. As a semiotic, not a dramatic enterprise, this chapter claims no expertise in performance studies. Performance studies are still at a developmental stage, and very little work has yet been done on the rehearsal process.

I want first to examine some general concepts and issues presented by a multi-medial text, including methodological approaches and problems, and then to analyse in detail the final scene of the play, in order to suggest what meanings are being made, and how. I will try to suggest how and why some meanings come to be selected at the expense of others, and I will discuss some of the implications these choices have.

Text and context

I am using the term 'text' in the general sense of 'any coherent complex of signs' (Bakhtin, 1986:103), that is, a configuration of semiotic acts, whereby certain meaning choices are made and realised in and through one or more semiotic systems. The rehearsals and performances of *Miss Julie* form a multi-medial text which is both process and product. As a multi-medial text, its meanings are constructed and encoded simultaneously at many levels, through many semiotic systems, enabling multiple possibilities for semiosis. The meanings encoded in different semiotic systems can and do conflict, forcing the encoder/decoder of the text to overcode meanings at a higher semiotic level or to undercode (Eco, 1979: 133, 135): that is, to construct new meanings using knowledge of existing codes (overcoding) or hypothesising, guessing where no such codes exist (undercoding) (Eco, 1970:136). It can be seen as a text in process, continually constituting and reconstituting itself in a recursive fashion through the rehearsal context; as a text in flux, not in the state of fixity we have come to expect from the term 'text' as it is used of written texts. The text can also be viewed as a product, in the context of its ultimate public performance. (However, it is difficult to pin down the ultimate performance as product. Not only were there two performances, each unique, but for the purposes of analysis I have taken as my 'ultimate performance' a videotape of the production which was made before the two public performances.) In spite of all these dimensions of possible variation, the *Miss Julie* project's textual coherence is maintained through recurring patterns of meaning choices.

As a performance text, the *Miss Julie* text has a complex relationship with its context. I am using 'context' in the Hallidayan sense of a situation type which is a semiotic construct (Halliday, 1978:125). Halliday suggests that this semiotic construct is structured in three ways: in terms of its *field* (the social activity which generates the text), its *tenor* (the role relationships of the participants) and its *mode* (the symbolic organisation, which relates the text to the social action and the role structure). As a fictional display text, the *Miss Julie* text is embedded in two contexts: the immediate fictional context constructed through the text, and the wider context of the rehearsal/performance situation. Both contexts constrain the meanings which can be produced, and are in turn constructed through the textual activity which defines them. As a further 'complication', discussions between the actors and director form a sort of parallel text. This is a metasemiotic discourse on the encoding and decoding of meanings within the play, through which the speaking subjects enact some of their conscious and explicit as well as unconscious and implicit orientations to meaning-making in the *Miss Julie* text. The relation between text and parallel text is therefore one of symbiotic intertextuality—a mutual exchange of meanings—although obviously a partial and unequal one, subject to many constraints.

I have been using metaphors such as 'meaning is constructed' and 'the text is constituted' in order to suggest that the meaning-making practices of subjects *construct* certain meanings and thereby the 'world' of particular texts. Rather than suggesting that such meanings *represent* some sort of reality independent of the text and transparently knowable, I am suggesting that the text allows for the construction of its own 'reality' and indeed contributes to the construction of social reality. Thus, gender, class and power in the *Miss Julie* text are not represented as stable entities but are constructed and reconstructed as shifting paradigms in relation to each other.

Method

The framework for the analysis of this theatrical text is necessarily eclectic; a text which is constituted through so many different semiotic media demands a variety of analytic approaches. The basic framework is semiotic; it draws upon the semiotic theory of Eco (1979), which encompasses both linguistic and non-linguistic sign systems. Two crucial concepts in Eco's theory are that of 'code' (a rule or set of rules coupling signals with meanings: Eco, 1979:36–38) and that of 'sign production' ('the kind[s] of labor required in order to produce and interpret signs, messages or texts': Eco, 1979:152). This chapter examines the construction and interplay of theatrical codes and the ways in which the practices of speaking subjects, their 'sign production', constrain the meanings which can be made.

In order to analyse the various systems through which the

theatrical text is constituted, it was necessary first to select those systems which seemed to me important or interesting, and then to adopt methods of analysis appropriate to the systems concerned. I have selected five of the non-linguistic systems for anaylsis: the kinesic, proxemic, aural, vestimentary (costume) and lighting systems. By kinesics, I mean the code of body movements and gesture, what meanings individuals encode with their bodies through motion and position. Proxemics refers to the spatial arrangement of the stage and the objects on it, including configurations of bodies. By the term aural sign system, I simply mean non-linguistic 'sound effects' (when these occur). 'Costume' and 'lighting' are self-explanatory. I have drawn to some extent upon Elam's work on the semiotics of theatre and drama; he isolates a number of codes which operate in theatrical texts, including kinesic, proxemic and vestimentary codes (Elam, 1980:57). However, the description and analysis are my own, consisting of descriptions of specific realisations within these systems as they seem relevant. A fully developed method for dealing with non-linguistic sign systems in rehearsal and performance texts has yet to be established.

The analysis of the linguistic system uses the social semiotics of Halliday (1978), which is able to suggest in very powerful ways the nexus between text and context. The verbal text is analysed using Halliday's semantically based systemic-functional grammar (1985), which provides a method for describing realisations within the linguistic system (the lexicogrammar) in ways which can then be related to the semantics and the context. The starting point for the analysis of the verbal text is the lexicogrammar (the choice of words and grammatical constructions), which in turn is seen as encoding the meaning potential (what the speaker can mean; the potential of the semantic system).

Halliday suggests that this encoding involves three functions: the *ideational function* (meaning as content, corresponding to the *field*), the *interpersonal function* (meaning as participation, corresponding to the *tenor*), and the *textual function* (meaning as texture, corresponding to the *mode*) (see Halliday, 1978:125). For each of these three 'metafunctions', there are a number of associated systems through which the lexicogrammatical realisations are produced. For the purposes of my analysis, I will be focusing on those which seem to be most relevant and revealing. With respect to the ideational function, I will be looking at the *lexical* choices (which construct certain semantic paradigms) and the *transitivity* choices (the types of processes—activities—and the participant roles associated with them). Within the interpersonal function, I will focus on the *mood, modality* and *polarity* choices. The system of mood encodes the speech roles taken by speakers towards hearers; whether they are stating something, asking a question, commanding or offering to perform an action. Halliday makes a useful distinction between the exchange of information (as in statements and questions), which he calls *propositions* and the exchange of goods or services (as in offers and commands), which he terms *proposals* (1985:68–71). The *modality* system overlays the mood system, and is used to express the speaker's attitude to a proposition or proposal, such as the *probability* or *possibility* of a proposition, and the *inclination* or *obligation* to perform a proposal.

I will not be focusing on the textual function, as the paradigms of gender and power are constructed mainly through the field of discourse (the ideational function) and the tenor of discourse (the interpersonal function). The textual function realises the mode of discourse (the dialogic conversational structure which constitutes dramatic dialogue). Within the textual function, analysis of the *thematic* system is often revealing of the concerns of the text, since the theme is 'the starting-point for the message' in the clause (Halliday, 1985:39). In the *Miss Julie* text the themes are mostly the human participants within the text (the protagonists). Other textual features include the use of deixis to construct the text in space and time and to link the text to its context, and the use of lexical cohesion and reference to establish the coherence of the text.

Figure 8 shows a sample of a functional analysis of the transitivity and mood systems in a short section of the text. (In order to write this chapter I analysed the complete verbal text of the final scene, but constraints of space preclude presenting the full analysis here.)

An important semiotic system which I have not attempted to analyse is the paralinguistic system, which is realised through features such as stress and intonation, voice quality and so on. An analysis of paralinguistic features would certainly reveal interesting information about the construction of interpersonal and textual meanings, but such an analysis is beyond the scope of the chapter.

Analysis of a theatrical text presents an important methodological problem: how to document and segment a text which is a continuum. While documentation and segmentation are necessary steps in analysis, no method of documentation (whether audio tapes, video tapes or still photography) can fully convey all aspects of the theatrical experience, and the segmentation of the text into significant units is necessarily selective. Imposing artifical boundaries must to some extent distort the processual nature of the text. This is a problem which performance analysts have yet to resolve satisfactorily.

However, for the purposes of my analysis I have segmented the verbal text according to Halliday's concept of the clause as the unit of meaning. I have therefore divided the text into discourse units consisting of main finite verb clauses, or minor clauses (clauses which have no finite verb). These are numbered consecutively. I have used the segmentation of the linguistic text as a reference point for the segmentation of the non-linguistic continuum, and have indicated the incidence or duration of kinesic or proxemic features according to the discourse units with which they co-occur. This sytem has obvious limitations, as the proxemic and kinesic systems can and do operate in the absence of any linguistic activity and are not necessarily homologous with the linguistic segmentation. However, in the case of this scene (and in the play in general), the kinesic and proxemic features were fairly closely tied to verbal utterances. This seems to be because of the naturalistic acting and directing codes, which take the verbal text as the basis for the construction of meanings in other semiotic systems.

Analysis

With such a complex and semiotically rich text for analysis, it was necessary to select a small part of it in order to look at what was going on. In this chapter I will look at the final scene of the play (Meyer, 1985:143–46). This scene was less well-rehearsed than the rest of the play, a factor which may have helped to highlight the effects of variations in the way the scene is played at different stages of the rehearsal to performance process, since a greater degree of fixity could be expected with increasing rehearsal time.

Before looking at the final scene, I will briefly give its context within the play. The action of the play takes place in a single evening, and in a single room, the kitchen of a country house. It concerns an aristocratic young woman, Miss Julie, and her father's servant, Jean. Miss Julie is an aristocrat who wishes to

Figure 8   A functional analysis of the transitivity and mood systems in a section of the *Miss Julie* text

88 I | can't | feel | anything,
- Transitivity: Senser | Mental process: affective | | Phenomenon
- Mood: Mood: declarative — Subject (I), Finite: -ve polarity, modal of ability (can't) | Residue (feel anything)

89 I | can't | repent,
- Transitivity: Behaviour | Behavioural process
- Mood: Mood: declarative — Subject (I), Finite: -ve polarity, modal of ability (can't) | Residue (repent)

90 can't | run away, | can't | die.
- Transitivity: Material process
- Mood: Mood: declarative — Finite: -ve polarity, modal of ability (can't) | Residue (run away)

91 can't | stay,
- Transitivity: Material process
- Mood: Mood: declarative — Finite: -ve polarity, modal of ability (can't) | Residue (stay)

92 can't | live -
- Transitivity: Material process
- Mood: Mood: declarative — Finite: -ve polarity, modal of ability (can't) | Residue (live)

93 can't | like a dog.
- Transitivity: Material process | Circumstance: manner (like a dog)
- Mood: Mood: declarative — Finite: -ve polarity, modal of ability (can't) | Residue

94 Help | me!
- Transitivity: Material process | Goal (me!)
- Mood: Residue

95 Order | me,
- Transitivity: Verbal process | Target (me,)
- Mood: Residue

96 and | I | 'll | obey | you | like a dog.
- Transitivity: Actor (I) | Material process (obey) | Beneficiary: Client (you) | Circumstance: manner (like a dog)
- Mood: Mood: declarative — Subject (I), Finite: future ('ll) | Residue

97 Do | me | this last service,
- Transitivity: Material process (Do) | Beneficiary: Client (me) | Effected participant (this last service,)
- Mood: Residue

98

save	my honour,
Behavioural process	Goal
Residue	

99

save	his name!
Behavioural process	Goal
Residue	

100

You	know	what I ought
Senser	Mental process: cognitive	Phenomenon
Mood: declarative		
Subject	Finite	
		Residue

101

to will myself to do, but	I	can't.
Phenomenon	Actor	(Material process)
	Mood: declarative	
	Subject: I	Finite: - ve polarity, modal of ability
Residue		

102

Will	me	to,	Jean,
Behavioural process	Goal		Behaviour
	Residue		

103

order	me!
Verbal process	Target
Residue	

descend to the level of the common people, and Jean is a lackey who wishes to rise in the world. Miss Julie is portrayed as sexually frustrated and confused; she has just broken off with her fiance and she has 'her monthly coming on' (Meyer, 1985:111). Jean is engaged to Christine, the cook, and is portrayed as sexually potent. After some flirtatious verbal sparring, a seduction takes place offstage. The couple come back on stage, each realises their own dilemma and each struggles for the fulfilment of their own desires and ambitions, either through or in spite of the other. However, these desires and ambitions are continually changing, as if Julie and Jean take up certain roles, play them out and then cast them off as ultimately unsatisfying or hollow. Finally, the pair decide to run away together, but the cook, Christine, discovers the plan and prevents it from being carried out. Thus, issues of gender and class can already be seen to be intricately bound up in each character's struggle for some sort of solution. At this point the final scene takes place (see Appendix C for the text of this). I will be looking specifically at the exchanges numbered from 29 to 171, which I have divided into two sections (29–72 and 73–171), punctuated by the ringing of the bell, signalling the return of Miss Julie's father, who has been visiting relatives. The division is not an arbitrary one, as rather different patterns of meaning take place before and after the bell rings.

I will first discuss briefly some features within the non-linguistic systems which do not vary greatly during this scene. Then I will look in turn at the meaning potential of the two sections (29–72 and 73–171), first as it is encoded in the lexicogrammar (the linguistic system) and then in the non-linguistic systems, and at the way in which these different systems interact.

There are certain elements within the non-linguistic systems which remain fairly constant, such as movable but non-dynamic proxemic features of the set and visual elements such as lighting and costume. In the final scene, a proxemic element which has been encoded early in the play, and which is a feature of both re-hearsals and performances, is the territoriality of the stage area. The stage area consists of the interior of a kitchen, with a large table at stage left, a pair of french doors at centre stage, and a scullery table and large stove at stage right (see the stage plan in Appendix C). The area at stage right is the centre of activity for Christine, as cook, while Miss Julie keeps to centre stage and stage left, as she is essentially displaced, a mistress in the servant's world. During rehearsals, Jean and Miss Julie both move towards each other at times and occasionally cross these territorial boundaries, but this changes gradually during the rehearsal to performance process. By the time the performance takes place, Miss Julie's movements are confined to centre stage and stage left, while Jean remains predominantly in the kitchen area (stage right). These proxemic features encode Jean's distancing (both physically and emotionally) of himself from Julie, his status as servant and the idea of *difference* between them (meanings which are also encoded in the verbal text).

The lighting is a visual element which is encoded in the context of performance, but not as a deliberate semiotic feature during rehearsals. The lighting for the performance is subject to the dramatic code of naturalism: it approximates 'natural light' falling through a doorway. The result is to light the centre of the stage and to leave the sides less well lit. As Miss Julie tends to keep closer to centre stage than Jean, she appears lighter. The semiotic feature of costume enhances this effect. Jean is dressed in a black suit while Miss Julie is wearing a long pale-blue dress, which appears almost white. These visual features encode many potential meanings—solidity versus frailty, evil versus innocence, masculinity versus feminity—but can clearly be seen as again encoding the idea of a difference between Jean and Julie.

The final scene from 29 to 72

In this section, as in the play as a whole, Jean and Miss Julie are constructed both through their own and through each other's speech; as subjects they are constructed in and through language.[1] The field of discourse is constructed partly through the transitivity patterns (the types of processes and the participants associated with them). In their own speech, Jean and Miss Julie construct themselves through the transitivity patterns as the active participants—as actors, sensers, behavers and sayers. (Of course, to talk of fictional personae as constructing themselves or making choices in their discourse in this way is a fallacy: it is the playwright Strindberg, via Meyer, the translator of the edition used, who constructs them as constructing themselves. But to avoid such a circumlocution I will talk of Jean and Julie as subjects who construct themselves.)

Miss Julie also constructs her father as a 'doer' or active participant. Both Jean and Miss Julie see themselves as separate participants, as the grammatical reference shows; the exclusive pronouns 'I' and 'you' are used, not the inclusive pronoun 'we', indicating separation between self and other. The relational processes, whereby one entity is identified in relation to another or assigned a value, are crucial in this part of the text. Jean uses relational processes to introduce the paradigms of gender and class, although in an oblique and indefinite way (*If I was a lady of noble birth* . . . , 37; *There's a difference between us*, 44). Miss Julie takes up these relations and elaborates them, defining herself with regard to them. Through her lexical choices, Miss Julie's discourse sets up a clear dichotomy between the intellect (containing mostly positive or neutral terms such as *clever, learned, thought* and *idea*) and the emotions (which are mostly negative: *hated, revenged, despise, blame*). Intellect is linked explicitly to the gender paradigm of maleness, and emotions are linked to that of femaleness (Miss Julie says *I haven't a thought I didn't get from my father, not an emotion I didn't get from my mother*, 62). (See Appendix C for a diagrammatic representation of these lexical sets and the way in which they interrelate and conflict.) So while it is Jean, the male, who introduces the notion of difference into the discourse, it is the female, Miss Julie, who elaborates it, not as a difference between herself and Jean, but as one embodied within herself. She is *half woman and half man* (58); she has no unified subjectivity (*Myself? I have no self*, 60–61). Even the rhetorical mode of her speech at this point, with its dialogic series of questions posed and answered, embodies this disunity.

During the rehearsal process, the elaboration of the 'difference' is taken up in the parallel text (a rehearsal discussion, involving the director and the actor playing Jean), and is constituted as 'feminine = emotional, romantic, honourable' and 'masculine = scientific, practical, intelligent'. In the rehearsal discussion, Miss Julie is aligned with the feminine (as it is constructed here) in a far less problematic way than she is in the verbal dramatic text. In the verbal text, Miss Julie's speech suggests very strongly that gender identity is socially constructed, as opposed to being naturally intrinsic to the biological individual.[2] However, the gender ambiguity constructed in Miss Julie's speech is encoded through the semiotics of costume more strongly in rehearsals than in performance. During rehearsals, the actress's dress and hair encode a tomboyish element which reinforces the gender ambiguity; her hair is cropped fairly short and she wears a long skirt but with a loose T-shirt. While not a deliberate dramatic encoding for performance, the actress's choice of rehearsal costume is still a realisation of her orientation to the meanings in the dramatic text. In the performance, Miss Julie is constructed as much more stereotypically and intrinsically feminine through her costume, thus not reinforcing the verbal text's problematising of gender. She wears a long pale-blue dress with a tight bodice, and her hair is long and piled up with a bow. The encoding of these meanings can be traced both to the rehearsal discussions (which contribute to the construction of meanings in the performance text) and to the director's orientation towards meanings and the codes he employs, which directly affect costume codes (as well as other codes in the performance).

The tenor of discourse (the system of role relationships) in this section is realised mainly through the mood, modality and polarity systems (see above, Method). Halliday's distinction between propositions and proposals is a useful one here. In this section, Jean's and Julie's discourses consist mostly of propositions (statements and questions). The speakers are constructed as manipulating the situation through the exchange of meanings rather than by attempts to get each other to act (as in proposals). In contrast to Jean, who uses few modals (auxiliary verbs expressing speaker's attitude), Miss Julie's speech is quite highly modalised. Miss Julie uses modals of ability with negative polarity to express her own (and her father's) inability to act (*I want to do it—but I can't. My father couldn't do it, either . . .*, 48–50). However, when questioning Jean, she uses positive propositions of ability and inclination (*Can you see any way out of this . . .*, 32; *What would you do in my place?* 34). This pattern of negative meanings constructed around herself and positive meanings constructed around others such as Jean is pervasive; others act and possess certain attributes, while she herself cannot act and defines herself by what she is not (*I can't . . .*, 49; *I have no self*, 61; *I haven't a thought*, 62). Her only positive modality is that of obligation, which carries the implication of external agency rather than self-will (*I shall have to bear the blame, carry the consequences*, 71).

As well as discussing the meaning potential of the verbal text, I want to focus on the non-linguistic systems, specifically the kinesics and proxemics, which are brought into play through performance. These systems play a crucial role in the construction of meanings. Early in the scene (34–40) Miss Julie asks Jean *What would you do in my place?*. Jean replies: *In your place? Wait, now. If I was a lady—of noble birth—who'd fallen? I don't know.*

Yes. I do know. The stage directions in the written text say Miss Julie 'picks up the razor and makes a gesture', saying *This?* (41). Such a condensed verbal and kinesic semiotic act requires a great deal of over- and undercoding on the part of both actors and audience in order to make sense of what is going on. The elliptical and deictic nature of the verbal act points us towards other semiotic systems. Within the kinesic system, gesture, gaze and the position of the razor are all crucial. The razor is a particulary powerful sign. It is (in Eco's terms) an *ostension*, a showing of the class of objects it indicates, and it is also an *index*, in that it points towards a meaning of which it is only a part (that is, its meaning as an instrument of suicide, just as it functioned earlier as an index of masculinity—we see Jean shaving with it). The use of gesture—what is done with the razor—makes these meanings more explicit. Gaze also functions in an important and indicative way; who is looking at the razor, and when, indicates the way in which we are to decode Jean's elliptical *Yes. I do know* (39–40).

In the first rehearsal run of this segment, Miss Julie has already reached for the razor and has begun playing with it at 37–38, thus ostending the idea of suicide before Jean's lines *I don't know. Yes. I do know.* Jean's gaze shows he has already seen her with the razor before he says *I don't know.* His gaze is not recorded by the camera when he says *Yes. I do know.* This is followed by Miss Julie putting the razor to her wrist as she says *This?*, thus making the idea of suicide very explicit through the use of gesture. However, the first run encodes an ambiguity over who was thinking of the razor at what point, an ambiguity intensified by the lacuna in the documentation—because of Jean's position outside the frame of the video we don't see his gaze at the crucial point.

In the second run, Jean clearly does not see Miss Julie pick up the razor. At 38, he is at the front of the stage with his hands over his face. The meaning encoded in this run is that it is Miss Julie who thinks of committing suicide with no input from Jean. The loss of lines 39–40 (*Yes. I do know.*), where Miss Julie comes in too early with her line *This?*, results in an even clearer construction of Jean as innocent of suggesting the idea. The run is interrupted at this point (41); the rehearsal discussion takes up the issue of 'whose idea is it first?' and explores ways of encoding Jean as suggesting to Miss Julie that she commit suicide.

The third run then takes place, and this time the idea of Miss Julie using the razor to commit suicide is clearly encoded as

Jean's unspoken suggestion. This is done through gesture and gaze; Jean paces in front of the table as if thinking, his eye falls on the razor, he pauses and says *Yes. I do know.* Miss Julie follows his gaze, reaches for the razor, places it against her wrist and says *This?.* Jean steps back and then walks over to the scullery area (stage right), a proxemic feature which puts a distance between him and Miss Julie, encoding his disassociation with her and the contemplated act.

The performance (that is, the one recorded on a split-screen video tape, which I have taken as my 'ultimate performance') does not retain the kinesic and proxemic features of the third rehearsal run. Jean does not pace across the stage but remains in the scullery area, and is bending over the table or has his face in his hands when Miss Julie reaches for the razor, which she does while Jean is still saying he doesn't know what he'd do in her place. Again, the crucial lines *Yes. I do know.* are omitted, again probably because Miss Julie comes in too early with her line *This?.* It is not until then that Jean looks up and sees her playing with the razor, thus he is encoded again in this performance as an innocent.

Gaze is therefore an extremely significant feature in the encoding and decoding of meanings; it is indicative of whether we are to see Jean or Miss Julie as suggesting the idea of suicide. It therefore has a vital effect on the positioning of Jean, either as a cold-blooded conniver or as someone acceding to someone else's impulsions. As we've seen, the razor as Jean's idea is encoded very clearly during the rehearsal process, but has reverted to being Miss Julie's idea in the performance. It is not clear whether this was a deliberate directing decision (the documentation of rehearsal discussions doesn't suggest this).

The final scene from 73 to 171

A sudden change in the discourse takes place with the ringing of the bell (after 72). This aural sign is, like the razor, indexical. It points to the return of Miss Julie's father, with all the possible implications we can over- and undercode from this. The most striking change occurs in the tenor of discourse, in the mood and modality choices that Miss Julie and Jean begin making. A wave-like pattern of propositions (consisting of statements of inability to act) followed by proposals (consisting of positive commands to act) occurs alternately in Miss Julie's and in Jean's speech.

Powerlessness is constituted both lexically and grammatically through the combination of active processes in the transitivity patterns and modals of inability (Miss Julie's *I can't repent, can't run away, can't stay, can't live, can't die!*, 89–93). In a similar way, Power/Action is constituted through the use of active processes combined with positive imperatives (Miss Julie's *Do me this last service, save my honour, save his name!*, 97–99). However, these commands have an ambiguity which I shall examine in more detail later.

As in the earlier part of the scene, Jean and Miss Julie construct themselves as active participants in their transitivity patterns. But Miss Julie very early rejects the role of senser (one who thinks, feels or perceives). Having stated that she *can't feel anything* (88), she does not construct herself as carrying out any further mental processes throughout the rest of the scene. By contrast, Jean continues to take the role of senser in his own discourse, but his mental processes are all intellectual rather than emotional, thus aligning him with the rational masculine paradigm set up earlier. Miss Julie also assigns Jean certain roles and activity types through her own discourse. She constructs him as acting, sensing, behaving and saying, roles which Jean tries to reject by expressing his inability to carry them out (*I can't*). It is also Miss Julie who sets up the relations of identification and attribution in this scene, both with respect to Jean and to herself, and also as a means of creating a desired 'reality' through discourse. She also reintroduces the relation *The last shall be first*, which was set up earlier by Christine in her sermon-like speech (22). However, this general summary of the main meaning-making practices in this scene can only convey a limited idea of the scene's dynamics, and tends to distort what is actually happening along the syntagmatic axis, as the text unfolds. In the following discussion, I'll follow this scene through in a more linear fashion, looking at it as process.

Miss Julie's speech begins with propositions expressing her powerlessness and inability to act, which then modulate to a series of proposals—commands directed at Jean. To order is to assume a powerful role, to attempt to force someone else to act in a certain way. But the nature of the activity which Miss Julie orders Jean to enact sets up a paradoxical flow of power. She is ordering him to order her (*Order me, and I'll obey you like a dog*, 95–96). Effectively, she is commanding him to be the powerful one, and assigning herself the status of helplessness or powerlessness (*Help me!*, 94; *Save me!*, 98; *Will me!*, 102). Such paradoxical behaviour encodes the contradictory role relationships between Jean and Miss Julie at this point. Miss Julie has institutionalised power over Jean by virtue of their respective class statuses. Jean's power over Miss Julie is that of a male over a female he has seduced—it seems that circumstances have given him a contingent power. However, it is not as simple as that. Jean's power also arises from his freedom from the class value of honour which constrains Miss Julie, a freedom which is just as institutionalised, as indeed is his gender-related freedom from blame in his share of the seduction.

In response to Miss Julie's commands to take control of her, Jean in turn expresses his inability to act and to assume such power over her, an inability which he links to his institutionalised servility (104–112).

Miss Julie's response is again to command (*Then pretend that you are he and I am you*, 113). At the same time, she realigns the critical participants so that Jean becomes *his lordship* and she becomes Jean. This effectively realigns the class status; Jean becomes aristocratic and endowed with power, and Miss Julie the powerless lackey. Miss Julie makes this even more explicit when she says *You acted so well just now, when you went down on your knees—then you were an aristocrat* (114–15). The proxemics for this scene, as they are encoded during the rehearsal process, make these constantly shifting paradigms of class and power even more contradictory. Julie's and Jean's relative positions in space encode this; during rehearsals Miss Julie begins by standing facing Jean, but later sits in the centre of the floor while Jean stands. The paradox is thus heightened: Miss Julie is an aristocrat, yet down on the floor; commanding, yet giving up power; while Jean is the lackey, but he stands; he's obeying, yet receiving power (see p. 206).

Miss Julie then introduces the metaphor of the hypnotist, suggesting to Jean that he assume this role. However, she effectively enacts this role herself, with a series of declarations which effect a desired reality through her discourse (*I am already asleep . . . and so peaceful*, 122–28). During the rehearsal process, this meaning is gradually made more explicit through gaze and eye contact. Miss Julie gazes steadily at Jean, forcing him to maintain eye contact, as if hypnotising him. When Jean fulfils her commands to act by handing her the razor and commanding her to go . . . *out to the barn—and—* (130), she is again unable to act, until Jean completes the realignment of the Last–First relation which she commands of him (*You are no longer among the first.*

Jean (John Howard) and Miss Julie (Laura Williams) in the final scene from Strindberg's *Miss Julie*, University of Sydney production at the Seymour Centre, Sydney, April 1986

You are—among the last!, 139–40). This is a crucial paradigm for Miss Julie, as it defines who shall be allowed to enter heaven. As Christine formulates it, There shall the last (in a worldly sense) be first (into heaven). At Miss Julie's prompting, Jean realigns these terms so that Miss Julie is no longer among the first (in a worldly sense) but among the last, and if she's among the last, she too can enter heaven.

However, before Jean can finally command her, he traces (from the ringing of the bell at 72–73) a chain of causality outside his control, leading to his own and Miss Julie's downfall. He does this in a series of material processes whose agent (participant who initiates or causes the action) is only partially and gradually revealed. It proceeds from the metonymic a hand, to the non-human something else, to the full human participant he (162–66). Although the he is unnamed, it refers to his lordship, as the ultimate authority and the presumed origin of the causal chain.[3] The actual ringing of the bell is an aural semiotic which functions both as an ostensive sign of his lordship taking up his role as agent, and as a connotative sign of authority and inevitability. Jean finally sees no alternative but to issue the command to Miss Julie to go.

During this final scene, there has been considerable shifting in the paradigms of gender, class and power. Through the construction of Jean as a subject, what was aligned as a masculine attribute, the intellect, has become paralysed and has been rejected as a means towards power; Jean says I don't know (104), I don't understand (106), and commands Miss Julie, Don't think, don't think! You take all my strength from me (151–53). At the same time, the 'feminine' attribute of the emotions has been paralysed, through Miss Julie; she says I can't feel anything (88) and at the same time cannot act in other ways. These explicitly constructed gender paradigms are thus negated. They are then replaced in a much less explicit way, through the different meaning-making practices which Jean and Julie, as gendered subjects, adopt in order to gain the power or will to act. Miss Julie achieves some sort of resolution of her dilemma by a process of analogy; she constructs analogic relations which realign participants and values in a way that permits Jean to command and her to obey. Jean, however, constructs his resolution differently, through a rational chain of cause and effect. Jean's power to command can be seen as ultimately hollow, as it is imposed on him externally, while Miss Julie's power is constituted by an act of volition, a powerful reality-changing act, which she makes Jean participate in. Thus, while on one level Miss Julie is a victim of male power, on another she contributes in a more powerful way than does Jean to her own end. This is, of course, a highly metasemiotic reading, but one which can be made, and one which is reinforced on other semiotic levels (such as the meaning encoded through Miss Julie's hypnotic gaze in the kinesics).

Conclusion

Finally (in terms of both the performance as 'final' product and the conclusion of the play), the construction of Jean and Julie seems to suggest a misogynist reading—one which sees the woman as self-destructive. Her construction as being, on one level, more powerful than Jean, tends to work against a construction of her as victim. In this reading, the blame or responsibility thus falls to her more than to Jean, who is not responsible for his own actions.

However, the written dramatic text does not construct this as a fixed and necessary order: the balance of power is ambiguous and fluctuates constantly as the text proceeds. The transformation of the written text into a rehearsal/performance text in turn opens up these paradigms further and allows for many possible meanings to be made.

During the rehearsal-to-performance process, the rehearsal context and the orientations towards meaning of the speaking subjects (actors, director, theatre workers) are all constitutive of the theatrical text. Meanings are selected and encoded through certain semiotic systems, in ways which foreground some meanings and de-emphasise others; this is often a deliberate and explicit semiotic act which takes place in the context of rehearsal discussions. The selection of some meanings and the omission (or de-emphasis) of others necessarily has ideological implications; but at the same time the complexity of the text allows for a plurality of ideological readings. Foregrounding of certain meanings can be achieved in a theatrical text either paradigmatically, by encoding a meaning within more than one level or system, or syntagmatically, by iterating it within the same system. Both strategies may be used, for example, the notion of 'difference' in the *Miss Julie* text is encoded paradigmatically by realisations simultaneously in the verbal text and in the proxemics (44–47), while the notion of Julie's inability to act is foregrounded syntagmatically by the repetition of 'can't' in the verbal text (89–93).

Foregrounding of meanings such as these is a strategy which may invite different readings. For example, the foregrounding of apparently misogynist meanings may be a strategy for inviting criticism of, or for reasserting the authority of such meanings. Alternatively, de-emphasising misogynist meanings may be a strategy for naturalising misogyny, or for attenuating its authority. Therefore, whether or not we read the *Miss Julie* text primarily as a misogynist text depends partly on the extent to which potentially misogynist meanings are foregrounded in its construction in rehearsals and performance, and partly upon the way in which we read such strategies (that is, upon our own orientation to meaning).

One aspect of the *Miss Julie* performance text which could be read as misogynist is the deliberate choice to encode the notion of 'femininity' through Miss Julie's costume. This constitutes a syntagmatic foregrounding which contributes to her construction as a gendered subject, and one which aligns her with the negative meanings constructed and associated with femininity in the verbal text. However, at the same time as these meanings are being foregrounded, the text still defies closure; there are conflicting meanings (such as the gender ambiguity encoded in Miss Julie's speech) at this and other points in the text. The construction of Miss Julie through her far less feminine costume during rehearsals points to the multiple possibilities encoding through different systems allows, and also highlights the implications of choosing to encode one meaning ('femininity') rather than another ('gender ambiguity') through a semiotic system such as costume. While such a strategy may invite a misogynist reading at one level, the conflicts within such a complex text work towards deconstructing it simultaneously at other levels. The reading of such a complex text is constrained but not ultimately defined by such foregrounding strategies (whatever their 'intention').

In conclusion, the paradigms of gender, class and power do not have fixed or static meanings, but dynamic meanings constructed through the interactions and interrelations of speaking subjects (constructed dramatis personae, actors, director and us, the audience). These meanings are set up initially through the written text, which retains a certain authority and fixity (probably because of the acting and directing codes involved, which seem to be oriented towards the primacy of the written text). However, the interaction between the verbal text and other semiotic systems which takes place during rehearsals and performances allows these meanings to be elaborated, made more explicit, shifted or even contradicted. These shifting and conflicting meanings defy any single 'reading' of this text in terms of its 'message'.

This chapter has drawn on conceptual dichotomies such as text/context and product/process; however, during the discussion of this complex text the boundaries of these dichotomies have tended to blur and even dissolve at times. This seems to me a necessary condition of the exploration of the systems and practices (both of production and reception) of this particular semiotic activity—the rehearsal/performance text.

12 Scientific constructions, cultural productions: scientific narratives of sexual attraction

Gisela T. Kaplan and Lesley J. Rogers

THERE IS today a great deal of evidence which moves away from the discrete polarisation into male and female categories which we have lived with for so long and which still constrains our thinking on the subject. People are assigned to the male and female sex according to the morphology of their genitalia. On the basis of this division there is an assumed biological underpinning which not only causes a host of secondary, physical differences between the sexes, but is assumed to cause sex differences in behaviour as well. As the understanding of the function of sex hormones and their effect on brain development has grown, it is becoming increasingly clear that the once-thought major biological differences between male and female are no longer so clear-cut, and that biology has responded to the cultural division placed upon the male and female sex (Bleier 1984; Rogers 1981).

Equally doubtful, therefore, must be the commonly held assumption that sexual attraction in heterosexual relationships results entirely from sex characteristics of the opposite sex. As

Hoult (1984) has pointed out, the biological model is inappropriate to an understanding of human sexuality, be it in terms of sexual actions per se, sexual orientation or gender identities. Sexual attraction has been channelled by most societies into a consciousness limited by cultural and social practices, although there are, of course, cultures which have placed less emphasis and different emphases on individual sex characteristics (Ford and Beach, 1951).

We suggest that the attraction of one person to another is guided by a variety of stimuli which are little concerned with any absolute male/female dichotomy. Overt gender signals may well reflect as closely as possible biological sex; however, there are covert signals and biological attributes which may either run counter to acceptable notions of masculinity and femininity or have nothing to do with either. We propose the thesis of an attraction to a mix of male and female characteristics.

We have argued elsewhere (Kaplan and Rogers, 1984) that sexual attraction is stronger to individuals who show a mix of male and female physical characteristics and of masculine and feminine behavioural traits. Most people have a mixture of male and female characteristics, both physical and behavioural. Recognition of this fact raises the question about what exactly we mean by 'male' and 'female' characteristics, and indeed whether the terms are at all useful or appropriate. In other words, a male may respond to a female not only because some of her physical and behavioural attributes are 'feminine' but because some of them are distinctly 'masculine', and vice versa. Bem (1974) has argued that behavioural masculinity and femininity should be measured as separate behavioural dimensions, not as opposite poles of a single continuum, as individuals may display behaviour which is both very masculine and very feminine. We wish to draw attention to the fact that the same intermingling of male and female characteristics may occur within an individual's physical features.

Our concept of the mix is thus not used as implying a levelling out of, and taking away from, maleness and femaleness. It is rather that both male and female attributes strongly assert themselves side by side and are received as stimuli in this way. Our concept is not to be confused with 'androgyny', commonly used to indicate a fusion of maleness and femaleness into a unified whole by way of minimising primary and secondary sexual attributes of both sexes (see Fig. 1 as an illustration of androgyny). The concept of androgyny certainly has its place,

The Little Fisherman by Pierre Puvis de Chavennes (1824–98)

but, if accepted as the only reference to a mix, obscures the real events precipitating and facilitating attraction of one individual to another.

It has long been known by artists of Eastern and Western cultures that the mix can be exploited very effectively in just about any art form. We will give some examples of artistic representation of the mix through the ages and in a number of cultures in order to demonstrate our suggestion that the persistent rendering of double gender messages is indeed related to the attraction to the mix, and the artist's awareness of such an attraction.

The painting of Bacchus by Caravaggio (Fig. 2) illustrates our definition of the sexual mix. The shoulder and arm muscles of Bacchus, as well as the exposed part of the chest, are strong displays of male characteristics. At the same time the gown draped over the right part of his torso, the graceful way of holding a goblet and especially the soft features of his face are indicative of female characteristics. According to Greek mythology, Bacchus (Dionysus) was the god of fertility and ecstasy and later also of wine. Interestingly, he was always considered the opponent and competitor of Apollo, the god of love. Bacchus was a lover of men but women loved him with such frenzy that they celebrated orgies in his honour. This aspect of the Bacchus myth, namely his extraordinary ability to sexually attract men and women alike, must have inspired Caravaggio. Very cleverly, he has worked into his painting an explanation of why Bacchus could be thought of as so attractive by both sexes. In very early representations Dionysus is depicted as a bearded man and in later centuries as a young man wearing an animal skin, accompanied by a panther. Instead of these male images, Caravaggio chose to endow him with male and female attributes and to let him rest on a pillow in this rather seductive pose, heightening further his sensuality and sexual attractiveness. In this painting, Caravaggio has rendered some of the complexities of human attraction that have little to do with stereotyped female/male models. The photograph of the singer 'Boy George', taken almost 400 years after Caravaggio's Bacchus was painted has been placed alongside the Bacchus in order to illustrate a rather striking similarity in posture and transmission of the mix.

The form in which the open enjoyment of the mix has been most often reified in non-Western and Western cultures alike is no doubt the theartrical arts. We are not suggesting that the open enjoyment of the male/female mix is the only factor which has

Bacchus by Michelangelo Merisi, known as Caravaggio (1560–1609)

The singer Boy George

led to theatre practices reflecting this interest. Complicated factors of economy, power, in many cases the oppression of women, and various other issues have contributed to the rise and maintenance of certain forms of stage performances and personalities. We need to take note, however, that, despite enormous differences of circumstances, of cultural context and time, there is much evidence in Western and non-Western cultures of a strong interest in plots and characters involving disguise across biological sex.

The theatre, in its capacity to present visual images in the context of action carried out in three-dimensional areas, has the advantage that anything happening on its chosen platform is, by definition, only an imitation of what it represents. The theatre is the place in which conscious illusions are created. The actors, as audiences know, are in real life not what they represent on stage. The make-believe world of the theatre, used for entertainment, for teaching and for political purposes, is also the place in which illusions to real life need not be rendered innocuous or carefully masked as they must be, say, in a scholarly work, a treatise or a report. It sets itself up as being removed from reality and therefore often takes the liberty of saying and exposing what might otherwise not be permissible. The non-verbal messages and visual stimuli can also be such that they become acceptable in the stage setting even if, in real life, they would be unacceptable or a threat. The enjoyment of the male/female mix falls perhaps most readily into this latter category.

Breeches roles for women and transvestite roles for men began to become part of the repertoire in Western culture once theatre was permitted and freed from the church's influence in the sixteenth and early seventeenth centuries. Michelene Wandor (1981:19) argues that transvestite theatre 'has flourished at times of changing attitudes to women in the theatre and to sexuality in society—the Restoration, the Industrial Revolution, the suffrage agitation and now, in the second half of the twentieth century. At such times clearly there is a tension between the surface appearance and how men and women are supposed to 'be' and the changing reality.' This explanation is an attractive one in a sense of highlighting that theatre may well respond to social changes by experimenting with extremes of such change, such as role reversals would be. However, examples of cross-dressing are not confined to the periods she specifies and are not less numerous, or at least not less important, in other periods.

One of the best known examples of an early breeches role is that of Viola, travelling as Cesario, in Shakespeare's *Twelfth Night*, written and performed in 1601, and based on an Italian comedy of 1531 (Halliday, 1964). Viola has been separated from her twin brother Sebastian during a shipwreck and is now in search of him, dressed up as Cesario. She goes on shore in Illyria and finds a job as page in the service of the Duke of Orsino who is suffering from unrequited love for Olivia, a rich countess. As Viola/Cesario takes on the role of go-between for the suitor, Olivia falls in love with Viola/Cesario while Viola herself has fallen in love with the duke. The audience is aware of Viola's disguise and can therefore relish the confusion in the relationships of Cesario and Orsino, and Cesario and Olivia: Olivia pining for the disguised Viola and the supposed Cesario blushing and making eyes at Orsino. The problem of the difference between appearance of clothes and physique is cleverly exploited by Shakespeare, and verbalised on several occasions. Orsino, for instance, is intrigued by Cesario and says:

> *they shall yet belie thy happy years,*
> *That say thou art a man: Diana's lip*
> *Is not more smooth and rubious; thy small pipe*
> *Is as the maiden's organ, shrill and sound;*
> *And all is semblative a woman's part.* (I, iv, 32–36)

The reference to sexual characteristics and the slippery use of metaphors to highlight the ambivalence of Viola/Cesario is readily understandable and engenders laughter in the audience. The question of reality and dream in relation to biological sex and gender role is later well put by Viola:

> *She loves me, sure. If it be so, as 'tis*
> *Poor lady, she were better love a dream.* (II, ii, 2–2)

The narrow confinement to socio-cultural roles has in fact not disappeared in the play: Olivia is capable of loving Viola but can do so only because she believes her to be a young, attractive male. However, the audience has a much broader perspective than the protagonists in the play, for it is aware of the crossing of roles. In a sense, Olivia loves an illusion, the nonexistent Cesario, but at the same time she loves this one particular and very much present image of Viola in men's clothes or of Cesario with feminine features. Ironically, this is what the Duke had predicted, if not for features of sex alone, but also for age, when he says to Viola:

> *. . . unfold the passion of my love;*
> *Surprise her with discourse of my dear faith:*
> *It shall become thee well to act my woes:*
> *She will attend it better in thy youth*
> *Than in a nuncio of more grave aspects.* (I, iv, 25–29)

This point is brought out later when Sebastian, Viola's twin brother, has been found and, luckily, is so much the image of Viola that he keeps being mistaken for her, i.e. for Cesario. He can replace Viola and now fulfil the role of Olivia's lover once Viola is discovered in her true sexual identity. Olivia can love Sebastian precisely because he is so much like her, and while he may well be second choice, he is the only choice Olivia has. Shakespeare has used women in men's roles quite often, for instance Julia in *The Two Gentlemen of Verona*, Portia in *The Merchant of Venice*, Helena in *All's Well That Ends Well*, or Rosalind's impersonation of Ganymede in *As You Like It*. It must also be remembered that women's parts were generally still taken by boys. Shakespeare's heroines in disguise were thus boys pretending to be women pretending to be men (Muir, 1970), a double entendre in the play with gender that the male-to-female disguise lacked at a time when all roles were filled by males.

Lesser known authors, and not just in England, used cross-dressing as an effective tool in their comedies throughout the seventeenth century. One such example occurs in *Arabella*, written in 1642 by the Duke of Brunswick. By no means does it reach the artistic standard of any of Shakespeare's plays, but it deals with cross-dressing in an interesting and complex way. Here, a man having had to disguise himself as a woman and a woman disguised as a man meet and fall in love. Finally, they are exposed and get married. The patterns of sexual attraction are quite complex, for the woman knows that she is a woman but believes the diguised man to be a woman, and vice versa. Lesbian, homosexual and narcissistic elements as well as a continuous exploitation of the attraction to the mix play into the plot, observable by the audience and intermittently suspected by the protagonists.

It seems that neither class differences nor the degree of social change at the time of the performance of a play are necessarily indices of the possible enjoyment of the mix or for the occurrence of cross-dressing in the theatre. The plays by Shakespeare were performed to a wide cross-section of the English (London) public, including the poorer people, the well-to-do merchants and the aristocracy (Salingar, 1970). The play by the Duke of Brunswick, by contrast, was limited to an aristocratic audience. While Elizabethan England showed signs of accelerated social mobility and change, the German dukedoms and principalities of the 1650s, where there was also a theatrical interest in cross-dressing, showed little change in social structures, although in practice the Thirty Years War had undermined some of the moral values held at the time (Kaplan, 1984).

If we do not confine ourselves to spoken stagecraft but include ballet, opera and also film in the performing arts, the evidence of cross-dressing and double-play with gender becomes even more pronounced. Opera, with its combination of acting and singing, was able to add auditory to the visual stimuli and thus take the disguise, gender confusion and cross-dressing a step further. In its beginnings, it did so by the introduction of castrati, singing at a voice level of soprano and contralto. Moreover, castrati sang both male and female roles. The castrati were very important figures in Western opera, right from its beginnings in 1607 when castrati first appeared in Monteverdi's *Orfeo* until around 1800 when their use was prohibited for humanitarian reasons. In these two centuries they often achieved prominence and they were increasingly afforded great power (often political) and wealth. The castrati are said to have been impressive figures on stage, tall and broad-chested (Heriot, 1956:27), and they were extremely popular in roles, even tragic ones, in which they portrayed female characters. They were in such demand in the eighteenth century that as many as 70 per cent of all male singers were estimated to have been castrati, at a time when there was no dearth of female singers (Heriot, 1956:31). Goethe (1749–1832), one of Germany's most eloquent poets at the time made special mention of these castrati: 'I reflected on the reason why these singers pleased me so greatly, and I think I have found it. In these representations, the concept of imitation and of art was invariably more strongly felt, and through their able performance a sort of conscious illusion was produced. Thus the double pleasure is given, in that these persons are not women, but only represent women' (cit. in Heriot, 1956:26). When Silberberg made a film of Wagner's opera *Parsifal* recently, he was obviously playing with this tradition but reversing the sex, a feat that could never be carried out in live theatre: here Parsifal, once having reached adolescence, is played by a woman but continues to be sung in a male voice. Interestingly, *Der Rosenkavalier* by Strauss (1911) uses sex-role disguise in much the same way that Shakespeare used it in his plays. The part of Octavian is played by a soprano and Octavian disguises himself as a woman in order to entrap and expose another male character.

In ballet, the role of Franz in Delibes' *Coppelia* was first danced by a woman when performed in 1870. Tchaikovsky's *Nutcracker Suite* contains a pantomime role of the Old Woman who Lived in a Shoe, to be danced by a male. Vladimir Yakovlav even wore a moustache in this role with the overt intention of showing the female-male mix (Warrack, 1973:258). Apart from these examples and the comedies which continued to use cross-dressing, the melodrama made its appearance on European stages at the close of the eighteenth century, at once including cross-dressing in its repertoire. In the twentieth century, the medium of film has continued to exploit, often in novel ways, the presentation of the mix. The film historian Homer Dickens, in his book *What a Drag*, has examined more than 200 cinematic treatments of cross-dressing in films from the 1920s onwards. Today, plays and films continue to be written and produced incorporating cross-dressing (Engel, 1985). Likewise, there are now a good number of individual performers and entertainers whose success is linked with or based on cross-dressing, like Boy George and Danny de la Rue.

We agree with Gabrielle Hyslop (1985) that cross-dressing was still, as late as the nineteenth century, often used as a comic device in the theatre that neither challenged nor undermined conservative values and traditional mores but reassured and reaffirmed them even if, within such a context, albeit limited, it may have contained a rebellion against conformity. This is as true for Shakespeare and the seventeenth-century playwrights as for Pixerécourt, the deeply conservative popular French dramatist who 'invented' melodrama (Hyslop, 1985).

Eastern Cultures also have well-entrenched theatrical traditions and cultural practices of cross-dressing and of the representation of the mix. Space does not permit us to delve into elaborations on these, let alone on other cultures around the globe, although examples are plentiful. We shall confine ourselves here to two examples, the Chinese traditional opera and the Japanese Kabuki theatre.

The main characters in the Kabuki Theatre are the female *onnogata* played by highly trained male actors. Even in present-day Japan these actors have a cult following. The Kabuki theatre originally developed in Kyoto in the early seventeenth century with an all-female cast. The word Kabuki denotes 'to be unusual' or 'out of the ordinary', with the connotation of sexual debauchery and, indeed, most actresses were also prostitutes. An injunction of 1629 would almost have ended the Kabuki theatre had it not been saved as an art form by some determined males who took over all the roles (Ernst, 1956), the female roles being played by beautiful young boys. These boys were so revered and admired that samurai fell in love with them and, after a public brawl between two samurai, this form of Kabuki theatre was also banned. The reopening of the theatre was granted on the condition that the *onnogata* cut their hair, wore wigs on stage and indicated to the audience by subtle hand movements that they were in fact males. It is in this latter form that the Kabuki theatre has survived to the present day.

As most Western observers of the Kabuki Theatre are unable to read the subtle hand and body movements indicating the maleness of the *onnogata*, the attraction of the male-female mix escapes them. Of course, this is not so for Japanese audiences, for whom the *onnogata* are special favourites, spurred on noisily with calls of enthusiasm, appreciation and support throughout the performance. Such extrovert enthusiam has to be regarded as significant in a society which tends to be otherwise very reserved in public expression of emotions of any kind. Since all other actors are equally well trained and experienced, it cannot be argued that the *onnogata* performers please particularly critical theatregoers. Here, obviously, it is important that these males have learned to portray the female convincingly. Aesthetic enjoyment aside, the admiration is likely to have a basis in the male-female double message.

In Chinese opera, we also find female impersonators. Their history within the Chinese opera, however, is considered to be longer than that of the *onnogata*, and the reasons for their appearance are likely to be different as well. Female impersonators have appeared in Chinese opera performances since ancient times, very often because emperors intermittently forbade stage appearances of males and females together (Mackerras, 1972:45) This was particularly so in the eighteenth century (Alley, 1957). The practice of males playing the female, or *tan*, roles has survived to the present day, although the restrictions placed upon the sex of actors are no longer applied. Many Western observers are unaware of this fact.

We do not know whether the actors of these female roles use or used any subtle signals to indicate their maleness to the Chinese audience or whether such special signals were in fact needed. For several ancient theatre performances the novelty and interest did not lie in the plot, which was already known (as for instance, in ancient Greek theatre) but in the way the story was told. We therefore tend to think that the audience, by whatever means, had the knowledge of the disguise. The Chinese opera has a stock of several stylised female roles: the young, the old, the naive and the dissolute as well as the female warrior. There are operas such as *The Iron Bow* in which we find the convoluted situation of a male actor playing the female role of Chen Xiuying who then, within the play, takes on the disguise of a man, goes to battle, overwhelming a battalion of troops in order to avenge 'her' husband!

The Chinese custom of forbidding men and women to perform together on stage also led to the formation of all-female acting troops. In these, the women played the male parts, *sheng*, but little is written about this reverse situation. However, there is a report that one actress in the female Shuang-chi'ng Company

A male performer of a female role in the Peking Opera

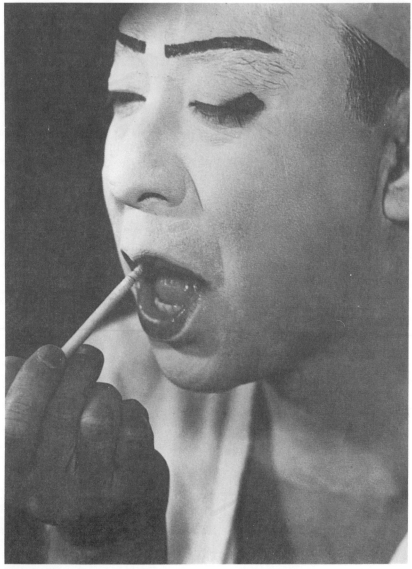

An *onnogata* actor (Onoe Baiko, VIII) applying his makeup

played the parts of beardless young men and scholar-lovers and in them she 'strongly resembled a man' (Mackerras, 1972:73).

While cross-gender disguise in Japan and China seems to have arisen, as it often did in Western countries, out of a need created by social conventions and restrictions at various times, we argue that its persistence beyond any of these restrictions up to the present day has been possible because, among other things, it generated an added attraction of its own, namely the attraction of the double message of male and female. The double message, which came about by default in its inception, was later kept alive by design.

It must be noted that in both the Kabuki Theatre and the Chinese Opera cross-gender disguise occurs in serious plots, while cross-dressing, in Western cultures, is a stock-in-trade of comedies, farces and melodramas. On Eastern stages, it has no trace of 'sending up' the female role as one may find in some modern drag shows. A similar serious interest in cross-gender disguise in the Western traditions has only occurred in the opera of the seventeenth century and marginally up to today.

Clearly, the function of cross-dressing in any of the performance arts, past and present, may have been different each time and we do not suggest minimising the complexity of this or simplifying historical perspectives and social contexts. We have also barely touched upon, and cannot here expand, on the fact that male-to-female and female-to-male cross-dressing may have signified very different things in terms of the interpretation of a given piece of performance art. However, on one level of psychological response, cross-dressing has undoubtedly an appeal to the audience, precisely because of the double message of the portrayal of the protagonists. It would be difficult to conceive of its continuing popularity through the ages otherwise.

If there has been a significant change in cross-dressing in the performing arts, it is that the use of the disguise has sometimes moved from merely being a theatrical *device* to becoming the very subject matter of the plot, as for instance in the film *Tootsie* or in such plays as *Torch Song Trilogy* and now *Eugenia Falleni*. The latter, written and performed first in 1986, is based on the true story of an Italian woman who came to Australia as a stowaway at the end of the nineteenth century, disguised as a man. She lived as a man and married twice, murdering her first wife after the discovery of her true sexual identity. Eugenia Falleni was sentenced to death, but her sentence was converted to life imprisonment and later she was released and died, after a few lonely years as a handyman, in Sydney in 1939. The story is tragic on several levels (Croft and McCallum, 1986). To such subject matter and to the treatment of cross-dressing, Homer Dickens (Engel, 1985) suggests that drag 'has gone from entertainment to reality'. But what reality? The action is still happening on the screen and on stage. The fascination and even titillation with the mix can be indulged in from the safety of the anonymity of a nameless audience and in the knowledge of the illusory and transient nature of a performance. The pleasure is not derived from a fusion of male and female attributes into one perfect form (as in androgyny) but from the assertion of both side by side. The intention of cross-dressing is ambivalence, cross-cutting categories that, in everyday life, are well-fixed and reified. On stage, for shows and popular culture even in the most repressed cultures, there is undeniable pleasure from the double entendre. In the real world, an exaggeration of the mix, of which most of us have some, might even be regarded as a threat or an abomination. There is as yet comparatively little tolerance for a shift away from rigidly defined gender roles in real life.

The challenge to the conventional restrictions of gender roles is of a very recent date. Some defenders and makers of this challenge are marked as outsiders, at least in our Western world, namely transvestites and transsexuals for whom the question of gender and sex with its contradictions and limitations is a matter of high priority and a necessary consciousness. For Jan Morris, a male-to-female transsexual, for instance, sex is a physical state while gender represents 'the inner consciousness—abstraction, not anatomy' (Morris, 1984). In a transvestite photographic exhibition, one photographer (Allen, 1984) writes:

> The primary emphasis of this exhibition is on the
> Transvestite, the man who yearns for femininity in his
> search for wholeness. Drag offers a way of playing
> with the illusion of femininity in consort with an
> audience that always knows the score. For the
> transsexual, it is the body's maleness itself that
> represents the ultimate illusion. If beauty is in the eye
> of the beholder, whether the beholder is in the outside
> world or a person looking into his or her mirror,
> beauty remains for all of us an illusion. The same can be
> said for masculinity and femininity. They are outward

*trappings that make a person appear to be male or
female.*

*And in the surgically advanced era in which we live,
anatomy itself becomes an illusion.*

*But the greatest illusion is that our sex determines
how we are supposed to conduct our lives.*

When long-cherished notions relating to the supposed 'naturalness' of behaviour according to biological sex are put into
question, doubts must arise about the 'truths' peddled about
biological sex and the whole societal framework constructed
around it. The experimentation with gender, with cross-dressing,
with role-reversals has now left the stage and become a social
issue, not for the sake of entertainment but for the sake of self-
assertion, (Glickman, 1985) not just for outsider or minority
groups but for any man or woman.

Evidence such as we have presented, which moves away from
the discrete polarisation into male and female characteristics,
points out that sexual attraction is indeed a much more complex
phenomenon than the simple male/female dichotomy suggests.
Recent scientific endeavours highlight the fact that the categorisations, for so long taken for granted, are not always meaningful,
especially when behavioural and physiological observations are
extrapolated from culturally existing forms which, in turn
obscure our understanding of the processes of sexual attraction.

Only recently have scientists come to realise that the male/
female dichotomy is not absolute. The scientific definition of
what is a male and what is a female has now become an issue,
facilitated by the development of techniques to genetically sex-
type individuals. It was consequently discovered that some
individuals are, for example, genetically male but female in
physical appearance (i.e. those with androgen insensitivity) and
that the cellular and hormonal factors once thought to be
distinctly different between the sexes are now known not to be so
clearly differentiated.

Our biology makes less distinction between the sexes than
does our social world. We know that biological factors contribute
to the determination of the physical characteristics of sex, the
construction of the genitalia and a number of other physical
traits. However, it is not a direct, invariant or unbroken chain of
causation from genotype (XX in the female or XY in the male) via
sex hormone levels to either the female or male phenotype
(physical type). Biology does not make a discrete choice between

227

one set of causal events which lead to a male phenotype or another set of events which lead to a female phenotype. Variation enters the system at all levels along the process of differentiation, and this results in a broad range of morphological (structural), physiological and behavioural characteristics in genetic 'males' and 'females'. Indeed, as vom Saal (1983) has stated, it is the very fact that sexual differentiation is affected by sex hormone levels that guarantees marked variation in phenotype.

The differentiation of sexual behaviour is no longer considered to be a unidimensional process (Olsen, 1983). Hormonal research has shown that 'masculinisation' and 'feminisation' are independent processes. 'Male'-type and 'female'-type behavioural characteristics can exist within the one brain.

Despite these findings, research scientists are only just beginning to see beyond the limits of channelled thinking, and it is not surprising that the tradition of psychomedical thinking is still largely locked within its narrow confines. There are some influential scientists in this area who still base their hypotheses on a simplistic interpretation of research with animals and on simplistic notions of human behaviour. Money and Ehrhardt (1972) and Dorner (1983) for example, have claimed that, in humans, sex differences in behaviour are caused by the action of hormones in the developing brain, and that the choice is to be either male or female. They have also claimed that abnormalities in sex hormone levels during development cause homosexuality, transvestism and, in the extreme case, transsexualism. These three variations on behaviour are placed along a continuum of increasing deviance caused by increasing hormonal imbalance, despite the fact that there is no evidence for the latter and that there is no continous behavioural variable which links the three behaviours. Behavioural variation, such as cross-dressing, is thus, in their view, a medical abnormality with a biological 'cause', to be confined, 'cured' and eliminated (Kaplan and Rogers, 1985).

The inquiry into the true nature of sexual attraction (at the perceptual end) has likewise been hampered by the male/female dichotomy and by the associated assumption of genitalia-based sexual identity. So far, most psychologists have considered sexual attraction only as a matter to be extrapolated from sexual practice (i.e. the response end) and thus have accepted, and mistaken, social norms for biological reality.

Despite such repressive theories, and despite the fact that many scientists have been tardy in recognising the lack of a sexually absolute dichotomy—as recently exemplified by the

BBC film *The Fight to be Male*—it is also known today that there is no proven biological cause for sex differences in behaviour. In any known mammalian species, 'maleness' and 'femaleness' and 'femininity' and 'masculinity' are not opposite ends of a polarity. This polarity has been a human construct, not one caused by biology but a conceptualisation which has been stamped upon biology. In other words, the male/female dichotomy is an illusion, a societal construct.

We have argued elsewhere (Kaplan and Rogers, 1984) that the separate dimensions of masculinity and femininity in one individual in behavioural terms, as Bem (1974) had suggested, can be extended to physical characteristics. As we showed, this makes biological sense as well. Individuals may possess some physical characteristics considered feminine and others masculine. The combined physical characteristics, including secondary sex characteristics, of males and females overlap significantly. Physical characteristics, moreover, in our social world, are linked to the choice of clothing that the individual uses for the portrayal of his/her identity. The form of dress can either exaggerate, conceal, or be incongruous (in cultural terms) with male or female physical characteristics (Kaplan and Rogers, 1984), as judged on the basis of the individual's particular makeup and the contemporary cultural norms (Harre, 1981).

It seems to us that the artist has stepped in at the point of the puzzling incongruity between social norms and actual behaviours and has intuitively formulated these irrationalities long before science began to investigate questions of maleness and femaleness or of sexual attraction systematically. The theatre presents human frailty and human folly. In comedies, we can laugh at the mistakes of the protagonists. In the case of mistaken identities and socially disapproved attraction, the question is whether we are laughing at the foolish error of mistaking the sex of an actor or whether we are not also laughing with the actors about the possibility that human attraction to a mix is happening despite and beyond the narrow, conventional dictates of the day. Art has asked for centuries what science has only recently begun to investigate.

In 1975 Gagnon declared that the issue of what, in behavioural terms, constitutes a man or a woman is an open question. Meanwhile, his question has expanded to include the phenotype, i.e. physical features as well, while the issue of sexual attraction has largely been left unprobed. It is our contention that sexual attraction is much more complex than traditional psychologists and physiologists suggest.

traction is much more complex than traditional psychologists and physiologists suggest.

Common sense should tell us that sexual attraction is not dependent on our creation of stereotyped females and males. On the contrary, had the human species not adapted to the reality of some degree of the mix, sexual attraction could not occur in most cases. However, sexual attraction is clearly not an area of common sense, nor, for that matter, are the constructs for social existence. We are convinced of the vast human capacity to respond to stimuli. The question is to what extent the human species has permitted itself to respond to these and in which context. By definition, selective perception, carefully guided by socialisation processes, neglects certain inputs. Artists and performers have used this negation of the complexity involved in the attraction to the mix to their advantage. Throughout history and today, the transcendence of gender identification, the purposeful confusion of expected elements of the male and female types in the theatre, in fine arts and in dance has had large followings, often by the same people who would, in real life, totally refuse to admit their fascination, even titillation with such a mix.

13 The privileging of representation and the marginalising of the interpersonal: a metaphor (and more) for contemporary gender relations

Cate Poynton

Il est, selon nous, dangereux d'établir d'avance une distinction entre des éléments grammaticaux d'un côté et certains autres qu'on appelle extra-grammaticaux de l'autre, entre un langage intellectuel et un langage affectif. Les éléments dits extra-grammaticaux ou affectifs peuvent en effet obéir aux règles grammaticales, en partie peut-être à des règles grammaticales qu'on n'a pas encore réussi à dégager. (Hjelmslev, 1928:240, cited from Stankiewicz, 1964:241)

M Y STARTING point is a range of linguistic phenomena which have not always been paid adequate attention descriptively and/or theoretically, looked at from the perspective of a systemic-functional model of language as social semiotic. From this perspective, the phenomena in question are identifiable as related in terms of structure and meaning, or function in context, under the general label of the interpersonal. They include: the organisation of conversation in terms of speech or conversational roles, including the relation of congruence or incongruence between speech function (speech act) choices, such as statement or command, and the grammatical (mood) choices which realise them; a range of aspects of lexical choice, including terms of address, slang, swearing and attitudinal lexis; and a range of 'expressive' phonological features, such as lengthening, speech rate, voice quality, pitch range in intonation contours and loudness or intensity, coding what has variously been referred to as feeling, emotion, evaluation or affect.

Many of these features have, of course, been identified as significant in the negotiation of social relations, especially in the influential work of Brown and Levinson on politeness (1978); in the literature on language and gender (see Thorne, Kramarae and Henley, 1983 for an extensive annotated bibliography), and in the now extensive literature on address, following in the footsteps of the pioneering work of Roger Brown and his colleagues (Gilman and Brown, 1958; Brown and Gilman, 1960: Brown and Ford, 1964. See Philipsen and Huspek, 1985 and Braun, Kohz and Schubert, 1986 for recent bibliographies). While such features have been recognised, however, and their social significance acknowledged, this has frequently been on terms which either ignore the place of this work within a theory of language, or else simultaneously acknowledge its significance and marginalise it by maintaining a rigorous boundary between the realms of 'syntax' and 'pragmatics', or 'linguistics' and 'sociolinguistics'.

Other interpersonal features have been identified as primarily personal, rather than interpersonal, under such labels as 'expressive' or 'emotive'. Central here are various 'expressive' aspects of phonology (stress, intensity, lengthening, etc.), of morphology (especially diminutive and augmentative affixation), and of lexis (slang, personal names, attitudinal lexis). Such features have not uncommonly been assigned a very marginal status indeed, if they have not been totally excluded as properly 'linguistic'. Concerning names, for example, Hudson suggests that, as the main markers of power and solidarity in English, they 'might fairly be described as peripheral to the system of English as a whole, in the sense that proper names used as vocatives . . . could be handled in a separate section of the grammar with little or no consequence for any other parts of it' (Hudson, 1980:125). And Markey makes a more far-reaching claim regarding their linguistic status, questioning whether names ought even to be regarded as linguistic items since they 'do not share the developmental properties of "normal" grammatical items ... [and] are peripheral to concerns which lie at the core of the theoretical investigation of language' (Markey, 1982:141). From a much more sympathetic perspective, Edward Stankiewicz, in a paper which describes a range of expressive phenomena in a number of European languages, notes that what he calls 'the emotive function ... and its peculiarities are still the least studied in linguistic works, despite repeated attempts on the part of some linguists to lift them from the limbo of grammatical appendices, footnotes or lists of exceptions.' (Stankiewicz, 1964:240). He sees part of the cause of this neglect as a tendency 'to confuse the instinctive nature of "sound-gestures" with what can properly be considered as the linguistic dimension of "expressiveness" or of the emotive function' (p.239), i.e. a failure to distinguish adequately between 'an "emotional" plane, which reveals itself in a variety of articulated or non-articulated "forms" of a symptomatic nature, that is through signals which are inextricably bound to the situation which evokes them and which they evoke, and the "emotive" plane, which is rendered through situationally independent, arbitrary symbols.' (p.240). He also suggests a historical basis for contemporary attitudes, going back to the 'neo-idealist' response to nineteenth-century Neogrammarianism: 'The mistrust of the phenomenon called "emotive language" can also be explained by the exaggerated attention it received in some linguistic quarters, which treated it as a panacea for all the shortcomings of nineteenth-century linguistics.' He goes on to give the following account:

> *The stylistic approach to emotive or 'expressive' language received a notable impetus with the crisis of the neogrammarian method ... The indictment of the deterministic and naturalistic program of the Neogrammarians took a variety of directions in the work of the so-called 'neo-idealistic' students of language ... All of them proclaimed the supremacy of individual innovation, the importance of psychological forces in the development of language, and the primacy of emotion over the 'intellectual', mechanical aspect of language and over the 'blindness' of the phonetic law ... The rejection of the neogrammarian*

method was accompanied by an interest in those areas
of grammar which seemed to 'leak'; i.e., in individual
deviations from the norm, in substandard speech, in
poetic language, in stylistics. All these areas of language
were supposed to provide evidence for the superiority
of emotive and subjective language over cognitive and
objective language. Despite the undeniable merits of
these scholars in accumulating stylistic and occasionally
linguistic material pertaining to emotive language, the
theoretical premises and philosophical mystique of the
linguistic 'expressionists' must be considered wrong-
headed from a modern point of view. The neo-
idealists . . . ignored or blurred the difference between
language and speech, code and message, or, in de
Saussure's terms, 'langue' and 'parole', directing the
attention only to the latter.

The methodological impressionism of the neo-
idealistic school, together with a programmatic
insistence on the primacy and non-systematic
character of emotion in the functioning and history of
language, have actually stood in the way of
recognising emotive language as a legitimate area of
linguistic research. Its treatment as a kind of 'contre-
grammaire', and its identification with individual
deviations, were self-defeating for linguistics as a
science. The harmfulness of this approach was voiced
early by Hjelmslev: 'Il est, selon nous, dangereux
d'établir d'avance une distinction entre des éléments
grammaticaux d'un côté et certains autres qu'on
appelle extra-grammaticaux de l'autre, entre un langage
intellectuel et un langage affectif. Les éléments dits
extra-grammaticaux ou affectifs peuvent en effet obéir
aux règles grammaticales, en partie peut-être à des
règles grammaticales qu'on n'a pas encore réussi à
dégager' ([Hjelmslev, 1928]:240).

To the opponents of the neogrammarian method,
'stylistics' seemed the road to the 'life' of language, to its
quivering essence, but, in effect, they did not abandon
the main tenets of the Neogrammarians: their
historicism which viewed language only in a state of
flux, their psychologism which recognized as 'real' only

the speech of the individual, and the atomistic
approach to linguistic facts. The question of emotive
language was, in fact, posited not with relation to
linguistic systems, but from the point of view of
contextual variation, of the possibilities of the
message. However, the expressive resources of the
message must be distinguished from the expressive
devices of the code, even if these do interact both
synchronically and diachronically. The confusion of
these two dimensions has not been avoided even by
some structural linguists, who are inclined to treat all
emotive phenomena as a problem of parole, rather
than of langue. (Stankiewicz, 1964:240–42)

The contemporary marginalising of interpersonal features is
hardly surprising given the negative value assigned to the
emotions, the realm of feeling, in contemporary Western culture
and the primacy of the referential within linguistics itself. The
effects have been unfortunate, most significantly in imposing
arbitrary limits on notions of 'language' as a human phenomenon
and of 'linguistics' as the study of that phenomenon. An arbitrary
separation of the two faces of language—as code and as social
practice, as system and process—has been fostered, with serious
consequences for the adequacy of accounts of the code itself,
long the primary focus of attention within linguistics. If, as
Stankiewicz notes, the neo-idealists of the early twentieth
century 'ignored or blurred the difference' between *langue* and
parole by focusing too exclusively on *parole*, then much of later
twentieth-century linguistics has gone the other way, exaggerat-
ing the difference between them by valuing the cognitive at the
expense of the emotive.

In terms of ontogeny, it seems clear that expressive and
interactive meanings emerge earlier than cognitive meanings (in
the sense of the referential or representational). Infants develop
repertoires of signs for expressing interest, pleasure, displeasure
and a desire for interaction itself, as well as for getting people to
do things for them, well before they start using language more
referentially by learning 'words' as 'labels'. The forms of these
signs, at this proto-language stage, are not yet those of the adult
language system that the child has yet to acquire, but they can be
shown to be both meaningful (i.e., functional in context) and
systematic (able to be mapped into sets of options organised
paradigmatically). They certainly form the basis for the range of

aspects of interpersonal meaning that the child later comes to be able to code simultaneously with representational or experiential meaning, by using the tri-stratal organisation of the adult linguistic system to map the structures realising interpersonal meaning onto the structures realising representational meaning, thereby producing a single, multifunctional output. (See Halliday, 1975; Painter, 1984 for detailed accounts).

Assumptions underlying marginalisation of the interpersonal

What, then, are the assumptions underpinning those models of language which have marginalised interpersonal structures and meanings? There are two interconnected aspects of such an exploration, one looking more narrowly at attitudes and beliefs focused specifically on language, the other looking more broadly at ideological aspects of Western epistemology, in particular the habit of dichotomising deconstructed so pungently by Derrida (1976, 1978), with its concomitant privileging of one term and dismissal of the other. The ideology of individualism is also involved.

In terms of thinking about language, the central issues would seem to be:

1 a too-exclusive focus on system at the expense of process (deriving from uncritical reliance on dichotomies such as *langue/parole*, competence/performance), one of the consequences of this imbalance being

2 the 'primacy attributed to referential meaning in the western positivist/empiricist tradition' (Quinn and Holland, 1987:14);

3 constituency-based notions of linguistic structure which allow no room for alternative kinds of structure;

4 assumptions about the unpredictability/lack of systematicity of interpersonal features, deriving from privileging the categorical at the expense of the probabilistic.

Saussure's distinction between _langue_ and _parole_ lies behind both the contemporary focus on system, as well as the separation of competence from performance and ultimately syntax from pragmatics. If one understands the <u>langue/parole</u> distinction as a dichotomy, then the twentieth-century tendency has been to choose to focus attention on one or other of the terms and, in making that choice, implicitly to evaluate them in relation to one another. If linguistics is defined as the study of <u>langue</u> then it is hardly surprising that <u>parole</u> becomes 'simply the evidence that you use and then throw away' (Halliday, 1987:603). Halliday, with Firth, finds little use for such dichotomies as <u>langue/parole</u> (and <u>competence/performance</u>) (Halliday, 1974). In a recent interview with Paul Thibault, he makes it clear that he wishes to value both terms, though the terms he prefers to use are not <u>langue/parole</u> but the Hjelmslevian <u>system</u> and <u>process</u>, or <u>system</u> and <u>text</u>:

> M.A.K.H.: . . . I would see text as instantiation of the system; the two must be mutually determining. Hjelmslev says that you could, in principle, have a system without process—a system without it generating any text, but you couldn't have the process without the system; he presents it as a one-way determination. <u>I prefer to think of these as a single complex phenomenon: the system only "exists" as a potential for the process, and the process is the actualization of that potential.</u> Since this is a language potential, the "process" takes the form of what we call text.

> P.J.T.: The Saussurean discussion of this relation has tended to disjoin system from text so that the ontological status of the system is privileged. The systemic-functional mode, as well as the earlier work of Firth and Hjelmslev, has quite a different view of this relation. The systemic-functional model is oriented to both "meaning" and "text". Can you explain this relation?

> M.A.K.H.: I've always felt that it was rather a distraction in Saussure that he defined linguistics as the study of <u>la langue</u>, with <u>parole</u> being simply the evidence that you use and then throw away. I don't see it that way. Firth, of course, was at the other end of the scale, in that for him the phenomenon was the text. He wasn't interested in the potential, but rather, as I think I put it in one of my papers, in the generalized actual, so that it was the typical texts that he was interested in.

> *Firth tended to privilege the text as against the system.*
> *I don't want to privilege either. (Halliday, 1987:603,*
> *emphases added).*

If, on the other hand, one treats the relationship between pairs of terms such as *langue/parole* as dialectic rather than dichotomous, then one has to pay attention to *both* system *and* its instantiation in particular contexts. Or one can look at the relation from the other direction (starting with *parole*), attending to actual instances of 'languaging' in the real world as *both* the only guarantee of the existence of any system *and* also as themselves affecting, and ultimately changing, the system. (And note that ultimately one has to pluralise 'system', or be trapped by one's own reified terminology in a way that has a great deal in common with nineteenth-century notions of 'nation' and 'people': a particular 'language', with its 'system', is just as much a fiction as a nation is an 'imagined community' (Anderson, 1983)—both are dreams or fantasies of desired unity in the face of actual diversity).

Chomsky's reformulation of *langue/parole* as *competence/ performance* not only involves a similar dichotomous view of the relation between system and process but also a strong emphasis on the cognitive, which he is quite explicit about (see especially chapter 1 of Chomsky, 1965). What isn't always understood is what has been lost by such an orientation, i.e. a concern not only for the affective/expressive but also, ironically, for the very social as against individual orientation to language that was one of the values of Saussure's *langue/parole* distinction. *Langue* was what we all shared as speakers, where *parole* was the individual use of that resource. What Chomsky does, with his cognitive orientation, is to tie the notion of system to the individual, albeit an individual who embodies the specifically human cognitive capacities evolved by the species. What this does, of course, is to sidestep the whole question of the social, and to ensure, because of the hegemony of Chomskian linguistics from the 1960s, that when linguists wanted to get back to the social (as increasingly they have from the 1970s), that there is a built-in hierarchy which gives priority to the cognitive and individual over the interpersonal and social.

Foregrounding the cognitive has a long history in Western ideas about language. Various commentators—almost invariably, however, from within those traditions or approaches to language with an interest in the social—have noted the preoccupation with the cognitive, referential, representational function of language: language representing and hence controlling the world. It is possible, however, to see the cognitive as constituting the 'central core' of language, and yet still to make a strong case for the inadequacy of a purely cognitivist orientation to language:

> *The linguist's primary concern with the cognitive elements of language is not surprising, because they constitute its central core. Yet even though the expressive elements are generally less apparent than the cognitive units, it would be deceptive to think that the former constitute a shapeless, subterranean stream buried under the structure of language. Absence of adequate descriptions is, as we know, not always determined by inaccessibility of empirical data; it is often the result of disinterest or of inadequacy of prevailing theories. And so long as linguists do insist on either/or solutions, or on a reductionism of all elements of language to a single cognitive level, they are bound to ignore those phenomena which do not fit their constructs, or to force the facts into ready-made schemes. (Stankiewicz, 1964:247)*

Within the neo-Firthian tradition, Ellis notes 'the excessively referential conception of extra-linguistic components', contrasting this to Firth's own emphasis on the importance of context (Ellis, 1966:89–90 n. 6) and Halliday identifies the firm commitment of linguists 'in the psycho-philosophical tradition' to language as 'an ideational system' (Halliday, 1979:71).

Among those working within pragmatics, Levinson, having referred to work on the 'functions of speech', notes the usefulness of this work in reminding us that 'contrary to the preoccupations of many philosophers and a great many semanticists, language is used to convey more than the propositional content of what is said' and several pages later is more explicit in acknowledging 'the philosophical and linguistic bias (no doubt reflected in this book) towards what Bühler (1934) called the <u>representational</u> and Jakobson (1960) the <u>referential</u> function of language' (Levinson, 1983:42,46).

Leech, in the earlier version of his work on the tact maxim (1980), though interestingly not in the later version (1983), takes up a related issue in seeing Austin's *How to Do Things with Words* as 'a milestone because it offered to release linguistic philosophy from the age-long tyranny of its preoccupation with the truth and falsehood of propositions' (Leech, 1980:79). But despite the very clear acceptance in the earlier version of different but parallel kinds of meanings, in the later version, in fact, he insists on a hierarchy, privileging the representational as more centrally linguistic (and seriously misrepresenting Halliday's work in the process).

Behind this widespread cognitively-oriented conception of language, shared by linguist and lay person alike, would seem to be two pairs of ideological dichotomies of profound importance to Western epistemology: the dichotomy of 'objective' and 'subjective' and that of 'reason' and 'emotion'. In both cases, the first term is highly valued and the second devalued. Both of these pairs of terms have had obvious significance as epistemological preconditions for the development of the physical sciences in the West, but have been invoked in other, social, areas of control, particularly in relation to the subordination of women. (Lloyd, 1984; Poynton, 1985:18–19).

These linked notions, of the objective and the rational, have undoubtedly served the interests of Western expansionist capitalism extremely well, by, on the one hand, assuming the value of control (by force, by knowledge, by language itself) and, on the other hand, by devaluing not only those uses of language directed towards the social but those people who habitually use and value the interpersonal, those who apparently talk 'for talk's sake' rather than for 'getting things done'. The dichotomy implied between talk 'for talk's sake' and talk for 'getting things done' is, of course, a false one: talk is *always* a mode of 'getting things done', a mode of action where what 'gets done' through the ongoing conduct of everyday social relations is the production/re-production of both social structure itself and individual social subjects, socially situated. But in the ideological world of conservative political values, where it is convenient to privilege the individual at the expense of the social, that is a most *in*convenient insight.

The primary groups whose linguistic practices have been systematically devalued by attitudes which assume the validity of such a dichotomy, between talk 'for talk's sake' and talk for 'getting things done', have been so-called 'primitive' peoples, those in whose societies a central role of language lies in its interactive role and its role in ritual and myth. Such attitudes proved disastrous for the Aboriginal people of Australia after European settlement, particularly when linked with the politically convenient nineteenth-century doctrine of *terra nullius* which asserted that, because the Aborigines had not made their mark on the land in ways that were recognisable to European eyes as settlement and use, therefore they had no claim to ownership of the land. What struck European eyes most forcibly was the poverty of Aboriginal material culture; what they were unable to understand, even to conceive of, was the possibility that 'almost all of the human creative energy of a culture over tens of thousands of years old had been invested in the development of the society's spiritual, intellectual, and social life' (Sutton, 1988:ix).

Within non-Aboriginal Australian society, and Western societies generally, it has been women and children whose selves and whose language have been marginalised and devalued. In the case of children, it is because however significant the representational must come to be for them, if they are to be taken seriously as adult human beings, it is not 'one of the earliest [functions of language] to come into prominence' and 'it does not become a dominant function until a much later stage in the development towards maturity' (Halliday 1973:16). And this is only the case if indeed, as Halliday goes on to note, in an oblique reference to the hegemony of representational notions of language, it ever does become the dominant *function* rather than the dominant *model* of language for anyone. Women and women's language have been devalued because competence in interactive genres, emphasising the interpersonal, is what they have been expected to demonstrate. Men's linguistic competence, on the other hand, has been expected to be in language as performance, as display, involving a significant focus on the representational, whether in the form of story-telling or the presentation of 'facts'. And such linguistic behaviour does have a high value in our culture. (Maltz and Borker, 1982; Poynton, 1985: 27–28).

A third reason for the marginalisation of the interpersonal is the long-standing assumption shared by many who have had a serious concern with language, particularly philosophers and linguists influenced by philosophy, that there is only one kind of linguistic structure: constituency structure. Hjelmslev, in the quotation heading this chapter, makes clear the possibility that 'affective elements' in language could well be subject to kinds of grammatical rules which have yet to be identified or described. Halliday (1979) has made a significant contribution to such an enterprise by distinguishing between three kinds of grammatical structure, coding three kinds of distinguishable semantic function. He distinguishes between (i) constituency structure, realis-

241

ing experiential meanings ('meaning in the reflective mode', p. 59); (ii) prosodic structure, realising interpersonal meanings ('meaning in the active mode', ibid); and (iii) culminative structure, realising textual meanings (meaning enabling 'the other two kinds [of meaning to] take on relevance to some real context', p. 60).

Halliday makes the following comment concerning differences in the attention paid to these different kinds of structure:

> *If we consider the major traditions in linguistic thought, we find, not at all surprisingly perhaps, that those in the psycho-philosophical tradition, who are firmly committed to language as an ideational system, have usually worked with constituency models of structure: American structuralist and transformationalist theories, for example. By contrast, linguists in the socio-anthropological tradition, like Firth, who are interested in speech functions and stress the interpersonal aspect of language, have tended to develop prosodic models. Those in the literary tradition, concerned primarily with texture and text structure, have developed models of a periodic kind: the structure of the paragraph (topic sentences, etc.), generic structures of various kinds, and of course the whole theory of metrics. (Halliday, 1979:71–73).*

He goes on to make explicit reference to the similar notions of 'Pike's (1959) important insight into language as particle, wave and field' and to note that :

> *Although Pike did not conceive of these in quite the same way, it seems very clear that this is what we have here:*
>
> *constituent (experiential) structures are particulate*
>
> *prosodic (interpersonal)   ″   ″ field-like*
>
> *periodic (textual)   ″   ″ wave-like*

I will not elaborate on the periodic (textual) type of structure here, since it is of no further relevance in this chapter, but will give a brief, introductory characterisation of the prosodic type of structure, characteristic of interpersonal meaning, in comparison with the constituency structure of experiential meaning.

Consider a possible utterance, perhaps said on the telephone as a prelude to terminating a conversation:

1. Someone is knocking on my door.

The experiential content of this utterance consists of Actor *someone*, Material Process *is knocking*, Circumstance: Location *on my door*. (See Halliday, 1985: chapter 5 for a detailed account of these categories). A representation of structure in constituency terms, bracketing the structural components as follows, seems perfectly appropriate:

(Someone) ((is) (knocking)) ((on) ((my) (door)))

But what about the following possible utterance, perhaps produced by the anxious and deferential student who was knocking on my door?

2. I was wondering if you could possibly spare me a few minutes, could you please.

Here, the experiential content is not only less straightforward to discern (for example what does one do about *was wondering*?), but the whole utterance is suffused with a set of interrelated features with the basic meaning of *maybe*, i.e. modality of probability, the social function of which in a sentence like this is to signal politeness or deference. The relevant features of the clause are:

- modal auxiliary (*could*)
- modalised tag (*could you*)
- modal adjunct (*possibly*)
- 'distant' tense choice: present in past, *was wondering*. (Compare other possible choices: the polite but less deferential present, *wonder*, or the more distant and hence more deferential past in past, *had been wondering* (see Halliday, 1985:177–84 for this system of tense description)
- grammatical metaphor. *I was wondering* is not in fact the alpha clause of a hypotactic clause complex, which is what it looks like at first glance, but a metaphorical way of realising modality, i.e. it means simply *maybe*. The tag, repeating the mood element of what looked like the beta clause, makes it clear that the subject of the whole clause is *you* not *I* (v. Halliday, 1985: chapter 10).

Added to these grammatical features, one should also include as relevant to the interpersonal impact the lexical choice of _spare_ as predicator in the verbal group (implying that the speaker recognises that this is an imposition and that the addressee is a busy person), the politeness marker _please_, and the massively incongruent relationship between the mood (tagged and modalised declarative) and the speech function of command (i.e. demand goods and services). A congruently realised command uses the imperative mood. (See Halliday, 1985: chapter 4).

These features are spread throughout the clause, several 'layers' thick (because the scope of modal choices is the whole clause not a single localised part of it), the reiteration of the fundamental interpersonal meaning of modality functioning like a prosody over the entire clause. The amount of repetition or reiteration (indicative of the strength or amplitude of the prosody) may not be precisely predictable from one relevant context to another, but the actual linguistic choices implicated (the systems 'at risk') certainly are.

Now consider a third example, involving the expression of attitude (the use of 'expressive' or 'emotive' language):

3. //1+Jesus those/filthy/bastards/fucking/<u>thrash</u>ed us//

Such a wording could have various phonological realisations. The symbols used to mark intonation here indicate one such possible realisation. As it is marked here there is only one point of tonic prominence, on _thrash_, a wide tone 1 (falling), (marked here as 1+), and no specific indication of what might be going on in the pre-tonic (which could be low level—making a very marked contrast with the high fall on _thrash_-, or rising). One obvious alternative is for _Jesus_ to constitute a single tone group, with the tonic on the first syllable _Je-_ and the vowel considerably lengthened. (See Halliday, 1970 for details of the notation employed here—but note that: // marks a tone group boundary; / marks a foot boundary.)

Again there is a cluster of relevant realisations which function together to realise the strong attitude involved here:

- attitudinal lexis (_filthy_, _bastards_, _thrash_)
- swearwords (_fucking_ as adjunct/ intensifier)
- thematised expletive (_Jesus_)
- exaggerated intonation contour
- other appropriate phonological features: intensity, rhythm, vowel lengthening (especially on _Jesus_), possibly voice quality.

Again, the choices implicated (the systems 'at risk') are predictable: in the case of attitude, they will be primarily phonological and lexical, in contrast with modality, which is realised grammatically. These two examples are intended to provide an illustration of what is meant by referring to interpersonal structure as prosodic. Suggestive analogies come from the fields of music and painting: Halliday would seem to have had both in mind in referring to interpersonal meaning as 'strung throughout the clause as a continuous motif or colouring' (Halliday, 1979:66). He goes on to say that 'the rationale behind this mode of realization' is that interpersonal meaning 'is the speaker's *ongoing* intrusion into the speech situation' and that 'the essence of the meaning potential of this part of the semantic system is that most of the options are associated with the act of meaning *as a whole*' (my emphases) (p.67).

Alongside the objections to interpersonal features as lacking in structure, because they are not analysable in terms of constituency, are assessments of them as unpredictable and hence not properly linguistic, i.e. part of the linguistic system. Robin Lakoff points out that 'interpersonal behaviour is frequently regarded as unpredictable and spontaneous. We do not feel that we are following rules or even a preordained pattern in the way we talk to others, move, respond emotionally, work, think' (Lakoff, 1979:53).

Lakoff is one of an increasing number of linguists interested in interpersonal phenomena, but the way she deals with this area is to make an unnecessary distinction between the linguistic and the stylistic, thereby contributing to perpetuating a view of the interpersonal as ultimately non-linguistic because outside the system, i.e. non-rule-governed. Lakoff certainly doesn't want to say that it is thereby uninteresting—on the contrary, she wants 'to construct a predictive system of rules of style, to establish for style something analogous to what linguists construct for language in the form of a grammar' (Lakoff, 1979:54). But making this kind of dichotomy between 'language' and 'style' certainly doesn't help to legitimise the study of the interpersonal as far as 'hard-core' cognitivist, *langue*-focused linguists are concerned.

The kind of rules needed for such an enterprise as Lakoff's, however, are not categorical but, rather, probabilistic; it is this which leads to the assessment of unpredictability. For many linguists, however, only the categorical is linguistically interesting, the probabilistic being dismissed as 'merely statistical' (Labov, 1972a:71). There is not only a clear bias in such views towards the linguistic system as against process, but a very different kind of conception of both the nature of the system itself and the relation between system and process from that of the systemic-functional model. (See Threadgold, 1988b for a grammatical analysis which uses the systemic-functional probabilistic approach to these questions.)

In this model, the system itself is modelled paradigmatically, i.e. as sets of options arranged in networks of related and/or dependent options. Each set of options, or system, is represented with its own entry condition/s, and the individual terms or features of each system have an inherent weighting or probability.

> ... the linguistic system as a system of paradigmatic oppositions is a system of possibilities. Choosing a particular feature in a system means what it does because of the features that were not chosen but could have been chosen. This is the qualitative aspect of the system, the system of 'either/or' relations. But the system is not only a system of possibilities, it is also a system of probabilities ... The choice of a particular feature also means what it does against the background of what are more likely and less likely choices. What is said is not only interpreted against a background of what could have been said but was not; it is also interpreted against the background of expectancies, against the background of what was more likely and what was less likely to be said. The grammar of a language is not only the grammar of what is possible but also the grammar of what is probable. (Nesbitt and Plum, 1988:8–9)

Instantiation in the text as process of such a paradigmatically conceived linguistic system is necessarily probabilistic, because it is context-dependent: this is as true for experiential structures as for interpersonal and textual structures (see Nesbitt and Plum, 1988:10–11 for a summary account of the notion of probabilistic realisation of context in language). Models of the system in essentially syntagmatic terms, i.e. as structures and rules about structures, and particularly context-independent models, give a greater significance to the categorical and necessarily see the probabilistic as indicating an inadequacy in the model itself.

At the same time as the presumed unpredictability of the

interpersonal is what appropriately excludes it from consideration as properly linguistic, it is precisely this which ensures that
the interpersonal (or, more accurately, the personal) is kept safe
from the control of 'rules', which have been seen as denying
autonomy and creativity. Lakoff (1979:53) does not accept that
the existence of implicit rules *does* deny autonomy and creativity, but in so stating her position she makes clear that these *are*
important values for her, as for many other linguists working in
the American tradition. Part of the context for seeing it as
necessary to assert the value of autonomy and creativity was
presumably a reaction to the behaviourism which Chomsky
(1959) criticised so trenchantly, but part of it is also an uncritical
acceptance of individualist ideology, a continuation of the
Romantic individualism of the nineteenth century, and its
particular early-twentieth-century manifestation within linguistics, the neo-idealist emphasis on the personal referred to
above.

The ideology of individualism in Western society is strongly
committed to notions of creativity, autonomy and free will—
notions which have not, it seems, been seen as antithetical to the
attempt to see linguistic 'competence' as rule-governed but
which for long largely precluded investigation of linguistic
'performance', particularly those aspects of it concerned with
interpersonal meaning. But a cognitively-oriented notion of
linguistic creativity, certainly when Chomsky was first dealing
with this notion, seems to be little more than a combinatorial
potential:

> *Although it was well understood that linguistic*
> *processes are in some sense 'creative', the technical*
> *devices for expressing a system of recursive processes*
> *were simply not available until much more recently. In*
> *fact, a real understanding of how a language can (in*
> *Humboldt's words) 'make infinite use of finite means'*
> *has developed only within the last thirty years, in the*
> *course of studies in the foundations of mathematics. Now*
> *that these insights are readily available it is possible to*
> *return to the problems that were raised, but not solved,*
> *in traditional linguistic theory, and to attempt an*
> *explicit formulation of the 'creative' processes of*
> *language. There is, in short, no longer a technical*
> *barrier to the full-scale study of generative grammars.*
> *(Chomsky, 1965:8)*

It is moreover, a combinatorial potential which is merely a 'means for expressing indefinitely many thoughts and for reacting appropriately in an indefinite range of new situations' (p.6), i.e. which maintains a rigid separation between language as expression and something else ('thoughts' in this case) which it is expressing. Such a perspective on the content–expression relation is quite antithetical to the views of Hjelmslev (1961) and those working within the systemic-functional model (where content and expression are both aspects of language itself, not one 'inside' and the other 'outside' language). It is a view cogently criticised in his paper on the 'conduit metaphor' (language seen as 'carrying' something else) by Michael Reddy (1979).

This is not to say that the combinatorial potential of language is not of the utmost significance, even for the very notion of 'the individual' that is seen as potentially threatened by any notion of 'rules' for social behaviour. People are, to a large extent, formed as individuals by what they do, including most significantly what they say, rather than simply 'being' who they are in some pure metaphysical sense. 'The individual' can be seen as an artefact of the particularity of the linguistic choices made by one person, choices both identifying and constituting them as a particular socio-historical entity. For those concerned about the apparent 'determinism' of such an account, with its apparent throwback to behaviourist ways of thinking about language, the individual so constructed is certainly unique: the combinatorial potential of the inherent probabilistic weightings of the system combined with the specificity of the linguistic demands made by the individual's personal history generates massive variability of forms and meanings. Our experience of ourselves as singular and unitary can then be seen as an artefact of the self-reflexive capacity of language (see the quotation from Benveniste below).

Language, the individual and the social

I now want to look at the systemic-functional notion of the interpersonal, incorporating as it does both the interactive and the personal, the social and the individual. There are two problematic, and interrelated, issues that need to be discussed. The first is the question of the relation between the individual and the social; the second is the question of the affective, the realm of feeling, emotion, passion, which seems irreducibly personal/individual at first glance (and having little to do with any self-re-

specting notion of linguistic system), but which employs resources from the linguistic system, resources which are
moreover structured in similar ways to the more overtly 'social',
i.e. interactive, resources.

I certainly take very seriously Halliday's view that 'the whole
question of the relationship between the individual and language
has to be seen as embedded in the social structure' (Halliday,
1974:117). The linguistic system itself is inherently social—it is
jointly produced, a shared resource (there would not only be no
possibility, but no point, in a single human producing a language
in social isolation). So too is the process of instantiation in text a
social phenomenon, for all forms of text, however innovative, are
built on pre-existing types of text, which are socially learned not
only as types of text but as meaningful forms of social action
(Martin, 1985).

The fundamental grammatical unit, the clause, is likewise a
social act. Halliday makes the point that 'an "act" of speaking is
something that might more appropriately be called an "interact":
it is an exchange ...' (Halliday, 1985:68), and the basis for that
exchange is the structural organisation of the clause from an
interpersonal perspective, by means of the system of mood:

> ... our traditional approach to grammar is not nearly
> as one-sidedly oriented towards the ideational function
> as sometimes seems to be assumed. For instance, the
> whole of the mood system in grammar, the distinction
> between indicative and imperative and, within
> indicative, between declarative and interrogative—this
> whole area of grammar has nothing whatever to do
> with the ideational component. It is not referential at all;
> it is purely interpersonal, concerned with the social-
> interactional function of language. It is the speaker
> taking on a certain role in the speech situation. This
> has been built into our interpretation of grammar, and I
> see no reason for departing from this and treating the
> social meaning of language as some kind of optional
> extra. (Halliday, 1974:97)

Mood options in the grammar make possible the organisation of
the clause in ways that are conventionally understood to constitute propositions (information-oriented moves) or proposals (ac-
tion-oriented moves), which are then open to negotiation.

One can only interact with others as an 'I' to the 'you' of
other/s, however, and this has profound consequences. At the

most literal level, 'I' signals the performer of a speech/conversation role (in fact, is constitutive of that performance), and is simultaneously 'this I', on this particular occasion, but also 'any speaker', from the viewpoint of the system rather than the text. At a more profound level, 'I' spoken as separate from 'you' seems a necessary condition for the development of the capacity of a speaker to posit themself as an individual, a self, a subject. Benveniste elaborates this in the following terms:

> It is in and through language that man [sic]
> constitutes himself as a subject, because language alone
> establishes the concept of 'ego' in reality, in its reality
> which is that of the being.
> The 'subjectivity' we are discussing here is the
> capacity of the speaker to posit himself as 'subject.' It is
> defined not by the feeling which everyone experiences
> of being himself (this feeling, to the degree that it can be
> taken note of, is only a reflection) but as the psychic
> unity that transcends the totality of the actual
> experiences it assembles and that makes the
> permanence of the consciousness. Now we hold that that
> 'subjectivity', whether it is placed in phenomenology
> or in psychology, is only the emergence in the being of a
> fundamental property of language. 'Ego' is he who
> says 'ego'. That is where we see the foundation of
> 'subjectivity', which is determined by the linguistic
> status of 'person.'
> Consciousness of self is only possible if it is
> experienced by contrast. I use I only when I am
> speaking to someone who will be a you in my address. It
> is this condition of dialogue that is constitutive of
> person, for it implies that reciprocally I becomes you in
> the address of the one who in his turn designates
> himself as I. Here we see a principle whose consequences
> are to spread out in all directions. Language is
> possible only because each speaker sets himself up as a
> subject by referring to himself as I in his discourse.
> Because of this, I posits another person, the one who,
> being, as he is, completely exterior to 'me,' becomes my
> echo to whom I say you and who says you to me. This
> polarity of persons is the fundamental condition in
> language, of which the process of communication, in
> which we share, is only a mere pragmatic consequence.

It is a polarity, moreover, very peculiar in itself, as it offers a type of opposition whose equivalent is encountered nowhere else outside of language. This polarity does not mean either equality or symmetry: 'ego' always has a position of transcendence with regard to you. Nevertheless, neither of the terms can be conceived of without the other; they are complementary, although according to an 'interior/exterior' opposition, and, at the same time, they are reversible. If we seek a parallel to this, we will not find it. The condition of man in language is unique.

And so the old antinomies of 'I' and 'the other,' of the individual and society, fall. It is a duality which it is illegitimate and erroneous to reduce to a single primordial term, whether this unique term be the 'I', which must be established in the individual's own consciousness in order to become accessible to that of the fellow human being, or whether it be, on the contrary, society, which as a totality would preexist the individual and from which the individual could only be disengaged gradually, in proportion to his acquisition of self-consciousness. It is in a dialectic reality that will incorporate the two terms and define them by mutual relationship that the linguistic basis of subjectivity is discovered. (Benveniste, 1958–71:224–25)

The 'I' who speaks is always an historically specific 'I', however, an 'I' who speaks with, at the very least, a gender, class, racial/ethnic and generational specificity. All these aspects of social identity are not simply given but are socially constructed in a complex of (i) culturally learned forms of interaction, (ii) structures of knowledge formed by the habitual forms of representation available to and used by the individual speaker, and (iii) structures of feeling about those structures of knowledge and interaction. The 'I' who speaks has, furthermore, a unique personal history, again with consequences for structures of feeling, knowledge and interaction and the relationships between them.

The expressive/emotive dimension of language is simultaneously social, in so far as it is part of the system, language as resource, but individual in so far as it is not only spoken by individuals but also 'speaks' those individuals, i.e. it is part of the means by which the particularity of individuals as historically specific individual subjects is not only made manifest but also socially constructed. What is particularly important about these expressive/emotive features is that they constitute a key semiotic resource for both producing structures of feeling, experienced at the level of the individual, and also for attaching feelings to the socially available forms of interaction and forms of representation. The attachment of feeling to representation is of particular importance for the circulation of ideologies, because it involves a virtual physical attachment of people to beliefs and values, thereby ensuring fierce commitment to those beliefs and values and resistance to attempts to 'take them away' by means of argument. The practice in contemporary polemical discourse of bolstering the legitimacy of arguments in support of one's own point of view by calling them 'rational' and delegitimising those of one's opponents by referring to them as 'emotional' doesn't help to clarify the complicated issues involved here.

The representational and the social

Western culture has a long history of valuing 'reason' and the 'rational' to the detriment of the 'emotional', with those apprenticed to the various fields of legitimated knowledge being conventionally required to suppress any evidence of 'personal feeling' in the name of 'objectivity'. What are regarded as inappropriate displays of feeling or emotion have been rigorously excluded from the highly prestigious forms of expository and descriptive discourse, especially scientific and philosophical discourse, i.e. those forms of speech and writing which are concerned with ideas, theories, understanding the material and social world we inhabit. This attempted exclusion of the affective has meant in practice the exclusion of overtly attitudinal lexis and of both the first-person pronoun I and instances and narratives deriving from the personal experience of that I ('the anecdotal'), as distinct from the scientific persona of that I (which in theory is indistinguishable from the scientific persona of any other I). This is presumably why the first person plural we is permissible: the text-producer is always presumed to speak not on their own behalf but as a representative, 'objective' voice. Note the discrepancy, however, between the legitimising of the individual in conservative political discourse and the refusal to grant it legitimacy in scientific discourse—politics can be seen to be about 'interests' but the West clings to a notion of science as about 'truth' rather than 'interests'). Current work in semiotic, feminist and critical theory (for example Belsey, 1980) has made abundantly plain that all producers of all texts are both themselves positioned (by their gender, class etc. affiliations, and by the very discourses they are articulating) and also attempt to position their listeners/readers as compliant, i.e. to regard that positioning as entirely uncontentious and unproblematic with respect to both the experiential content of the text and the implicit social relationship between producer and receiver of the text.

The systematic exclusion of the first-person singular pronoun, attitudinal lexis and the anecdotal does anything but guarantee that 'scientific' texts are suitably 'objective', however, since these are only the most overt markers of 'feeling' and the 'personal'. Even the most innocuous-seeming representations need to be understood to be just that: representations, employing a wealth of grammatical resources to obscure that fact (see Threadgold, 1988c for an analysis of neo-classical aesthetics in these terms). This is the territory of what Whorf (1956) called *cryptotypes* and Halliday (1985) calls *grammatical metaphor*. The effect of such grammatical patterns is to de-problematise the representations involved, both in terms of the objective/subjective dichotomy (where 'I can organise this data into three categories' becomes 'There are three categories') and in terms of the disguising of ideology/evaluation (where 'I think this is the way things ought to be' becomes 'Our children's futures depend on the maintenance of the traditional values of honesty, integrity and the freedom of the individual', to give a rather crude example).

The structural continuity of expressive/emotive features at various linguistic levels is a crucial issue in building towards an understanding of the individual–social nexus in all its ramifications. As long as the quintessential expressive/emotive features were seen as phonological (and both outside the purview of segmental approaches to phonology and, by definition, 'meaningless'—i.e. non-referential), it was possible to maintain the fiction that these were purely individually expressive (only really, of course, by not asking the question of why these supposedly 'individual' manifestations were systematic within particular languages, or by blurring the boundary between involuntary 'noises', such as snorts, and more systematic features). It was even possible to be extraordinarily reluctant to admit that they existed at all as elements of the linguistic system itself, as in the case of phonaesthesia or sound-symbolism, that very theoretically inconvenient conjunction of phonological segments with the referential. (Jakobson, 1978; Jakobson and Waugh, 1979; Jespersen, 1922–33; Sapir, 1915–51, 1929–51; Wescott, 1976, 1980). Once you admit the essential continuity of the phonological with the morphological (or with an intermediate morphophonemic level), or with the lexical, then the way is open to acknowledging the interconnection of the 'expressive' with the representational. It is lexis that is the real key, looking both ways: 'down' to the personal by means of attitudinal/evaluative items, 'up' to the social in terms of the representational which is simultaneously referential and ideological.

Phenomena like insult/abuse (Labov, 1972b; Leach, 1964; Mitchell-Kernan, 1972; Murray, 1979, 1983; Winslow, 1969) and slang (Wescott, 1976, 1980) are well understood within linguistics to be social, not simply individual—even when 'social' is interpreted to mean 'anti-social', acting in the interests of a minority group rather than mainstream society. What does not appear to be as well understood is that such affectively loaded linguistic phenomena simultaneously function to code social attitudes and values and to attach individuals to the social order constituted by that set of attitudes and values.

It is important to identify the relation of language to feeling/ the emotions/the passions as a significant issue demanding attention. One obvious future direction is to develop connections between linguistics and psychoanalytic theory that go beyond the kind of linguistic analysis of therapy sessions of Labov and Fanshel (1977), however locally revealing these may be, or which, from the psychoanalytical side, approach the linguistic from too general a perspective, eschewing any serious consideration of the nature and implications of empirical data (for example Kristeva, 1980, 1984). The work of the group of people, mainly based in Sydney, drawing on the systemic-functional model of language in work they call simply social semiotics (for example Kress, 1985, Kress and Threadgold, 1988, forthcoming; Lemke, 1988, forthcoming a, b; Thibault, 1986; Threadgold, 1986, 1988a, b, c), has been notable for the multiple connections being made with work in semiotic, critical, feminist and social theory. Psychoanalytic theory needs to be added to this repertoire for any serious exploration of the interconnections between language, the individual and the social.

Future work will need to build towards an adequate understanding of this individual–social nexus by exploring precisely the structural continuity of emotive/expressive features at various linguistic levels and relating these findings to issues being raised in psychoanalytic and other theoretical areas. Meanwhile, what the denial of the linguistic legitimacy of the interpersonal has consistently refused to see (probably a historically necessary refusal, if Western control over the external world—with its dubious benefits as well as its undoubted gains—was to be achieved as it has been) is that linguistic representations of the world are *not* the kind of value-free representations that many thought they were and ought to be, that representations to a significant degree are simply that: representations, constructions, indicative just as much of what people think the world *should* be like as of how it actually *is*.

Appendix A Extra illustrating material for chapter 5

1 Extract from A Talkyng of þe Loue of God (translation)

But my sweet lover, enough were Your poverty and Your great disgrace without other sufferings, but it never seemed enough to You fully to buy my love altogether, as long as Your life lasts. Ah sweet Jesus, mercy! What a high price You set on me, never was a valueless thing bought half so dear. For Your whole life on earth was always spent in much toil for me, unworthy wretch, and always more and more, so that before Your death You exerted Yourself so much and worked so hard that You sweated red blood: factus est sudor eius sicut guttae sanguinis in terram decurrentes. For, as Saint Luke says in his holy gospel, You were in so great labour that Your sweat ran like drops of blood down upon the ground. But what tongue can tell, what heart can consider, for sorrow or for pity, that cruel beating, that dragging about and abusing that You disgracefully endured, when You were first laid hands on, when Judas Iscariot treacherously brought hellhounds to seize and bring You to their leaders; and how they bound You so harshly and so firmly that the blood sprang out at Your finger-nails, as saints relate and as it is written in books. And they bound You so fast and led You roughly forth, piteously beating You on back and on shoulders and on either side. And before the leaders buffeted You and mocked You and blindfolded Your eyes, struck a blow and made You their fool and spat in Your face many a time and often, and made it so disgusting, so pale and so livid with beating and buffeting and spitting and spewing. Without any mercy they maltreated You so. They grinned at You and wagged their heads and put out their tongues and raved at You disgracefully and ridiculed You. How afterwards before Pilate You were naked bound to a pillar and scourged so cruelly that You could not turn at all, nor in any way avoid their painful lashes. There You were for my love with hard knotty scourges flogged and beaten so painfully and so cruelly that Your fair complexion, which was so bright and so fresh, was utterly defiled and soiled, Your skin torn and rent to pieces. There flowed on each side a stream of water and of red blood. You, Lord, endured all their pleasure with such a meek mood. Then there was put on Your head a crown of sharp thorns so that wherever there was a thorn the red blood streamed out. Then they also beat down the crown on Your head and put it straight and pressed it and made it sit fast so that the sharp thorns went into the brain, put a reed in Your hand instead of a king's sceptre, in scorn and in contempt, and bent their knees for You and said: 'Hail to You, King' and spat straight in Your face. And after all that villainy they would not stop there, but wickedly and unjustly sentenced You to death.

Ah dear Lord, what shall I do now? Now can I no longer live for sorrow and for grief, now that my dear love shall suffer death. Now I may mourn vehemently, now I may weep bitterly, now I may sigh heavily and lament constantly. Ah, now they lead Him away to Mount Calvary, to the place of execution, to kill Him there. Ah my dear love! He carries the cross on His bare shoulder for the love of me. His body is so tender. His bones long and lean. Stooping He goes so that it is a piteous thing to see. Ah my sweet love, the blows they deal You, the grief they cause You! On either side they wickedly and violently push You on, crying horribly, to Your death hastily. And You endured everything with love for me, unworthy wretch. Lord, who are almighty, give me for Your mercy remembrance of that villainy and make me feel in my heart how Your wounds smart. Ah sweet Jesus, dear life, how many men follow You now to gape at You in scorn. Your friends are sad and sorrowful at heart. Your enemies follow mockingly and delight in their victory and decry You basely in the sight of this whole world. Alas, now they have brought Him there where they will kill Him. Now they cast Him down and lay Him on the cross. Now they stretch His limbs, His sinews burst asunder, His limbs break out of joint so that none of them can hold out. Alas, my dear love, how can man, instead of feeling compassion, cause You all that woe in return for so great favours, You who are so beautiful, so fair and so noble. And You endured so meekly all that they chose to do. Ah Jesus, now they drive the blunt large nails through Your fair hands and Your goodly feet. Now Your skin bursts, Your sinews and Your bones. My heart breaks in my breast in pity of Your complaints. Ah Jesus darling, where is any weeping, where is a spring of tears to pour out on my cheeks? May I never cease [to weep] either by day or by night, now that I see Your fair limbs so piteously treated. The blood of Your wounds springs so brightly and flows on Your white skin, so ruthful to see. Your

mother looks at it, that pure virgin. Her sorrow weighs more heavily on
You than Your own, as I think. Ah, now they set up the cross and set up
the rood-tree and Your body all covered with blood hangs on it. Ah
Jesus, now they put the cross in the socket. Your limbs leap out of joint,
Your bones part asunder, Your wounds are torn open because of being
gullied out so wide. Lord, that You were woe begone at that time! Ah my
dear love, when You had lost all Your blood, You became quite dried up
and began to be very thirsty. They offered You vinegar and gall to drink.
But when You tasted of it, You would take no more. Ah my sweet love,
in addition to Your other woe, they raved at You, when You hung on the
cross, so gentle and so meek, as if You were a meek lamb, when, to Your
shame, foully grinning, disgracefully shaking their heads in contempt
and in scorn, they said in reproach: 'Lo, where He hangs who could save
other people and fails to save Himself.' Alas Lord, our love is little worth
that cost You so dear. And yet we do not allow You to have it here but
follow our lusts in the devil's company, as if he were better than You and
more worthy. Alas, alas, the pity of it, that I must see You, my love, so
cruelly tortured and that it is all my fault. Badly tortured and rent to
pieces, spat upon and shamefully dishonoured, to save us in the straits
we were in, that was Your only cause. Ah Jesus, sweet love, how can I
now live, now that I see You, dear life, the love of my heart, my darling,
my longing, my blessed Lord, my beloved, with arms white and fair,
stretched so tightly, without any mercy, naked on the cross, so that all
Your holy bones can be counted. There You hung piteously, so cold and
so bloody. All raw and stained is Your sweet body. Ah sweet Jesus, dear
love, now You die for me hanging on the rood-tree and let fall Your head,
that it is a pity to see. The white of Your eyes is turned upwards. Ah
Jesus, now the sun grows dark, now the earth trembles and the stones
burst. Now the temple splits asunder with sorrow for my love. Now the
dead rise up in witness of Your Godhead and walk in Jerusalem, as was
written before. Alas, no thing mourns, no thing feels grief for my dear
love, who suffered a painful and dishonourable death on the cross
without guilt of sin. Ah my dear love, my sorrow, my bliss, only love of
my life, who died such a cruel death for the life of this whole world, the
most painful and miserable that ever anybody suffered or might die in
for the love of men. Ah sweet Jesus, of Your grace, let me now die in
Your blissful arms from all the love of this world into the love of You, so
that only Your love be for ever all my delight. (Westra, 1950:47–53)

2 Extract from þe Wohunge of Ure Lauerd

Ah! Jesu, sweet Jesu, thou that wast shamefully treated for love of me,
grant that the love of thee be all my delight. Sufficient were poverty and
shame, without other torments; but it seemed never to thee, my life's
love, that thou mightest fully purchase my friendship whilst life lasted

thee. Ah! a dear bargain hadst thou in me; never was so unworthy a thing bought so dearly. All thy life on earth was in affliction for my sake, ever longer the more so. But before thy death so infinitely thou wast afflicted and so sorely, that thou didst sweat red blood; for, as St. Luke saith in the Gospel, thou wast in so great an affliction that the sweat, as drops of blood, ran down to the earth. But what tongue may tell, what heart may think, for sorrow and for ruth, of all the buffets and the grievous blows that thou didst suffer in thy first capture, when that Judas Iscariot brought the hell-bairns (children of hell) to take and to bring thee before their princes; how they bound thee so cruelly fast that the blood was wrung out at thy finger-nails (as saints believe), and led thee sorrowfully bound, and struck harsh blows on thy back and shoulders, and before the princes buffeted and beat thee; how afterwards before Pilate thou wast bound naked and fast to the pillar, so that thou mightest nowhere turn (wrench thyself) from the blows. There thou wast, for love of me, with knotty whips beaten, so that thy lovely body might be torn and rent asunder; and all thy blissful body streamed in one blood-stream. Afterwards on thine head was set the crown of sharp thorns, so that with every thorn the red blood poured out from thine holy head. Afterwards also wast thou buffeted and struck on the head with the sceptre of reed, that was previously in thine hand given thee in scorn. Ah! what shall I do now? Now my heart may break, my eyes flow all with water. Ah! now is my beloved doomed to die. Ah! now they lead him forth to mount Calvary to the place of execution. Ah, lo! he bears his rood upon his bare shoulders; and would that those blows had struck me with which they battered and thrust thee quickly forward toward thy doom! Ah! beloved, how they follow thee; thy friends sorrowfully with lamentation and sorrow, and thy enemies mockingly in scorn and to bring trouble on thee. Ah! now they have brought him thither. Ah! now they raise up the rood, and set up the accursed tree. Ah! now they strip my beloved. Ah! now they drive him up with whips and with scourges. Ah! how can I live for grief, seeing my beloved upon the cross, and his limbs so drawn asunder that I may tell each bone in his body. Ah! how do they now drive the iron nails through thy fair hands into the hard rood, [and] through thy gracious feet. Ah! now from those hands and feet so lovely, streams the blood so ruefully. Ah! now they offer my beloved, that saith he thirsts, eisel, sourest of all drinks, mixed with gall, that is the bitterest thing (two bale-drinks in blood-letting, so sour and so bitter), but he drank not of it. Ah! now sweet Jesu, yet in addition to all thy woe they increase it by shame and mockery, they laugh thee to scorn where thou hangest on the rood. When thou, my lovely beloved, with outstretched arms, hangedst on the rood, it was rueful to the righteous, but laughter to the wicked. And thou, before whom all the world might dread and tremble, wast a laughing-stock and a mockery to the wicked folk of this world. Ah! that lovely body that hangest so sorrowfully, so bloody, and so cold! Ah! how shall I now live, for my beloved dies now for me upon the dear cross. He hangs down his head and his soul departs. But it seems to them that he is not yet fully tormented, nor will they let the sorrowful body rest in peace. They lead forth Longius with the broad sharp spear. He pierces his side, cleaves the heart, and there comes flowing out of the wide wound the blood that redeemed [us] and the water that washed the world from guilt and from sin. Ah! sweet Jesu, thou openest for me thy heart, that I may know (thee) truly and read therein true love-letters, for there I may openly see how much thou lovedest me. With wrong should I refuse thee my heart, since thou hast brought heart for heart. (Morris, 1886:280, 282)

3 'Quia Amore Langueo' (Lambeth MS 853)

(1)

In a valey of þis restles mynde
I souȝte in mounteyne & in myde,
Trustynge a trewe loue for to fynde.
Vpon an hil þan y took hede;
A voice y herde—& neer y ȝede—
In huge dolour complaynynge þo,
"Se, dere soule, how my sidis blede,
Quia amore langueo."

(2)

Vpon þis hil y fond a tree;
Vndir þe tree a man sittynge,
From heed to foot woundid was he,
His hertë blood y siȝ bledinge:—
A semeli man to ben a king,
A graciouse face to loken vnto;—
I askide whi he had peynynge,
He seide "quia amore langueo."

(3)

I am true loue, þat fals was neuere;
Mi sistyr, mannis soule, y loued hir þus;
Bi-cause we wolde in no wise disceuere,
I lefte my kyngdom glorious
I purueide for hir a paleis precious;
Sche fleyth, y flolowe, y souȝte hir so,
I suffride þis peynë piteuous
Quia amore langueo.

(4)

My fair spouse, & my louë briȝt,
I saued hir fro betynge, & sche haþ me bet;
I cloþid hir in grace & heuenli liȝt,
þis bloodi scherte sche haþ on me sette,
For longynge of loue ȝit wolde y not lett;
Swetë strokis axë þese; lo,
I haue loued hir euere as y hir het,
Quia amore langueo.

(5)

I crowned hir wiþ blis, & sche me with þorn;
I ledde hir to chaumbir, & sche me to die;
I brouȝte hir to worschipe, & sche me to scorn;
I dide her reuerence, & sche me vilonye.
To loue þat loueþ, is no maistrie;
Hir hate made neuere my loue hir foo,
Axë me no questioun whi,
Quia amore langueo.

(6)

Loke vnto myn hondis, man!
þese gloues were ȝoue me whan y hir souȝte;
þei ben not white, but rede & wan,
Onbroudrid with blood my spouse hem brouȝte.
þei wole not of, y loose hem nouȝte,
I wowe hir with hem where-euere sche go;
þese hondis for hir so freendli fouȝte,
Quia amore langueo.

(7)

Merueille nou3te, man, þou3 y sitte stille;
Se, loue haþ sched me wondir streite,
Boclid my feet, as was hir wille,
With scharp naile, lo, þou maiste waite.
In my loue was neuere desaite,
Alle myn humours y haue opened hir to,
Þere my bodi haþ maad hir hertis baite,
Quia amore langueo.

(8)

In my side y haue made hir neste;
Loke in! how weet a wounde is heere,
þis is hir chaumbir, heere schal sche reste,
þat sche & y may slepe in fere.
Heere may sche waische, if only filþe were,
Heere is sete for al hir woo;
Come whanne sche wole, sche schal haue chere,
Quia amore langueo.

(9)

I wole abide til sche be redy,
I wole hir sue if sche seie nay;
If sche be richilees, y wole be gredi,
And if sche be daungerus, y wole hir praie.
If she wepe, þat hide y ne may,
Myn armes her hired to clippe hir me to;
Crie oonys; y come: now, soule, asay,
Quia amore langueo.

(10)

I sitte on þis hil, for to se fer,
I loke into þe valey, my spouse to se;
Now renneþ sche a-wayward, 3it come sche me
    neer,
For out of my si3te may sche not flee.
Summe wayte hir prai to make hir to flee,
I renne bifore, and fleme hir foo;
Returne my spouse a3en to me,
Quia amore langueo.

(11)

Fair loue, lete us go pleye!
Applis ben ripe in my gardayne,
I schal þee cloþe in a newe aray,
þi mete schal be mylk, hony & wiyn.
Fair loue, lete us go digne,
þi sustynaunce is in my crippe, lo!
Tarie þou not, my faire spouse myne,
Quia amore langueo.

(12)

Iff þou be foul, y schal þee make clene;
If þou be sijk, y schal þee hele;
If þou moorne ou3t, y schal þee meene;
Whi wolt þou not, faire loue, with me dele?
Foundist þou euere loue so leel?
What woldist þou, spouse, þat y schulde do?
I may not vnkyndeli þee appele,
Quia amore langueo.

(13)

What schal y do with my fair spouse,
But a-bide hir of my gentilnes
Til þat sche loke out of hir house
Of fleischli affeccioun? loue myn sche is.
Hir bed is maade, hir bolstir is blis,
Hir chaumbir is chosen; is þer non moo.
Loke out on me at þe wyndow of kyndenes,
Quia amore langueo.

(14)

My loue is in hir chaumbir: holde 3oure pees,
Make 3e no noise, but lete hir slepe:
My babe, y wolde not were in disese,
I may not heere my dere child wepe.
With my pap y schal hir kepe.
Ne merueille 3e not þou3 y tende hir to;
þis hole in my side had neuere be so depe,
But quia amore langueo.

<table>
<tr><td align="center">(15)</td><td align="center">(16)</td></tr>
</table>

(15)	(16)
Longe þou for loue neuere so hiʒ,	Wexe not wery, myn ownē wijf!
My loue is more þan þin may be;	What mede is it to lyue euere in coumfort?
þou wepist, þou gladist, y sitte þee bi,	In tribulacioun y regne moore rijf
ʒit woldist þou oonys, leef, loke vn-to me!	Ofttymes þan in disport.
Schulde y alwey fedē þee	In wele & in woo y am ay to supporte;
With children mete? nay, loue, not so!	Myn ownē wijf, go not me fro!
I wole preue þi loue wiþ aduersite,	þi meede is markid whan þou art mort,
Quia amore langueo.	Quia amore langueo.

(Furnivall, 1886: 180–88)

Appendix B French-English passages from Zola's *Une Page d'Amour* illustrating chapter 6

Passage 1

... ses cheveux châtains puissamment noués / les mèches de ses cheveux s'envolaient / Elle passa une jupe ... jeta un châle sur ses épaules / le médecin parut en veston, sans cravate, elle l'entraîna, elle ne le laissa pas se vetir davantage / Le médecin avait boutonné son veston pour cacher son cou nu. Hélène était restée enveloppée dans le châle qu'elle avait jeté sur ses épaules. Mais Jeanne en se débattant, tira un coin du châle, déboutonna le haut du veston / Elle rencontra le châle de sa mère, elle s'y cramponna ... le châle était complètement tombé de ses épaules, découvrant la naissance de la gorge / son chignon dénoué laissait pendre des mèches folles jusqu'à ses reins ... ses bras nus / le médecin ... son veston ouvert ... son col de chemise que Jeanne venait d'arracher / Il avait

She slipped on a petticoat and threw a shawl over her shoulders The wind ... tossed about her dishevelled hair ... her nut-brown hair twisted into a knot / the doctor appeared in a short coat and without a neck-cloth, she dragged him away without allowing him to finish dressing / The doctor had buttoned up his coat to hide his bare neck, and Hélène's shoulders had been enveloped till now in her shawl; but Jeanne in her struggles had dragged away a corner of the shawl, and unbuttoned the top of the coat / she touched her mother's shawl and fiercely clung to it ... the shawl had quite slipped off her shoulders, displaying her throat and bosom. Her back-hair had become undone, and some wanton tresses swept down to her hips ... her arms free and uncovered / the

effleuré de la joue son *épaule nue* . . . son souffle rencontra le souffle d'Hélène / *Le châle avait encore glissé, la gorge se découvrait, les bras restaient nus.* Une grosse *natte,* couleur d'or bruni, *coulait* sur l'épaule et se perdait entre les seins. Et, dans son *jupon mal attaché, échevelée et en désordre,* elle gardait une majesté, une hauteur d'honnêteté et de pudeur qui la laissait chaste sous ce regard d'homme, où montait un grand trouble / il avait le *cou nu* / Hélène, d'une main lente *remonta son châle et s'enveloppa,* tandis que le docteur *boutonnait le col de son veston* (Zola, 1973:49–57).

doctor . . . his unbuttoned coat . . . his shirt-collar that Jeanne's clutch had torn away / He touched with his cheek her naked shoulder . . . he could have heard the throbbing from the mother's breast . . . his breath mingled with Hélène's. The shawl had again slipped off, and the arms and bosom were completely bare. A thick tress of hair waved over her shoulder, and was lost between her breasts. With everything on her person disarranged, she stood in the petticoat, that scarcely clung to her, a model of queenliness, chastity, and modesty, even beneath the gaze of this man within whom were already awakening confused sensations / his neck was bare / Hélène slowly wrapped her shoulders in the shawl, while the doctor hastened to button his coat at the neck (Zola, 1895:9–19).

Passage 2

C'était comme si elles se fussent arrêtées au seuil d'un monde dont elles avaient l'éternel spectacle, en refusant d'y descendre. (Zola, 1973:102).

It was as if they had stopped on the threshold of a world that lay forever outspread before them, and refused to enter it (Zola, 1895:65).

Les deux fenêtres de la chambre étaient grandes ouvertes, et Paris, dans l'abîme qui se creusait au pied de la maison, bâtie à pic sur la hauteur, déroulait sa plaine immense (Zola, 1973:94)

The two windows of Hélène's room were wide open. Down below, the vast plain for Paris stretched out, in the abyss that lay at the foot of the house, perched right on the edge of the hill (Zola, 1895:56).

En haut, dans sa chambre, dans cette douceur cloîtrée qu'elle retrouvait, Hélène se sentit étouffer. La pièce l'étonnait, si calme, si bien close, si endormie sous les tentures de velours bleu, tandis qu'elle y apportait le souffle court et ardent de l'émotion qui l'agitait. Etait-ce sa chambre, ce coin mort de solitude où elle manquait d'air? Alors, violemment, elle ouvrit une fenêtre, elle s'accouda en face de Paris (Zola, 1973:154)

Upstairs in her room, in that familiar atmosphere of cloistered quiet, Hélène felt herself stifled. She was amazed to find the room so calm, so confined, so drowsy under its blue velvet hangings, while she herself was panting and afire with turbulent emotion. Was this really her room, this lonely, lifeless, airless place? Then, violently, she threw open a window and leaned there to look out at Paris (Zola, 1895:94).

Paris . . . était insondable et changeant comme un océan, candide le matin et incendié le soir, prenant les joies et les tristesses des cieux qu'il reflétait, Un coup de soleil lui faisait rouler des flots d'or, un nuage l'assombrissait et soulevait en lui des tempêtes. Toujours, il se renouvelait; c'étaient des calmes plats, couleur orange, des coups de vent qui d'une heure à l'autre plombaient l'étendue, des temps vifs et clairs allumant une lueur à la crête de chaque toiture, des averses noyant le ciel et la terre, effafant l'horizon dans la débâcle d'un chaos. Hélène goûtait là toutes les mélancolies et tous les espoirs du large; elle croyait même en recevoir au visage le souffle fort, la senteur amère; et il n'était pas jusqu'au grondement continu de la ville qui ne lui apportait l'illusion de la marée montante, battant contre les rochers d'une falaise (Zola, 1973:95).

Paris . . . was unsoundable and various as an ocean, innocently bright in the morning and aflame at night, assuming the joyous or melancholy mood of the skies it reflected. A burst of sunshine would set it rippling with floods of gold, a cloud would darken it, awakening stormy turbulence. It was constantly new; in a dead calm it would glow orange, under a sudden squall turn leaden grey from end to end, bright clear weather would set the crest of every house-top sparkling, while rainstorms drowned heaven and earth and wiped out the horizon in chaotic disaster. For Hélène it held all the melancholy and all the hope of the open sea; she even fancied she felt the sharp breath and the tang of the sea against her face; and the very sound of the city, its low continuous roar, brought her the illusion of the rising tide beating against the rocks of a cliff (Zola, 1895:47–48).

Passage 3

*... elle ne voulait pas montrer
ses jambes, et elle demanda une
ficelle, avec laquelle elle noua
ses jupes au-dessus de ses
chevilles / Pas un pli de ses
jupes n'avait bougé / Une natte
de son chignon se dénouait /
La natte dénouée battait sur son
cou / Malgré la ficelle qui les
nouait, ses jupes flottaient et
découvraient la blancheur de
ses chevilles / Sa natte s'était
échevelée;* la ficelle devait se
relâcher, et ses jupons avaient
des bruits de drapeau / *elle
serra ses jupes autour de ses pieds*
(Zola, 1973:90–93).

Laughingly, she declared she
must not expose her legs, and
asked for some cords to tie her
skirts securely round her
ankles / Not a fold of her
skirts was out of place, but a plait
of hair had slipped down /
The loosened plait of hair rustled
against her neck. Despite the
cord which bound them, her
skirt waved about, revealing
the whiteness of the ankles /
The tress of hair was flying in
disorder, the cord that confined
her skirts had given way
somewhat, and they rustled in
the wind like a flag /
She ... drew her skirts round her
feet (Zola, 1895:51–54).

Passage 4

*... le passage des Eaux, un
étrange escalier étranglé entre les
murs des jardins voisins, une
ruelle escarpée qui descend sur
le quai des hauteurs de Passy.
Au bas de cette pente...* (Zola,
1973:73).

... the Passage des Eaux, a
strange looking steep lane like a
stair-case, smothered between
garden-walls, leading down from
the heights of Passy to the
quay. At the bottom of this
descent... (Zola, 1957:29).

266

Appendix C Strindberg's *Miss Julie*: supporting material for chapter 11

Verbal text of final scene (Meyer, 1985: 143–146)

CHRISTINE [1]Are you coming with me to the church now? [2]You need a good sermon after what you've done.

JEAN [3]No, I'm not going to church today. [4]You can go by yourself, and confess what you've been up to.

CHRISTINE [5]Yes, I will, and [6]I'll come home with my sins forgiven, and yours too. [7]The blessed Saviour suffered and died on the cross for all our sins, [8]and if we turn to Him with a loyal and humble heart He'll take all our sins upon Him.

JEAN [9]Including the groceries?

MISS JULIE [10]Do you believe that, Christine?

CHRISTINE [11]With all my heart, as surely as I stand here. [12]I learned it as a child, Miss Julie, [13]and I've believed it ever since. [14]And where the sin is exceeding great, there His mercy shall overflow.

MISS JULIE [15]Oh, if only I had your faith! [16]Oh, if—!

CHRISTINE [17]Ah, but you can't have that except by God's special grace, [18]and that isn't granted to everyone—

MISS JULIE [19]Who has it, then?

CHRISTINE [20]That's God's great secret, Miss Julie. [21]And the Lord's no respector of persons. [22]There shall the last be first—

MISS JULIE [23]Then He has respect for the last?

CHRISTINE (CONTINUES) [24]And it is easier for a camel to pass through the eye of a needle than for a rich man to enter the Kingdom of Heaven. [25]That's how it is, Miss Julie. [26] Well, I'll be going—[27]and as I pass the stable I'll tell the groom not to let any of the horses be taken out before his lordship comes home, just in case. [28]Goodbye. (SHE GOES).

JEAN   [29]Damned bitch! [30]And all for a greenfinch!

MISS JULIE (DULLY)   [31]Never mind the greenfinch. [32]Can you see any way out of this, any end to it?

JEAN (THINKS)   [33]No.

MISS JULIE   [34]What would you do in my place?

JEAN   [35]In your place? [36]Wait, now. [37]If I was a lady—of noble birth—who'd fallen—? [38]I don't know. [39]Yes. [40]I do know.

MISS JULIE (PICKS UP THE RAZOR AND MAKES A GESTURE)   [41]This?

JEAN   [42]Yes. [43]But *I* wouldn't do it, mind. [44]There's a difference between us.

MISS JULIE   [45]Because you're a man and I'm a woman? [46]What difference does that make?

JEAN   [47]The difference—between a man and a woman.

MISS JULIE (HOLDING THE RAZOR)   [48]I want to do it—[49]but I can't. [50]My father couldn't do it, either, the time he should have.

JEAN   [51]No, he was right. [52]He had to be revenged first.

MISS JULIE   [53]And now my mother will be revenged again, through me.

JEAN   [54]Have you never loved your father, Miss Julie?

MISS JULIE   [55]Yes—enormously—[56]but I've hated him too. [57]I must have done so without realizing it. [58]But it was he who brought me up to despise my own sex, made me half woman and half man. [59]Who is to blame for what has happened—my father, my mother, myself? [60]Myself? [61]I have no self. [62]I haven't a thought I didn't get from my father, not an emotion I didn't get from my mother—[63]and this last idea—that all people are equal—I got that from him, my fiancé whom I called a wretched little fool because of it. [64]How can the blame be mine, then? [65]Put it all on to Jesus, as Christine did—[66]no, I'm too proud to do that, and too clever—thanks to my learned father. [67]And that about a rich person not being able to get into heaven, that's a lie, [68]and Christine has money in the savings bank so she won't get there either. [69]Whose fault is it all? [70]What does it matter to us whose fault it is? [71]I shall have to bear the blame, carry the consequences—

JEAN   [72]Yes, but—

THERE ARE TWO SHARP RINGS ON THE BELL. MISS JULIE JUMPS UP. JEAN CHANGES HIS COAT.

JEAN   [73]His lordship's home! [74]Good God, do you suppose Christine—? (GOES TO THE SPEAKING TUBE, KNOCKS ON IT, AND LISTENS.)

MISS JULIE   [75]Has he been to his desk?

JEAN ⁷⁶It's Jean, milord. (HE LISTENS. THE AUDIENCE CANNOT HEAR WHAT IS SAID TO HIM) ⁷⁷Yes, milord. (HE LISTENS). ⁷⁸Yes, milord. ⁷⁹Immediately. (HE LISTENS) ⁸⁰At once, milord. (LISTENS) ⁸¹Very good, my lord. ⁸²In half an hour.

MISS JULIE (DESPERATELY FRIGHTENED) ⁸³What does he say? ⁸⁴For God's sake, what does he say?

JEAN ⁸⁵He wants his boots and his coffee in half an hour.

MISS JULIE ⁸⁶In half an hour, then—! ⁸⁷Oh, I'm so tired! ⁸⁸I can't feel anything, ⁸⁹I can't repent, ⁹⁰can't run away, ⁹¹can't stay, ⁹²can't live— ⁹³can't die. ⁹⁴Help me! ⁹⁵Order me, ⁹⁶and I'll obey you like a dog. ⁹⁷Do me this last service, ⁹⁸save my honour, ⁹⁹save his name! ¹⁰⁰You know what I ought to will myself to do, ¹⁰¹but I can't. ¹⁰²Will me to, Jean, ¹⁰³order me!

JEAN ¹⁰⁴I don't know—¹⁰⁵now I can't either—¹⁰⁶I don't understand— ¹⁰⁷it's just as though this coat made me—¹⁰⁸I *can't* order you—¹⁰⁹and now, since his lordship spoke to me—¹¹⁰I can't explain it properly, but—¹¹¹oh, it's this damned lackey that sits on my back—¹¹²I think if his lordship came down now and ordered me to cut my throat, I'd do it on the spot.

MISS JULIE ¹¹³Then pretend that you are he, and I am you. ¹¹⁴You acted so well just now, when you went down on your knees—¹¹⁵then you were an aristocrat—¹¹⁶or—haven't you ever been to the theatre and seen a hypnotist? (JEAN NODS) ¹¹⁷He says to his subject: 'Take the broom!', ¹¹⁸and he takes it, ¹¹⁹He says: 'Sweep!' ¹²⁰and he sweeps—

JEAN ¹²¹But the subject has to be asleep.

MISS JULIE (IN AN ECSTASY) ¹²²I am already asleep—¹²³the whole room is like smoke around me—¹²⁴and you look like an iron stove—which resembles a man dressed in black, with a tall hat—¹²⁵and your eyes shine like coals, when the fire is dying—¹²⁶and your face is a white smear, like ash—(THE SUN'S RAYS HAVE NOW REACHED THE FLOOR AND ARE SHINING ON JEAN) ¹²⁷It's so warm and good—! (SHE RUBS HER HANDS AS THOUGH WARMING THEM BEFORE A FIRE) ¹²⁸And so bright—and so peaceful—!

JEAN (TAKES THE RAZOR AND PLACES IT IN HER HAND)¹²⁹ Here's the broom. ¹³⁰Go now—while it's light—out to the barn—and—(HE WHISPERS IN HER EAR)

MISS JULIE (AWAKE) ¹³¹Thank you. ¹³²Now I am going to rest. ¹³³But just tell me this—those who are first—they too can receive grace? ¹³⁴Say it to me—even if you don't believe it.

JEAN ¹³⁵Those who are first? ¹³⁶No, I can't! ¹³⁷But, wait—Miss Julie— ¹³⁸now I see it! ¹³⁹You are no longer among the first. ¹⁴⁰You are—among the last!

MISS JULIE ¹⁴¹That's true. ¹⁴²I am among the last of all. ¹⁴³I am the last. ¹⁴⁴Oh! ¹⁴⁵But now I can't go! ¹⁴⁶Tell me once more—¹⁴⁷say I must go!

JEAN ¹⁴⁸No, now I can't either. ¹⁴⁹I can't!

MISS JUNE ¹⁵⁰And the first shall be last.

JEAN   [151]Don't think, [152]don't think! [153]You take all my strength from me, [154]you make me a coward. [155]What? [156]I thought the bell moved! [157]No. [158]Shall we stuff paper in it? [159]To be so afraid of a bell! [160]Yes, but it isn't only a bell—[161]there's someone sitting behind it—[162]a hand sets it in motion—[163]and something else sets the hand in motion—[164]you've only got to close your ears, close your ears! [165]Yes, but now he's ringing louder! [166]He'll ring till someone answers—[167]and then it'll be too late. [168]The police will come—and then—!

TWO LOUD RINGS ON THE BELL

JEAN (CRINGES, THEN STRAIGHTENS HIMSELF UP)   [169]It's horrible. [170]But it's the only possible ending. [171]Go!

MISS JULIE WALKS FIRMLY OUT THROUGH THE DOOR

Lexical Sets and Interrelations

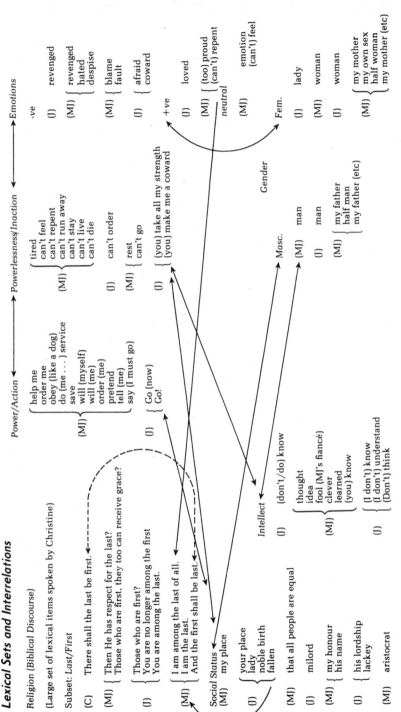

Note — Character in whose speech a lexical item occurs is designated by (J) = Jean, (MJ) = Miss Julie, (C) = Christine.

Floor plan of the set and seating layout for the English Department's Theatres Studies Project *Miss Julie* 1986. At the Downstairs Space Seymour Centre, seating capacity as shown = 88.
(Plan courtesy of Theatre Studies Service Unit, University of Sydney)

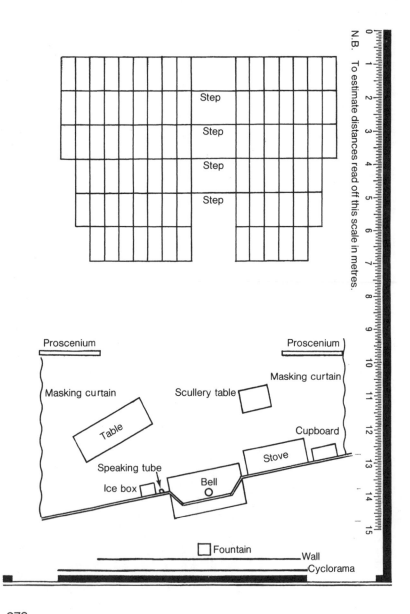

Endnotes

1 Introduction

Terry Threadgold

1 The verb 'elide from' is used here to indicate the conscious and deliberate exclusion, in all discussion, of the private from the public world.

2 Foucault and Irigaray

Rosi Braidotti

1 The reference is to one of J. Derrida's books, *La Carte Postale*, literally 'post-card'.
2 My analysis of the intersection between feminism and modernity is in disagreement with the 'post-modern' diagnosis, as in Jardine (1985).
3 University of Chicago Press, 1983.
4 *The Use of Pleasure* New York: Pantheon Books, 1985.
5 For an account of recent Italian feminism see Braidotti (1986).
6 Both titles were translated by Cornell University Press in 1985.
7 On this particular point I disagree with the reading of Irigaray proposed by E. Gross in 'Irigaray and Sexual Difference' *Australian Feminist Studies* 2, 1986.

4 Inscriptions and body-maps

Elizabeth Grosz

With special thanks to the Humanities Research Centre at the Australian National University, and to the feminists gathered there for the theme of 'Feminism and the Humanities'. Without the generous support of the centre and various individuals, this paper could not have been written. I would like to acknowledge the invaluable help of Susan Sheridan, Virginia Blain and Meaghan Morris.

1 Franz Kafka's short story, 'The Penal Settlement', describes an 'exquisite' punishment machine that will serve as an emblem of the concerns of this chapter: the socio-material, representational inscription of bodies. Kafka's machine is an ingenious device made of three parts: first, a 'Bed', onto which the prisoner is tied; second, the 'Designer', which determines what messages will be inscribed; and, third, 'the Harrow'. It executes the sentence on the prisoner's body, using a moving layer of needles to print the Designer's message:

> As soon as the man is strapped down, the bed is set in motion. It quivers in minute, very rapid vibrations ... You will have seen similar apparatus in hospitals; but in our Bed, the movements all correspond very exactly to the movements of the Harrow ... Our sentence does not sound severe. Whatever commandment the condemned man has disobeyed is written on his body: 'Honour thy superiors' ... (although he doesn't know the sentence) he'll learn it corporeally, on his person ... An ignorant onlooker would see no difference between one punishment and another. The Harrow appears to do its work with uniform regularity ... the actual progress of the sentence can be watched, [for] the Harrow is made of glass ... When the Harrow ... finishes its first draft of the inscription on the back, the layer of cotton wool (on the Bed) begins to roll and slowly turns the body over, to give the Harrow fresh space for writing. Meanwhile the raw part that has been written on lies on the cotton wool, which is especially prepared to staunch the bleeding and so makes all ready for a new deepening of the script ... So it keeps on writing deeper and deeper for the whole 12 hours ... But how quiet he grows at just about the 6th hour! Enlightenment comes to the most dull-witted. It begins around the eyes. From there, it grows, it radiates. A moment that might tempt one to get under the Harrow with him. Nothing more happens after that, the man only begins to understand the inscriptions ... You have seen how difficult it is to decipher the script with one's eyes; but our man deciphers it with his wounds. To be sure, that is a hard task; he needs 6 hours to accomplish it. By that time, the Harrow has pierced him quite through and casts him into the grave ... Then the judgement has been fulfilled and we bury him. (Kafka, 'The Penal Settlement', *Metamorphosis and other Short Stories*)

Three elements of Kafka's description and relevant to my chapter. He links punishment to the operations of knowledges. Penal punishment requires a certain epistemic backup for knowledges are both the preconditions of power's concrete operations, and are also amenable to revision and transformation by information gathered from the processes of supervision, observation and inscription of the prisoner's suffering body. Second, Kafka explicitly describes the machine as a discursive or *writing* instrument. Like the stylus, pen or typewriter, this writing-machine is an instrument of material inscription producing propositions, texts and discourses: the surface to be inscribed in this case is human flesh and skin rather than the blank page of the book, and the consequence of this inscriptive procedure is not only a text, but a particular type of human subject. Third, messages or inscriptions are etched on the body's surface, without the prisoner knowing the crime with which he is charged, or the punishment he is to be apportioned. These punitive practices create an 'enlightenment', a *consciousness* or psychic effect solely by materially marking the prisoner's body. Kafka allows us to focus on relations between bodies, textuality, and consciousness (or mind).

5 The discursive construction of Christ's body

Jennifer Ash

1 The development of eucharistic doctrine and theology in the history of the Christian faith is extremely complex. An excellent discussion of the situation in the medieval period is given in Macy 1984.
2 See the texts presented in the appendix.
3 See Breuer and Freud, 1893–95; Freud 1905, 1912. Hysteria as a 'feminine' phenomenon has recently been the focus of feminist theorising—especially psychoanalytic theorising; see Irigaray, 1985a, 1985b; Cixous and Clement, 1986; also the excellent collection of articles in Bernheimer and Kahane, 1985.
4 For the discussion which follows see Lacan, 1977, but especially Irigaray, 1985a, 1985b; see also Threadgold, 1988a which provides an overview and analysis of much recent work being done on woman's relation to language. Doane, 1981:30ff gives a neat summary of the situation in terms of psychoanalytic theorising.
5 See Lacan, 1982. Like hysteria, anorexia has become an issue of concern for feminism. I found the analysis and discussion of anorexia in Celemajor, 1986, 1987 particularly useful and satisfying, and have incorporated arguments presented there in the material which follows. See also Bordo, 1988 and Probyn, 1988.
6 Women's religious experience—whether orthodox or heterodox—in the late medieval period has become the subject of much energetic research in the last few years. Consequently an exhaustive bibliography is not really possible, or sensible, given the scope of this chapter. However, I would like to make a few suggestions for those interested: Baker, 1978, Beckwith, 1986; Bell, 1985; Bolton, 1976, 1978; Goodich, 1981; Bynum, 1982, 1984, 1987; Erickson, 1976; Kieckhefer,

1984; McDonnell, 1969; McLaughlin, 1974, 1979; McNamara and Wemple, 1977; Nichols and Shank, 1984; Petroff, 1977, 1986; Schulenburg, 1978, 1984; Stargardt 1985.

7 A phrase borrowed from Michele Montrelay ('Inquiry into Femininity' *Semiotexte* 4, 7, 1981, pp.228–35, special issue: *Polysexuality*).

8 This is the title of a Middle English mystical text. For the argument presented here see Lacan, 1982.

9 *Inedia.* The word is used in Bynum (1987) to mean the condition of not eating.

6 The feminine as a semiotic construct: Zola's Une Page d'Amour

Maryse Rochecouste

1 This chapter is adapted from ch. 3 of my book (Rochecouste, 1988).

2 By 'bovarysme' I mean the neurotic malady caused by unrealisable romantic ideals and yearnings, as experienced by Madame Bovary.

3 Or 'falling' sickness—which gives free rein to catamorphic postures.

4 I have discussed this symbolism in an earlier study (Rochecouste, 1979:22, 35).

5 I am extending to textual indices Keir Elam's (1980:76) concept: 'Related indices of speaker-gesturer intention include what can be named *attitudinal* markers, indicative not of the act intended but of the attitude adopted (towards the world, the addressee, the propositional content of the utterance) in speaking. Head nods, finger wags, eyebrow movements, and so on, come close in function, in determined communicative situations, to the linguistic modalities usually expressed by means of 'modal operators' such as 'want', 'must', 'can', 'may', 'impossible', indicating the speaker's propositional attitudes.'

6 See appendix B, passage 1 for the parallel French-English texts.

7 Schor (1976:189) rightly identifies the mysterious 'unknown' which needles Hélène's curiosity as to her libido.

8 Zola (1971:95) actually uses the word 'initiation'.

9 Despite the fact that she has experienced marriage, motherhood and widowhood, she is still not sexually awakened.

10 See Figure 5, adapted from Pavis' model (1976:51), and the parallel French-English texts in appendix B, passage 2.

11 See appendix B, passage 3.

12 An interesting parallel is to be found in Jeanne's clockwork doll, the iconic portrayal of Hélène; like the heroine, its broken-down mechanism causes it to somersault backwards, but thanks to Rambaud's patient mending, it walks and talks again—mechanically. In the course of her childish games, Jeanne even 'feeds' it the

symbolic apple, fruit of the Fall—a clear symbolic representation of Hélène eating from the Tree of Knowledge. This reification process is also extended to Jeanne's other doll, her 'rag doll', which can also be seen as portraying Hélène, especially when it is described as follows, at the very moment of her first rendezvous with Henri: 'the pink limbs, stuffed with sawdust, had become as loose and ungainly as old clothes' (Zola 1973:281, my translation).

13 See appendix B, passage 4.

14 See O'Toole (1982:159) in which the 'erotic elements in land-scape . . . the . . . integration of natural scene and character . . . the male quality of the . . . townscape . . . matched by the predominant-ly female anatomy of the country scene' are discussed. Borie's (1971:214) instructive comments about the Seine are also helpful in deciphering the hidden meaning behind Zola's sexualisation of the urban landscape.

15 The thematic recurrence and catamorphic significance of the vestmental code when Hélène returns to the apartment is to be noted. The reversed procedure, that is, the ritual of undressing and dressing follows, doubled by the symbolic washing of the hands.

7 The films of Marguerite Duras

Michelle Royer

1 Shoshana Felman 'Woman and madness: a critical phallacy', p.4 as cited by Rosalind Jones (1985) in *Making a Difference* p.97

2 Luce Irigaray, interview with 'Liberation' 21 March 1979, as cited by Rosi Braidotti in *Refractory Girl* 23, March 1982, p.11.

9 Homosexualities

Michael Hurley

The author wishes to thank Liz Jacka and Leigh Raymond for comments on earlier drafts of this chapter.

1 Pers. comm.

2 I might add here that in relation to men, 'Wilde' and the twentieth century, I am modifying Sedgwick's more general argument that 'homosexual panic' is used to construct a (male) heterosexuality in which male homosocial desire is routed through women (Sedgwick 1985:114–17).

3 The reference is to Yeats' poem 'The Circus Animals' Desertion'.

11 *Strindberg's* Miss Julie

Susan Yell

1 See, for example, Bal (1984) for a discussion of the construction of subjectivity through language.

2 Lemke (1988:11) argues for the social construction of the gendered individual, pointing to anomalies between 'biological sex' and 'social gender'.

3 I am grateful to Dr Rosemary Huisman for a discussion in which she drew my attention to these features.

Bibliography

Adams, P. (1979) 'A Note on Sexual Division and Sexual Differences' *m/f* 3, pp. 51–58

Addleshaw, P (1895) 'The Woman Who Did' *Academy* 2 March, pp. 186–87

Allen, G. (1895) *The Woman Who Did* London: John Lane

Allen, M.P. (1984) Fantasia Fair *Outreach Newsletter* repr. in *Australian Seahorse Bulletin* June Issue

Alley, R. (1957) *Peking Opera* Peking: New World Press

Anderson, B. (1983) *Imagined Communities: reflections on the origin and spread of nationalism* London: Verso

Ang, I. (1985) *Watching Dallas: Soap opera and the melodramatic imagination* trans. Della Coutling, London: Methuen

Aristotle (1976) *Nichomachean Ethics* trans. J.A.K. Thomson and H. Tredinnick, Harmondsworth: Penguin

Armstrong, K. (1987) *The Gospel According to Woman: Christianity's Creation of the Sex War in the West* London: Pan Books

Bachelard, G. (1964) *L'Eau et Les Rêves* Paris: Corti

Baker, D. ed. (1978) *Medieval Women* Oxford: Blackwell

Bakhtin, M.M. (1981) *The Dialogic Imagination: Four Essays* trans. C. Emerson and M. Holquist, ed. M. Holquist, Austin: University of Texas Press

——(1986) 'The Problem of Text in Linguistics, Philology and the Human Sciences: an Experiment in Philosophical Analysis in *Speech Genres and Other Late Essays* trans. Vern W. Mc.Gee, Austin: University of Texas Press

Bal, M. (1984) 'The Rhetoric of Subjectivity' *Poetics Today* 5,2, pp.337–76

——(1985) *Narratology: Introduction to the Theory of Narrative* trans. Christine van Boheemen, Toronto: University of Toronto Press

Barker, F. (1984) *The Tremulous Private Body: Essays on Subjection* London and New York: Methuen

Barthes, R. (1977) *Image/Music/Text* trans. Stephen Heath, London: Fontana

——(1981) *Elements of Semiology* trans. Annette Lavers and Colin Smith, New York: Hill and Wang

Bataille, G. (1986) *Erotism: Death and Sensuality* trans. M. Dalwood, San Francisco: City Lights

Beane, W.C. and W.G. Doty eds. (1975) *Myths, Rites, Symbols: A Mircea Eliade Reader* New York: Harper & Row

Beckwith, S. (1986) 'A Very Material Mysticism: The Medieval Mysticism of Margery Kempe' in D. Aers (ed.) *Medieval Literature: Criticism, Ideology and History* Brighton: Harvester Press

Beer, P. (1974) *Reader, I Married Him* London: Macmillan

Beilby, R. and C. Hadgraft (1979) *Ada Cambridge Tasma and Rosa Praed* Oxford: Oxford University Press

Bell, R. (1985) *Holy Anorexia* Chicago and London: University of Chicago Press

Belsey, C. (1980) *Critical Practice* London: Methuen

Bem, S.L. (1974) 'The Measurement of Psychological Androgyny' *Journal of Consulting and Clinical Psychology* 42, pp. 155–62

Bemis, K. (1978) 'Current Approaches to the Etiology and Treatment of Anorexia Nervosa' *Psychological Bulletin* 85, 3

Benjamin, J. (1984) 'Master and Slave: the Fantasy of Erotic Domination' in Ann Snitow et al. (eds) *Desire: the Politics of Sexuality* London: Virago

Bennett, T. (1979) *Formalism and Marxism* London: Methuen

——(1984) 'Texts in History: The Determinations of Readings and Their Texts' *Australian Journal of Communication* 5–6.

Benveniste, E. (1958–71) 'Subjectivity in Language' in *Problems in General Linguistics* trans. M.E. Meek, Coral Gables, Florida: University of Miami Press, pp.223–30

Bernheimer, C. and C. Kahane eds (1985) *In Dora's Case: Freud—Hysteria—Feminism* London: Virago

Berry, G.L. (1980) 'Children, television and social class roles: the medium as an unplanned educational curriculum' in E.L. Palmer and A. Dorr *Children and the Faces of Television* New York: Academic Press

Blachford, G. (1981) 'Male Dominance and the Gay World' in K. Plummer (ed.) *The Making of the Modern Homosexual* London: Hutchinson

Bleier, R. (1984) *Science and Gender* New York: Pergamon Press

Blumer, H. (1969) *Symbolic Interactionism, Perspective and Method* New Jersey: Prentice-Hall

Bolton, B. (1976) 'Mulieres Sanctae' in S.M. Stuard (ed.) *Women in Medieval Society* Philadelphia: University of Pennsylvania Press

——(1978)' Vitae Matrum: a further aspect of the Frauenfrage' in D. Baker (ed) *Medieval Women* Oxford: Basil Blackwell.

Booth, M. (1983) *Camp* London: Quartet

Bordo, S. (1988) 'Anorexia Nervosa: Psychopathology as the Crystallization of Culture' in I. Diamond and L. Quinby (eds) *Feminism and Foucault: Reflections on Resistance* Boston: Northeastern University Press

Borie, J. (1971) *Zola et les Mythes, ou de la nausee au salut* Paris: Seuil

Bφrreson, K.E. (1981) *Subordination and Equivalence: The Nature and Role of Women in Augustine and Thomas Aquinas* trans. C.H. Talbot, Washington: University Press of America

Boskind-Lodahl, M. (1976) 'Cinderella's Stepsisters: A Feminist Perspective on Anorexia Nervosa and Bulimia' *Signs* 11

Braidotti, R. (1981) Feminism et Philosophie, Doctoral dissertation in Philosophy, University Pantheon—Sorbonne

——(1982) 'Femmes et Philosophie—questions a suivre' *La Revue d'en Face* 13

——(1985) 'U-Topies des non-lieux post modernes' *Cahiers du Grif* 30

——(1986) 'The Italian Women's Movement in the 1980s' *Australian Feminist Studies* 3

Braun, F., A. Kohz and K. Schubert (1986) *Anredeforschung. Kommentierte Bibliographie zur Sociolinguistik der Anrede* (Research on forms of address. Annotated bibliography on the sociolinguistics of address) Tubingen: Narr

Breuer, J. and S. Freud, (1955) *Studies on Hysteria* (1893–1895) The Standard Edition of the Complete Pyschological Works vol. 2, trans. J. Strachey, London: Hogarth Press.

Britton, A, (1978–9) 'For Interpretation, against Camp' *Gay Left* no. 7, Winter, pp. 11–14

Brooke-Rose, C. (1985)'Woman as a Semiotic Object' in S. Suleiman (ed.) *The Female Body in Western Culture: Semiotic Perspectives* 6, 1–2, pp.9–20

Brooks, P. (1984) *Reading for the Plot: Design and Intention in Narrative* New York: Alfred A. Knopf

Brown, B. and G. Whitlock (1985) 'Talking about The Well of Loneliness' *Hecate* vol. X, no. 2 (1984) pp. 7–39

Brown, P. and S. Levinson (1978)'Universals in Language Use: politeness Phenomena' in E.N. Goody (ed.) *Questions and Politeness: strategies in social interaction* Cambridge: Cambridge University Press, pp.56–324

Brown, R. and A. Gilman (1960) 'The Pronouns of Power and Solidarity' in T.A. Sebeok (ed.) *Style in Language* Cambridge, Mass.: M.I.T. Press, pp.253–76

Brown, R. and M. Ford (1964)'Address in American English' in D. Hymes (ed.) *Language in Culture and Society: a reader in linguistics and anthropology* New York: Harper & Row

Brubacker, R. (1984) *The Limits of Rationality* London: George Allen & Unwin

Bugge, J. (1975) *Virginitas: An Essay in the History of a Medieval Ideal* The Hague: Martinus Nijhoff

Bullough, V. L. (1973) 'Medieval Medical Scientific Views of Women' *Viator* 4

Bynum, C. W. (1982) *Jesus as Mother: Studies in the Spirituality of the High Middle Ages* Berkeley and Los Angeles: University of California Press

——(1984) 'Women Mystics and Eucharistic Devotion in the Thirteenth Century' *Women's Studies* 11

——(1986a)" ... And Woman His Humanity": Female Imagery in the Religious Writing of the Later Middle Ages' in C. Bynum, S. Harrell, P. Richman (eds) *Gender and Religion: On the Complexity of Symbols* Boston: Beacon Press

——(1986b) 'The Body of Christ in the Later Middle Ages: A Reply to Leo

Steinberg' *Renaissance Quarterly* 39

——(1987) *Holy Feast and Holy Fast: The Religious Significance of Food to Medieval Women* Berkeley and Los Angeles: University of California Press

Byrne, D. (1896) *Australian Writers* Bentley

Caine, B., E.A. Grosz and M. de Lepervanche, [eds] (1988) *Crossing Boundaries* Sydney: Allen & Unwin

Cameron, D. (1985) *Feminism and Linguistic Theory* London: Macmillan

Cameron, Mrs Lovett (1895) *The Man Who Didn't* London

Campioni, M. and E. Gross (1983) 'Love's Labours Lost: Marxism and Feminism' *Beyond Marxism? Interventions after Marx* Sydney: Intervention, pp.113–42

Celemajer, D. (1986) Psychoanalysis, Anorexia and the Constructions of the Body, BA thesis, University of Sydney

——(1987) 'Submission and Rebellion: Anorexia and a Feminism of Body' *Australian Feminist Studies* 5

de Certeau, M. (1979) 'Des outils pour ecrire le corps' *Traverses* 14–15

Chomsky, N. (1959) 'Review of Skinner (1957)' *Language* 35, pp.26–58

——(1965) Aspects of the Theory of Syntax Cambridge, Mass.: M.I.T. Press

Cixous, H. (1975) *La Jeune Née* Paris: UGE

——(1976) 'La sexe ou la tete' *Cahiers du Grif* 13, October

——(1977) 'Entretien avec Françoise van Rossum-Guyon' *Revue des sciences humaines* 168

——(1983) 'Tancrede continue', *Etudes Freudiennes* 21–22, pp.115–52

Cixous, H. and C. Clement (1986) *The Newly Born Woman* trans. B. Wing, Minneapolis: University of Minnesota Press

Cleeve, L. (1895) *The Woman Who Wouldn't* London

Colledge, E. and J. Walsh [eds] (1978) *A Book of Showings to the Anchoress Julian of Norwich* 2 vols, Toronto: Pontifical Institute of Medieval Studies

Commonwealth Schools Commission (1984) *Girls and Tomorrow: The Challenge for Schools* Canberra

Constable, G. (1982) *Attitudes Toward Self-Inflicted Suffering in the Middle Ages* Brookline, Massachusetts: Hellenic College Press

Coward, R. (1984) *Female Desire. Women's Sexuality Today* London: Granada Publishing

——(1985) 'Female Desire and Sexual Identity' in M. Diaz-Diocaretz and I. Zavala (eds) *Women, Feminist Identity and Society in the 1980s* Amsterdam: John Benjamins

Cranny–Francis, A. (1988) 'Out Among The Stars in a Red Shift: Women and Science Fiction' *Australian Feminist Studies* 6, Autumn

Croft, J. and J. McCallum (1986) *Eugenia Fallini* program notes, Armidale, University of New England, Drama Department, 23–26 October

Cross, V. (1903) *Six Chapters in a Man's Life* London: Walter Scott Publishing Co.

——(1895) 'Theodora: A Fragment' *The Yellow Book* 4, pp. 156–88

Crosse, V. (1985) *The Woman Who Didn't* London: John Lane

Cunningham, G. (1978) *The New Woman and the Victorian Novel* London: Macmillan

Curthoys, A. (1988) *For and Against Feminism: A personal journey into feminist theory and history* Sydney: Allen & Unwin

Daniels, K. (1972–73) 'Rejecting the New Woman: Problems with Nineteenth Century Publishers' *Refactory Girl* 1, pp.5–7

Denzin, N.K. (1978) *The Research Act* 2nd edn, New York: McGraw Hill

Derrida, J. (1967) *L'Ecriture et la differance* Paris: Seuil

——(1976) *Of Grammatology* trans. G.C. Spivak, Baltimore: Johns Hopkins University Press

——(1972) *Marges* Paris: Minuit

——(1978) *Eperons* Paris: Flammarion

——(1978) *Writing and Difference* trans. A. Bass, London: Routledge & Kegan Paul

Diamond, I. and L. Quinby (1988) *Feminism and Foucault: Reflections on Resistance* Boston: Northeastern University Press

Diaz-Diocaretz, M. and I. Zavala eds (1985) *Women, Feminist Identity and Society in the 1980s* Amsterdam: John Benjamins

Dickens, H. (1982) *What a Drag* Sydney: Angus & Robertson

Doane, M.A. (1981) 'Women's Stake: Filming the Female Body' *October* 17

Dorner, G. (1976) *Hormones and Brain Differentiation* Amsterdam, Oxford, New York: Elsevier

Dowling, L. (1979) 'The Decadent and the New Woman in the 1890s' *Nineteenth Century Fiction* 33, pp.434–53

DuPlessis, R. Blau (1985) *Writing Beyond the Ending: Narrative Strategies of Twentieth Century Women Writers* Bloomington: Indiana University Press

Durand, G. (1969) *Les Structures Anthropologiques de L'Imaginaire. Introduction a l'archetypologie generale* Paris: Bordas

Duras, M. (1975) 'Interview by Susan Husserl-Kapit' *Signs* winter 1975, reprinted in E. Marks and I. de Courtivron (eds) *New French Feminisms* Hassocks, Sussex: Harvester Press

Dutton, G. (1976) *The Literature of Australia* Ringwood: Penguin

Dyer, R. (1986) *Heavenly Bodies, Film Stars and Society* London: BFI/Macmillan

Eagleton, T. (1985) The Subject of Literature, paper delivered to the annual conference of the National Association of English Teachers, Nottingham, unpublished manuscript

Eco, U. (1976) *A Theory of Semiotics* London and Basingstoke: Macmillan

——(1979) *A Theory of Semiotics* Bloomington: Indiana University Press

Elam, K. (1980) *The Semiotics of Theatre and Drama* London and New York: Methuen

Ellis, J. (1966) 'On contextual meaning' in C.E. Bazell, J.C. Catford, M.A.K. Halliday and R.H. Robins (eds) *In Memory of J.R. Firth* London: Longmans, pp. 79–95

Engel, P. (1985) 'Androgynous Zones' *Harvard Magazine* Jan–Feb pp. 24–32

Erickson, C. (1976) *The Medieval Vision: Essays in History and Perception* New York: Oxford University Press

Ernst, E. (1956) *The Kabuki Theatre* New York: Grove Press

Fawcett, M. G. (1895) 'The Woman Who Did' *Contemporary Review* 67, May pp.627–33

Fedkew, P. (1982) 'Marguerite Duras: Feminine Field of Hysteria' *Enclitic* 6

Felman, S. (1981) 'Rereading Femininity' *Yale French Studies* special issue, pp. 19–44

Fernando, L. (1977) *'New Women' in the Late Victorian Novel* University Park and London: Pennsylvania State University Press

Fiske, J. (1982) *Introduction of Communication Studies* London & New York: Methuen

Ford, C.S. and F.A. Beach (1951) *Patterns of Sexual Behaviour* New York: Harper & Row

Foster, V. (1984) *Changing Choices. Girls, School, Work* Sydney: Hale & Iremonger

Foucault, M. (1977) *Discipline and Punish. The Birth of the Prison* London: Allen Lane

——(1978) *The History of Sexuality* vol. 1 London: Allen Lane

——(1980) *Herculine Barbin: being the Recently Discovered Memoirs of a Nineteenth Century Hermaphrodite* New York: Pantheon Books

——(1985) *The Use of Pleasure.* vol. 2 of The History of Sexuality New York: Pantheon Books

Freud S. (1905) 'Fragment of an Analysis of Hysteria (Dora)' *The Pelican Freud Library* (1976–85) vol. 8, Harmondsworth: Penguin

——(1911) 'Psychoanalytic Notes on an Autobiographical Account of a Case of Paranoia' (Dementia Paranoides)' in *The Standard Edition of the Complete Works*, Vol. XII, trans. and ed. James Strachey (1958) London: The Hogarth Press

——(1912) *Selected Papers on Hysteria and other Psychoneuroses* trans. A.A. Brill, New York: Journal of Nervous and Mental Disease Publishing Company, reprinted (1970) New York: Johnson Reprint Corporation

Furnivall, F.J. [ed] (1866) *Political, Religious Love Poems* (re-edited 1903) EETS OS 15 London: Kegan Paul, Trench, Trubner & Co.

Gagnon, P. (1975) 'Sex Research and Social Change' *Archives of Sexual Behaviour* 4, pp. 111–41

Gallop, J. (1982) *The Daughter's Seduction: Feminism and Psychoanalysis* Ithaca, New York: Cornell University Press

Gatens, M. (1983) 'A Critique of the sex/gender distinction' in J. Allen and P. Patton (eds) *Beyond Marx? Interventions after Marx* Sydney: Intervention

——(1988) 'Towards a Feminist Philosophy of the Body' in Caine et al. (eds) *Crossing Boundaries*

Gilbert, S.M. and S. Gubar [eds] (1979) *Shakespeare's Sisters: Feminist Essays on Women Poets* Bloomington: Indiana University Press

Gillard, P.M. see P.M. Palmer

Gilman, A. and R. Brown (1958) 'Who says "tu" to whom' *ETC: A Review of General Semantics* 15, pp.169–74

Glickman A. (1985) 'Androgyny is in at Harvard—sort of' *Harvard Magazine* Jan–Feb, p.33

Goethe (1951) *Faust* Part I trans. Philip Wayne, Harmondsworth: Penguin

Green, H. M. (1966) *A History of Australian Literature* Sydney: Angus & Robertson

Greenfield, C. (1983) 'On Readers, Readerships and Reading Practices' *Southern Review* 16 March

Greimas, A. G. (1987) 'Elements of Narrative Grammar' in *On Meaning: Selected Writings in Semiotic Theory* trans. P. Perron and F. Collins, Minneapolis: University of Minnesota Press, ch. 4, pp.63–83

Gross, E. see Grosz, E.

Gross, E. (1986) 'Irigaray and Sexual Difference' *Australian Feminist Studies* 2, pp.63–78

Grosz, E. (1986) *Irigaray and the Divine* Sydney: Local Consumption

——(1987) 'Notes Towards a Corporeal Feminism' in *Feminism and the Body* special issue, eds J. Allen and E. Grosz *Australian Feminist Studies* 5, pp.1–16

——(1988) 'The In(ter)vention of Feminist Knowledges' in Caine et al. (eds) *Crossing Boundaries*

Grosz, E. and M. de Lepervanche (1988) 'Feminism and Science' in Caine et al. (eds) *Crossing Boundaries*

Hall, E.T. (1968) 'Proxemics' *Current Anthropology* 9, 2–3, pp.83–108

Halliday, F.E. (1964) *A Shakespeare Companion 1564–1964* Harmondsworth: Penguin

Halliday, M.A.K. (1970) *A Course in Spoken English: Intonation* Oxford: Oxford University Press

——(1973) 'Relevant models of language' in *Explorations in The Functions of Language* London: Edward Arnold. pp. 9–21

——(1974) 'Discussion with M.A.K. Halliday' in H. Parrett *Discussing Language* The Hague: Mouton, pp. 81–120

——(1975) *Learning How to Mean: explorations in the development of language* London: Edward Arnold

——(1978) *Language as Social Semiotic* London: Edward Arnold

——(1979) 'Modes of meaning and modes of expression: types of grammatical structure, and their determination by different semantic functions' in D.J. Allerton, E. Carney and D. Holdcroft (eds) *Function and Context in Linguistic Analysis* Cambridge: Cambridge University Press

——(1985) *An Introduction to Functional Grammar* London: Edward Arnold

——(1987) 'An interview with Michael Halliday by Paul J. Thibault' in R. Steele and T. Threadgold (eds) *Language Topics: essays in honour of Michael Halliday* volume 2. Amsterdam: Benjamins

Hamon, P. (1983) *Le Personnel du Roman. Le Systeme des Personnages dans les "Rougon-Macquart" d'Emile Zola* Geneve: Dros

Harre, R. (1981) 'The Dramaturgy of Sexual Relations' in M. Cook (ed.) *The Bases of Human Sexual Attraction* London: Academic Press

Hasan, R. (1986) 'The Ontogenesis of Ideology: An Interpretation of Mother Child Talk' in T. Threadgold et al. (eds) *Semiotics-Ideology-Language* Sydney: SASSC pp. 125–46

Hawkes, T. (1971) *Structuralism and Semiotics* London: Methuen

Heath, S. (1981) *Questions of Cinema* London: Macmillan

Hegel, G.W.F. (1977) *The Phenomenology of Spirit* trans. A.V. Miller, Oxford: Oxford University Press

Henriques, J. W. Hollway, C. Urwin, C. Venn and V. Walkerdine (1984) *Changing the Subject* London: Methuen

Heriot, A. (1956) *The Castrati in Opera* London: Secker & Warburg

Hjelmslev, L. (1961) *Prolegomena to A Theory of Language* trans. F.J. Whitfield, Madison: University of Wisconsin Press

Hobbes, T. (n.d.) *Leviathan* ed. M. Oakeshott, Oxford: Basil Blackwell

Hollway, W. (1984) 'Gender difference and the production of subjectivity' in Henriques et al. *Changing the Subject*

Hoult, T.F. (1983) 'Human Sexuality in Biological Perspective: theoretical and methodological considerations' *Journal of Homosexuality* 9, 2–3, pp.137–55

Hudson, R.R. (1980) *Sociolinguistics* Cambridge: Cambridge University Press

Huizinga, J. (1965) *The Waning of the Middle Ages* trans. F. Hopman, Harmondsworth: Penguin

Hunter, I. (1982) 'The Concept of Context and the Problem of Reading' *Southern Review* 18, 1

——(1983) 'Reading Character' *Southern Review* 16

——(1984a) 'Literary Discipline' Part IV of 'Text in Itself: a Symposium' *Southern Review* 17, 2

——(1984b) 'After Representation: recent discussions of the relation between language and literature' *Economy and Society* 13, 4

Hurley, M., (1985) Rosa Praed's Affinities, paper presented to ASAL annual conference, Armidale

Hyslop, G. (1985) 'Deviant and Dangerous Behaviour' *Journal of Popular Culture* 19, pp.65–77

Irigaray, L. (1985a) *Speculum of the Other Woman* trans. G. Gill, Ithaca, New York: Cornell University Press

——(1985b) *This Sex which is Not One* trans. C. Porter, Ithaca, New York: Cornell University Press

——(1985c) *Parler n'est jamais neutre* Paris: les editions de minuit

——(1986) *Divine Women* trans. S. Muecke, Sydney: Local Consumption

Jackson, R. (1981) *Fantasy: The Literature of Subversion* London: Methuen

Jakobson, R. (1978) *Six Lectures on Sound and Meaning* with a preface by Claude Lévi-Strauss, trans. J. Mepham, Hassocks, Sussex: Harvester Press

Jakobson, R. and L. Waugh (1979) *The Sound Shape of Language*

Brighton, Sussex: Harvester Press

Jameson, F. (1981) *The Political Unconscious: Narrative as a Socially Symbolic Act* London: Methuen

Jardine, A. (1985) *Gynesis* Ithaca, New York: Cornell University Press

——(1987) 'Men in Feminism: Odor di Uomo or Compagnons de Route?' in Jardine and Smith (eds) *Men in Feminism*

Jardine, A. and P. Smith eds (1987) *Men in Feminism* New York and London: Methuen.

Jesperson, O. (1922–1933) 'Symbolic value of the vowel I' in *Linguistica: selected papers in English, French and German* Copenhagen: Levin & Munksgard/London: Allen & Unwin, pp.283–303

Johnson, B. (1981) Translator's Introduction to J. Derrida *Dissemination* Chicago: University of Chicago Press

Jolley, E. (1983) *Miss Peabody's Inheritance* Brisbane: University of Queensland Press

Jones, A.R. (1985) 'Inscribing Femininity: French theories of the feminine' in G. Greene and K. Kaln (eds) *Making a Difference* New York: Methuen

Kafka, F. (1969) 'The Penal Settlement' *Metamorphoses and Other Short Stories* Harmondsworth: Penguin

Kamuf, P. (1987) 'Femmeninism' in Jardine and Smith (eds) *Men in Feminism*

Kaplan, G.T. (1984) The Politics of Survival, PhD thesis, Monash University

Kaplan, G.T. and L. Rogers (1984) 'Breaking out of the dominant paradigm: a new look at sexual attraction' *Journal of Homosexuality* 10, 3–4, pp.71–75

——(1985) 'The definition of male and female: biological reductionism and the sanctions of normality' in *Feminist Knowledge as Critique and Construct* Geelong: Deakin University, Section 7, pp.1–43.

Keller, E. Fox (1985) *Reflections on Gender and Science* New Haven and London: Yale University Press

Kieckhefer, R. (1984) *Unquiet Souls: Fourteenth Century Saints and their Religious Milieu* Chicago and London: Chicago University Press

King, N. (1985) 'The Teacher must exist before the pupil' The Newbolt Report on the Teaching of English in England, 1921, unpublished paper

Kramer, L. (1980) 'Pseudoxia Endemica' *Quadrant* July

Kress, G. (1985) *Linguistic Processes in Sociocultural Practice* Geelong: Deakin University Press

——(1989 forthcoming) '1: Genre' in R. Andrews (ed.) *Narrative and Argument* Stony Stratford: Open University Press

——(forthcoming) *A Social Theory of Language* London: Polity Press

Kress, G. and T. Threadgold (1988) 'Toward a Social Theory of Genre' *Southern Review* 21, 3, pp.218–43

——(forthcoming) *Genre: a study in power, pedagogy and polyphony* London: Polity Press

Kristeva, J. (1976) 'Signifying Practice and Mode of Production'

Edinburgh Review 1, pp.64–75

——(1977) *Polylogue* Paris: Seuil

——(1980) *Desire in Language: A Semiotic Approach to Literature and Art* trans. T. Gora, A. Jardine and L. Roudiez, New York: Columbia University Press/Oxford: Basil Blackwell

——(1981) 'La femme, ce n'est jamais ça' *Tel Quel* 1974, reprinted in E. Marks and I. de Courtivron (1981) *New French Feminisms* Hassocks, Sussex: Harvester

——(1984) *Revolution in Poetic Language* trans. A Waller, New York: Columbia University Press

Kroker, A. and M. Kroker (1988) *Body Invaders: sexuality and the postmodern condition* London: Macmillan

Labov, W. (1972a) 'The isolation of contextual styles' in *Sociolinguistic Patterns* Philadelphia: University of Pennsylvania Press, pp. 70–109

——(1972b) 'Rules for ritual insults' in *Language in The Inner City: studies in the Black English vernacular* Philadelphia: University of Pennsylvania Press, pp. 287–53

Labov, W. and D. Fanshel (1977) *Therapeutic Discourse: psychotherapy as conversation* New York: Academic Press

Lacan, J. (1977) *Ecrits: A Selection* trans. A. Sheridan, London: Tavistock

——(1982) *Feminine Sexuality: Jacques Lacan and the ecole freudienne* eds. J. Mitchell and J. Rose, trans. J. Rose, London: Macmillan

Lagorio, V. (1985) 'Variations on the Theme of God's Motherhood in Medieval English Mystical and Devotional Writings' *Studia Mystica* 8

Lakoff, R.T. (1979) 'Stylistic Strategies within a Grammar of Style' in J. Orasanu, M.K. Slater, and L.L. Adler (eds) *Language, Sex and Gender: does 'la difference' make a difference?* New York: Annals of the New York Academy of Sciences, vol. 327, pp.53–78

Lauretis, T. de (1986) *Feminist Studies: Critical Studies* Bloomington: Indiana University Press

——(1987) *Technologies of Gender* Bloomington: University of Indiana Press

Leach, E. (1964) 'Anthropological perspectives on language: animal categories and verbal abuse' in E. Lenneberg (ed.) *New Directions in the Study of Language* Cambridge, Mass.: M.I.T. Press, pp.23–64

Leavis, Q. (1932) *Fiction and The Reading Public* London: Penguin

Leech, G.N. (1980) *Explorations in Semantics and Pragmatics* (Pragmatics and Beyond, No. 5) Amsterdam: Benjamins

——(1983) *Principles of Pragmatics* London: Longmans

Leff, G. (1976) *The Dissolution of the Medieval Outlook* New York: New York University Press

Lemay, H. R. (1982) 'Human Sexuality in Twelfth- through Fifteenth-Century Writings' in V. Bullough and J. Brunage (eds) *Sexual Practices and the Medieval Church* Buffalo, New York: Prometheus Books

——(1985) 'Anthonius Guainerius and Medieval Gynecology' in J. Kirshner and S. F. Wemple (eds) *Women of the Medieval World* Oxford: Basil Blackwell

Lemke, J. L. (forthcoming) 'Heteroglossia and social theory' in *Bakhtin:*

Radical Perspectives New York Bakhtin Circle
——Meaning and Power: social semiotics and political conflict, unpublished manuscript
——(1988) 'Towards a social semiotics of the material subject' in T. Threadgold (ed.) *Sydney Association for Studies in Society and Culture Working Papers* 2, 1 Sydney: SASSC
Levine, D. N. (1981) 'Rationality and Freedom: Weber and Beyond' *Sociological Enquiry* 51, pp. 5–25
Levinson, S. (1983) *Pragmatics* (Cambridge Textbooks in Linguistics) Cambridge: Cambridge University Press
Lingis, A. (1984) *Excesses. Eros and Culture* New York: State University of New York
——(1985) *Libido* New York: State University of New York
Lloyd, G. (1984) *The Man of Reason: 'male' and 'female' in Western Philosophy* Minneapolis: University of Minnesota Press
Lonzi, C. (1974) *Sputiamo su Hegel* Milano: Rivolta Femminile
——(1977) *Egia politica* Milano: Rivolta Femminile
Lumsden, C.J. and E.O. Wilson (1981) *Genes, Mind and Culture: the coevolutionary process* Cambridge, Mass. and London: Harvard University Press
Lynch, M. (1987) 'The Body: Thin is Beautiful' *Arena* 79
Lyotard, J-F (1979) *La Condition Post-Moderne* Paris: Minuit
——(1980) 'One of the Things at Stake in Women's Struggles' *Substance* 20
——(1984) *The Post-Modern Condition: A Report on Knowledge* trans. G. Bennington and B. Massumi, Manchester: Manchester University Press
Macdonnell, D. (1986) *Theories of Discourse: An Introduction* Oxford: Basil Blackwell
Mackerras, C.P. (1972) *The Rise of the Peking Opera 1770–1870* Oxford: Clarendon Press
MacNeill, I. (1984) 'Too Soon, Too Late' Gay Information, 14–18
McDonnell, E.W. (1969) *The Beguines and Beghards in Medieval Culture* New York: Octagon Books
McLaughlin, E. C. (1974) 'Equality of Souls, Inequality of Sexes: Woman in Medieval Theology' in R.R. Ruether (ed.) *Religion and Sexism: Images of Woman in Jewish and Christian Traditions* New York: Simon & Schuster
——(1975) "Christ My Mother": Feminine Naming and Metaphor in Medieval Spirituality" *Nashotah Review* 15, 3
——(1979) 'Woman, Power and the Pursuit of Holiness in Medieval Christianity' in R.R. Reuther and E. McLaughlin (eds) *Women of Spirit: Female Leadership in the Jewish and Christian Traditions* New York: Simon & Schuster
McNamara, J.A. and S.F. Wemple (1977) 'Sanctity and Power: The Dual Pursuit of Medieval Women' in R. Bridenthal and C. Koonz (eds) *Becoming Visible: Women in European History* Boston and London: Houghton Mifflin
Macy, G. (1984) *The Theologies of the Eucharist in the Early Scholastic*

Period Oxford: Clarendon Press

Maltz, D.N. and R.A. Borker (1982) 'A cultural approach to male–female miscommunication' in J.J. Gumperz (ed.) *Language and Social Identity* Cambridge: Cambridge University Press

Marcuse, H. (1968) 'Industrialisation and Capitalism in the Work of Max Weber' in Marcuse *Negations* trans. J.J. Schapiro, Harmondsworth: Penguin

Markey, T. L. (1982) 'Crisis and cognition in onomastics' *Names* 30, pp. 129–42

Marks, E. and I. de Courtivron (1981) *New French Feminisms* Hassocks, Sussex: Harvester Press

Marrow, J.H. (1979) *Passion Iconography in Northern European Art of the Late Middle Ages and Early Renaissance* Belgium: Van Ghemmet

Marshall, J. (1981) 'Pansies, Perverts and Macho Men: changing conceptions of male sexuality' in K. Plummer (ed.) *The Making of the Modern Homosexual* London: Hutchinson

Martin, J.R. (1985) 'Process and text: two aspects of human semiosis' in J.D. Benson and W. S. Greaves (eds) *Systemic Perspectives on Discourse* vol. 1 Norwood, New Jersey: Ablex

Martin, L. K. (1982) In the Mind's Eye: The Expression of Perceived Space and Time in the Novels of Emile Zola and in the Art of his Contemporaries, PhD thesis, University of Wisconsin

Martinez, I. (1983) 'The Lesbian Hero Bound: Radclyffe Hall's portrait of sapphic daughters and their mothers' *Journal of Homosexuality* 8, 3–4

Marx, K. (1975) Letters from *Deutsch-Franzosische Jahrbucher* (1844) in Marx and Engels *Collected Works* vol. 3, London: Lawrence and Wishart

Masterman, L. (1983) 'Media Education: Theoretical Issues and Practical Possibilities' *Metro* 60, pp.5–10

Metz, C. (1977) *Le Signifiant Imaginaire* Paris: Union Generale d'Editions

Meyer, M. trans. (1985) *Strindberg Plays: One* London: Methuen

Miller, E. Morris and F. McCartney (1956) *Australian Literature* Sydney: Angus & Robertson

Miller, N.K. (1986) *The Poetics of Gender* New York: Columbia University Press

Millett, K. (1977) *Sexual Politics* London: Virago

Mitchell-Kernan, C. (1972) 'Signifying, loud talking and marking' in T. Kochman (ed.) *Rappin' and Stylin' Out* Urbana, Ill: University of Illinois Press

Modjeska, D. (1981) *Exiles at Home* Sydney: Angus & Robertson

Modleski, T. (1982) *Loving with a Vengeance: mass-produced Fantasies for Women* New York and London: Methuen

Mogul, S. L. (1980) 'Asceticism in Adolescence and Anorexia Nervosa' *The Psychoanalytic Study of the Child* 35

Moi, T. (1985) *Sexual/Textual Politics* London: Methuen

Money, T. and A. Ehrhardt (1972) *Man and Woman: Boy and Girl* Baltimore and London: Johns Hopkins University Press

Morris, M. (n.d.) 'The Practice of Reviewing' *Framework* 22–23

——(1987) 'In any event' in Jardine and Smith (eds.) *Men in Feminism*

——(1988) *The Pirate's Fiancee: Feminism, Reading, Postmodernism* New York and London: New Left Books

——(1988) 'A-mazing Grace: Notes on Mary Daly's Poetics' in Morris Miller, E. and F. McCartney (1956) *Australian Literature* Sydney: Angus & Robertson

Morris, R. ed. (1886) *Old English Homilies* EETS OS 29 London: Oxford University Press

Muir, K. (1970) 'Changing Interpretations of Shakespeare' in *Pelican Guide to English Literature* Ringwood: Penguin, pp.282–301

Muraro, L. (1984) *Guglielma Manfreda* Milano: La tartaruga

Murray, S.O. (1979) 'The art of gay insulting' *Anthropological Linguistics* 21, 5, pp.211–23

——(1983) 'Ritual and personal insults in stigmatised subcultures: gay-black-Jew' *Maledicta* 7, pp. 189–211

Nelson, B. (1973) 'Zola and the ambiguities of passion: *Une Page d'Amour*' *Essays in French Literature* 10, pp.1–22

Nesbitt, C. and G. Plum (1988) 'Probabilities in a Systematic-Functional Grammar: the clause complex in English' in R.P. Fawcett and D. Young (eds) *New Developments in Systemic Linguistics* vol. 2 London: Francis Pinter, pp. 6–38

Nichols, J. and L.T. Shank (1984) *Medieval Religious Women* vol. 1 Kalamazoo: Cistercian Publications

Nietzsche, F. (1969) *On The Genealogy of Morals* New York: Vintage Press

——(1988) *The Will to Power* trans. W. Kaufman and J. Hollingdale, New York: Vintage Books

Nightingale, V. (1985) Subversion and Repression in Australian Soaps: the position of the Audience, paper presented at ANZAAS Conference, University of New South Wales, August

Oberman, H. (1978) 'Fourteenth Century Religious Thought: A Premature Profile' *Speculum* 53

Olsen, K.L. (1983) 'Genetic Determinants of Sexual Differentiation' in J. Balthazart, E. Prove and R. Gilles (eds) *Hormones and Behaviours in Higher Vertebrates* Heidelberg, New York and Toronto: Springer-Verlag

O'Toole. L.M. (1982) *Structure, Style and Interpretation in the Russian Short Story* New Haven and London: Yale University Press

Painter, C. (1984) *Into the Mother Tongue: A Case Study in Early Language Development* London: Frances Pinter

Palmer, P.M. (1985) 'New methods, new reasons: television and children's leisure time' *Media Information Australia* 37, pp.55–58

——(1986) *Girls and Television* Sydney: Social Policy Unit, Ministry of Education

Pateman, C. (1988) *The Sexual Contract* Oxford: Polity Press

Pateman, C. and E. Gross (1986) *Feminist Challenges* Sydney: Allen & Unwin

Pavis, P. (1976) *Problemes de Semiologie Theatrale* Canada: Presses de l'universite de Quebec

Petroff, E. (1979) *Consolation of the Blessed* New York: Alta Gaia

——(1986) *Medieval Women's Visionary Literature* New York and Oxford: Oxford University Press

Philipsen, G. and M. Huspek (1985) 'A bibliography of sociolinguistic studies of personal address' *Anthropological Linguistics* 27, pp. 94–101

Plummer, K. (1981) *The Making of the Modern Homosexual* London: Hutchinson

Poole, R. (1985a) 'Morality, Masculinity and the Market' *Radical Philsophy* 39, pp.16–23

——(1985b) 'Structures of Identity: Gender and Nationalism' in P. Patton and R. Poole (eds) *War/Masculinity* Sydney: Intervention Publications

Poynton, C. (1985) *Language and Gender: Making the Difference* Geelong: Deakin University Press

Praed, R. (1886) *Affinities: A Romance of Today* London: Routledge

Probyn, E. (1988) 'The Anorexic Body' in A. and M. Kroker (eds) *Body Invaders: Sexuality and the Postmodern Condition* Basingstoke and London: Macmillan pp. 201–212

Quinn, N. and D. Holland (1987) 'Culture and Cognition' in D. Holland and N. Quinn (eds.) *Cultural Models in Language and Thought* Cambridge: Cambridge University Press, pp. 3–40

Rabinowitz, P. (1987) *Before Reading: Narrative Conventions and the Politics of Interpretation* Ithaca, New York: Cornell University Press

Radway, J.A. (1984) *Reading the Romance: Women, Patriarchy and Popular Culture* Chapel Hill and London: University of North Carolina Press

——(1986) *The Progress of Romance: The Politics of Popular Fiction* London: R.K.P.

Reddy, M. (1979) 'The conduit metaphor: a case of frame conflict in our language about language' in A. Ortney (ed.) *Metaphor and Thought* Cambridge: Cambridge University Press.

Rich, A. (1985) 'Notes Towards a Politics of Location' in Diaz-Diocaretz and Zavala (eds) *Women, Feminist Identity and Society in the 1980s*

Rizzuto, A-M., R.K. Peterson and M. Reed (1981) 'The Pathological Sense of Self in Anorexia Nervosa' *Pyschiatric Clinics of North America* 4

Rochecouste, M. (1979) Le Decor Mythique de *Nana*. Premiere etape, BA thesis, Monash University

——(1988) *The Role of Parallel Catamorphic Systems in the Structure of Zola's 'Rougon-Macquart'* Hildesheim, Zurich, New York: Georg Olms Verlag

Roderick, C. (1948) *In Mortal Bondage* Sydney: Angus & Robertson

Rogers, L.J. (1981) 'Biology: Gender Differentiation and Sexual Variation' in N. Grieve and P. Grimshaw *Australian Women: Feminist Perspectives* Oxford: Oxford University Press, pp.44–57

——(1988) 'Biology, the popular weapon: sex differences in cognitive function' in Caine et al. (eds) *Crossing Boundaries*

Rose, J. (1986) *Sexuality in the Field of Vision* London: Verso

Rousselle, A. (1988) *Porneia: On Desire and the Body in Antiquity* trans. F. Pheasant, Oxford: Basil Blackwell

Rowland, R. (1988) *Woman Herself* Oxford: Oxford University Press

Ruehl, S. (1982) 'Inverts and Experts: Radclyffe Hall and the Lesbian Identity' in R. Brunt and C. Rowan (eds) *Feminism, Culture and Politics* London: Lawrence & Wishart

Rule, J. (1975) *Lesbian Images* NY: Crossing

vom Saal, F.S. (1983) 'The interaction of circulating oestrogens and androgens in regulating mammalian sexual differentiation' in J. Balthazart et al. (eds) *Hormones and Behaviour in Higher Vertebrates* Berlin, Heidelberg, New York, Toronto: Springer Verlag

Salingar, L.J. (1970) 'The Elizabethan Literary Renaissance' in *Pelican Guide to English Literature* Ringwood: Penguin

Sapir, E. (1915–1951) 'Abnormal types of speech in Nootka' in D. G. Mandelbaum *Selected Writings of Edward Sapir in Language, Culture and Personality* Berkeley and Los Angeles: University of California Press, pp. 179–96

——(1929–1951) 'A study in phonetic symbolism' in D.G. Mandelbaum (ed.) *Selected Writings of Edward Sapir in Language, Culture and Personality* Berkeley and Los Angeles: University of California Press

Scarry, E (1985) *The Body in Pain: The Making and Unmaking of the World* New York and Oxford: Oxford University Press

Schaffer, K. (1988) *Women and the Bush: forces of desire in the Australian cultural tradition* Cambridge: Cambridge University Press

Schiller, G. (1972) *Iconography of Christian Art* vol. 2 trans. J. Seligman, London: Lund Humphreys

Schor, N. (1969) Le Cycle et le Cercle: temps, espace, et revolution dans quatre romans de Zola, PhD thesis, Yale University.

——(1976) 'Le Sourire du Sphinx: Zola et l'enigme de la femininite' *Romantisme* 13–14, pp.149–61

Schulenberg, J.T. (1978) 'Sexism and the Celestial Gynaeceum—from 500–1200' *Journal of Medieval History* 4

——(1984) 'Strict Active Enclosure and its Effects on the Female Monastic Experienc (500–1100)' in Nichols and Shank (eds) *Medieval Religious Women* vol. 1

Sedgwick, E. Kosofsky (1985) *Between Men: English Literature and Male Homosocial Desire* New York: Columbia University Press

Seidel, G. (1988) *The Nature of The Right* Amsterdam: John Benjamins

Sharkey, M. (1983) 'Rosa Praed's Colonial Heroines' *Australian Literary Studies* 10

Sheridan, S. (1982) 'Ada Cambridge and the Female Literary Tradition' in S. Dermody, J. Docker, D. Modjeska (eds) *Nellie Melba, Ginger Meggs and Friends* Melbourne: Kibble

——(1988) 'Feminist Readings: the case of Christina Stead' in Caine et al. (eds) *Crossing Boundaries*

Showalter, E. (1985) *The New Feminist Criticism* London: Virago

Sontag, S. (1978) *Against Interpretation* New York: Delta

Sours, J. A. (1981) 'Depression and the Anorexia Nervosa Syndrome'

Psychiatric Clinics of North America 4

Spender, D. (1980) *Man Made Language* London and Melbourne: Routledge & Kegan Paul

Stankiewitz E. (1964) 'Problems of emotive language' in T.A. Sebeok, A.S. Hayes and M.C. Bateson (eds) *Approaches to Semiotics* (Transactions of the Indiana University Conference on Paralinguistics and Kinesics) The Hague: Mouton, pp. 239–76

Stargardt, U. (1985) 'The Beguines of Belgium, the Dominican Nuns of Germany, and Margery Kempe' in T.J. Heffernan (ed.) *The Popular Literature of Medieval England* Knoxville: University of Tennessee Press

Stead, C. (1934) *Seven Poor Men of Sydney* Sydney: Angus & Robertson, 1981

Steedman, C. (1986) *Landscape for a Good Woman* London: Virago

Steinberg, L. (1983) *The Sexuality of Christ in Renaissance Art and Modern Oblivion* New York: A Pantheon/October Book

Stokes, S. (1928) 'How I won my Victoria Cross' in *Pilloried* London, pp.78–83

Suleiman, S. ed. (1985) *The Female Body in Western Culture: Semiotic Perspectives Poetics Today* 6, 1–2, 1985

——(1985) '(Re)Writing the Body: the Politics and Poetics of Female Eroticism' *Poetics Today* 6, 1–2, pp. 43–66

——ed. (1986) *The Female Body in Western Culture: Contemporary Perspectives* Cambridge, Mass. and London: Harvard University Press

Summers, A. (1975) *Damned Whores and God's Police: The Colonisation of Women in Australia* Harmondsworth: Pelican

Sutton, P. ed. (1988) *Dreamings: The Art of Aboriginal Australia* Ringwood, Victoria: Viking (Penguin Australia)

Tagg, J. (1988) *The Burden of Representation: Essays on Photographies and Histories* Basingstoke and London: Macmillan

Thibault, P.J. (1986) *Text, Discourse and Context: a social semiotic perspective* (Monographs, Working Papers and Prepublications 3, 1986) Victoria University, Toronto: The Toronto Semiotic Circle

Thorne, B., Kramarae C. and Henley N. (1983) *Language, Gender and Society* Rowley, Mass: Newbury House

Threadgold, T. (1986) 'Semiotics—ideology—language' in Threadgold et al. (eds) *Semiotics—Ideology—Language*

——(1987a) 'The Semiotics of Halliday, Voloshinov and Eco' *American Journal of Semiotics* 4, 3, pp.107–42

——(1987b) 'Rossi-Landi's Higher Dialectical Level: Alienation, Relativity and Ideology' *Il Protagora* IV Serie per Ferruccio Rossi-Landi, a cura di S. Petrilli, pp.81–98

——(1988a) 'Language and Gender' *Australian Journal of Feminist Studies* 6, pp.41–70

——(1988b) 'Stories of Race and Gender: An Unbounded Discourse' in D. Birch and L. M. O'Toole (eds.) *The Functions of Style* London: Frances Pinter

——(1988c) 'Changing the Subject' in R. Steele and T. Threadgold (eds)

Language Topics: Essays in Honour of Michael Halliday vol. 2, Amsterdam: Benjamins

——(1989, forthcoming) 'Paradigms of Culture and Semiosis: Grammatiks for Cryptogrammars or Metalanguages for the ineffable?' in W. Koch (ed.) *The Evolution of Culture* proceedings of the Villa Vigoni conference, Lake Como, September 1988 Bochum: Studienverlag Brockmeyer

Threadgold, T., E.A. Grosz, G. Kress and M.A.K. Halliday eds. (1986) *Semiotics-Language-Ideology* Sydney: SASSC

Ubersfeld, A. (1978) *Lire le Theatre* Paris: Editions Sociales

Ulmer, G. (1980) 'The Discourse of the Imaginary' *Diacritics* 10

Waller, J. (1983) 'Goldenhair' in S. Goode (ed.) *The Penguin Book of Homosexual Verse* London: Penguin

Wandor, M. (1981) *Understudies, Theatre and Sexual Politics* London: Eyre Methuen

Ward, B. (1987) *Miracles and the Medieval Mind* rev., Philadelphia: University of Pennsylvania Press

Warner, M. (1985) *Alone of All Her Sex* London: Picador

——(1987) *Monuments and Maidens: The Allegory of Female Form* London: Picador

Warrack, J. (1973) *Tchaikofsky* London: Hamish Hamilton

Watkins, R.N. (1983) 'Two Visionaries and Death: Catherine of Siena and Julian of Norwich' *Numen* 30

Watney, S. (1987) *Policing Desire: Pornography, AIDS and the Media* London: Comedia/Methuen

Weber, M. (1919) 'Science as a Vocation', reprinted in Weber 1977

——(1922) 'Bureaucracy', excerpts from *Economy and Society* Part III, ch. 6, reprinted in Weber 1977

——(1922–23) 'The Social Psychology of World Religions', reprinted in Weber 1977

——(1964) *The Theory of Social and Economic Organisation* [= Economy and Society Part I] trans. T. Parsons, New York: The Free Press

——(1977) *From Max Weber: Essays in Sociology* trans. H.H. Gerth and C. Wright Mills, London: Routledge & Kegan Paul

——(1984) *The Protestant Ethic and the Spirit of Capitalism* trans. T. Parsons, London: George Allen & Unwin

Weedon, C. (1987) *Feminist Practice and Poststructuralist Theory* Oxford: Basil Blackwell

Weeks, J. (1977) *Coming Out: Homosexual Politics in Britain from the nineteenth Century to the Present* London: Quartet

——(1981) 'Discourse, Desire and Sexual Deviance: some problems in a history of homosexuality' in K. Plummer (ed.) *The Making of the Modern Homosexual* London: Hutchinson

——(1985) *Sexuality and its Discontents* London: Routledge & Kegan Paul

Westcott, R.W. (1971) 'Labio-velarity and derogation in English: a study in phonosemic correlation' *American Speech* 46, pp.123–37

——(1976) 'The phonology and morphology of American English slang' in R.J. di Pietro and E.L. Blansitt jr. (eds) *The Third Lacus Forum* Columbia, South Carolina: Hornbeam Press, pp.108–119

——(1980) *Sound and Sense: linguistic essays on phonosemic subjects* (Edward Sapir Monograph Series in Language, Culture, Cognition) Lake Bluff, Illinois: Jupiter Press

Westra, M. S. (1950) *A Talking of þe Loue of God* The Hague: Martinus Nijhoff

White, P. (1979) *The Twyborn Affair* London: Jonathan Cape

Whorf, B. L. (1956) *Language, Thought and Reality: selected writings of Benjamin Lee Whorf* ed. J.B. Carroll, Cambridge, Mass.: M.I.T. Press

Williams, R, (1971) *The Long Revolution* first published 1962, London: Penguin

Williamson, D. (1989) *Authorship and Criticism* Sydney: Local Consumption Publications

Winslow, D.J. (1969) 'Children's derogatory epithets' *Journal of American Folklore* 82, pp.255–63

Woolf, V. (1963) *A Room of One's Own* London: Penguin

Wotherspoon, G. (1984) 'Thirties Images' *Gay Information* 14–18, pp.46–50

Zholkofsky, A.K. (1978) 'The Window in the Poetic World of Boris Pasternak' trans. L.M. O'Toole, *New Literary History* Winter, 9, 2, pp.279–314

Zola, E. (1895) *A Love Episode* ed. E.A. Vizetelly, London: Hutchinson & Co

——(1957) *A Love Affair* trans. J. Stewart, London: Paul Elek

——(1973) *Une Page d'Amour* [1878] chronologie, introduction, notes et archives de l'oeuvre par Colette Becker, Paris: Flammarion.

Index

aboriginal, 240
actantial, 108–10, 112
Adams, P., 34
Addleshaw, P., 143
Allen, Grant, 141–53 *passim*
Alley, R., 222
anamorphic, 108, 109, 118, 119
Anderson, B., 238
androgyny, 212–14, 226
anorexia, 94–6
Aristotle, 58, 89–90
art, 10, 21
Ash, J., 31, 33
attitude, 201, 244 *passim*, 254; *see also* emotion
auditory stimuli, 219
aural semiotic, 193, 207
Austin, J.L., 239
auto-reproduction, 27

Bachelard, G., 121
Bakhtin, M.M., 191
ballet, 219–20
Barker, F., 25
Barthes, R., 107, 131, 179
BBC, 'The Fight to be Male', 229
Beane, W.C. and W.G. Doty, 113
Beckwith, S., 91
Bell, R., 94
Belsey, C., 253
Bem, S.L., 212, 229

Benjamin, W., 57
Bennett, T., 157, 159
Benveniste, E., 250–1
binarism, 1, 4–5, 7, 11, 19, 28–30, 133–4, 139, 199–200, 204–6, 210; binary constructions, 34; binary oppositions, 4, 19; dichotomy, 1, 5; male/female dichotomy, 72, 211–12, 227–9; *see also* dichotomy
biology, 4, 8, 23, 25–7, 66, 71–4, 200, 211, 216, 226–8 *passim*; as cultural construction, 31
Birch, D., and M.O'Toole, 20
birth, 26
Blachford, G., 164
Bleier, R., 211
body, 3–4, 13–16, 23, 62, 65 *passim*, 70 *passim*, 75–90, 193; biological body, 31; body politic, 26–7; Christ's body, 28, 31, 75; corporeal inscription (as construction), 24; genitalia, 211–12; male body, 19; psychical body, 31; sex-hormone levels, 228–30; Foucault on, 39–40
Booth, M., 162
Borie, J., 124, 126
Borresen, K.E., 89
Braidotti, R., 9, 17, 24

297